The Best of Everything After 50

The Best of Everything After 50

The Experts' Guide to Style, Sex, Health, Money, and More

by Barbara Hannah Grufferman

Illustrated by Sarah Gibb

RUNNING PRESS
PHILADELPHIA · LONDON

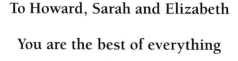

To Howard, Sarah and Elizabeth

You are the best of everything

Library of Congress Control Number: 2009943380

ISBN 978-0-7624-3740-5

Cover and interior design by Corinda Cook
Illustrations by Sarah Gibb
Edited by Jennifer Kasius
Typography: Berkeley, Onyx, and Univers

Running Press Book Publishers
2300 Chestnut Street
Philadelphia, PA 19103-4371

Visit us on the web!
www.runningpress.com

Contents

Introduction

I wrote this book for me.

I was perfectly fine with turning fifty—except that it snuck up on me. Once I got over the shock and realized that I was really and truly going to be fifty, I wanted to do it right. While I really believe I'm getting better as I get older, I also know that my body and lifestyle have changed with the years and I haven't really paid attention to how those changes will affect me in the long-term. I needed a new plan for dealing with my new reality. I had questions about big things (How can I prevent heart disease?) and less frightening but still important ones (Can I still wear 7 For All Mankind jeans?).

Knowledge is power, right? So I went on a quest to find the answers. I searched the Internet, bookstores, and magazines, but it soon turned into information overload. Everybody had an opinion—and most of them conflicted with each other. Then one day, it hit me. I didn't want lots of information; I wanted the *best* information—bottom line—about what I needed to know now about my skin, hair, makeup, health, sex, clothes, exercise, money and more. Talking to my friends, it was clear we were all looking for the same thing—a simple guide to living well over fifty that would give us the answers we needed in a simple format.

I wanted a straightforward book that put all of the most useful information in one place with common sense but without fuss or too much jargon. "Tell me what I need to know and tell me now" is part of the collective consciousness of women over fifty. We want to streamline our lives down to the essential elements. I know, because I am this woman, too.

The book didn't exist, so I decided to write it myself.

I searched out the top experts in all of these fields—and more—and asked them my questions, put myself in their hands, did their programs (to make sure they really worked), and then shared everything I learned with all my women friends.

The result is this book.

It poses the questions, explains the research, introduces the experts, and offers answers, solutions, and advice. I've used myself as the test case to make sure that all of this advice is effective and I give real-life examples of what I do, and what other savvy women I know are doing—and tell you what is working for us.

At the end of every chapter there is a concise list of important findings that recaps the advice, and includes the essential "must-dos" and "must-haves." Every chapter also includes a list of other resources for more in-depth information. The book ends with the best of the best for women over fifty: "The Plan" which puts everything into a manageable outline.

The Best of Everything After 50 will be your go-to reference guide to our changing bodies and lifestyles. You'll find yourself picking it up whenever you have a question about health, your heart, skin care, makeup, style, money, sex, organizing your life, losing weight, getting in shape, and so much more. Your questions will be the same as mine, I guarantee.

I learned a great deal from my wonderful experts, but the most important lesson of all is this: if you're healthy, you feel good. If you feel good, you look good. If you feel good, look good, have your finances under control, and a vision for your future, you feel even better. If you've got all that plus the knowledge about how to stay that way (with some good sex thrown in), you feel amazing. And if you feel amazing, who cares about age?

That is what it means to have the best of everything.

Chapter 1

Feelin' Alright

Don't Worry, Be Healthy

I have an early childhood memory of counting backward from 100—and then waking up much later to the sing-song voice of my mother asking, "Would you like some ice cream?" While I was happy about the ice cream, I still don't know why my tonsils had to be removed. The little buggers had never given me any problems, and yet . . . out they came. To this day, even my mother isn't sure why. During the fifties and sixties, countless American children had their tonsils removed—it was practically a rite of passage. This is no longer the case. We know much more now than we did then, are more informed, and most of us have access to better health care. Questioning a doctor's opinion and seeking out a second one is more the norm. It can still be confusing, though, especially as we get older.

Superwoman

I entered my adult years with the same high expectations of good health that I had as a kid. Why not? I had taken my Flintstones vitamins every morning for years. I felt invincible and inde-structible in my twenties and thirties—even my forties.

But what if . . . ?

After I crossed the threshold of fifty, I started to look around a little more. Some people my age were having strokes, contracting cancer, struggling with depression, gaining weight, and developing diabetes. It's not that people who were younger didn't have some of these health concerns. After fifty, it suddenly seemed all too common. I started asking myself the "what if" questions: What if I really get sick, or have a heart attack? Can I get Alzheimer's? What if I get cancer? Do I already have cancer and don't even know it?

The more I thought about it, the more questions I had: Can some of these illnesses be prevented? Am I doing everything right to protect myself? Am I at risk for something serious? How would I know? Are there tests I should be getting? What, where, and how often? I'm over fifty. What can I do to make sure that as I get older, I live a good, healthy life?

We can't control getting older. We can control how we do it.

I was determined to find out how we could age gracefully, with dignity and relatively good health. Like many other women, I had gone for a long time without doing simple things that could positively affect my health and well-being. Life had kept me busy taking care of others, but kept me from doing the right things for myself. Sleeping enough and exercising daily had seemed like an indulgence, even as I made sure my family was well-fed and well-rested. Was I too late to make a difference in my own health?

A Promise to Ourselves

Yes, we are going to get older. Let's control how we do it, so we can be productive, fit, and strong women, no matter what our age. There are measures we can take now that will help us to enjoy our later years, not just endure them. Starting today, starting now, make this our goal: everything we do, we will do in a way that will benefit us and our current—and future—selves. We will prioritize our quality of life, not

compromise it. It's not exactly starting over, but starting on a new path. It's a thoughtful, mindful approach to healthy living. We can do it.

But how?

When in doubt, do more research, but try not to drive yourself crazy.

After giving myself weeks of nightmares by exhaustively researching each and every possible disease and illness and bodily malfunction that could hit a woman over fifty, I woke up one morning and thought: "Enough already." I was making myself crazy, nervous, and a hypochondriac. Not a good way to start on my new life plan. Instead of obsessing over unlikely scenarios and struggling with medical jargon, I needed to get real information about the most probable problems and, more importantly, the best defenses. I needed to call in the experts.

I scheduled my annual physical exam and asked my doctor for a double session so he could talk me through everything I really needed to know—and do—going forward.

It's time to take control.

Dr. Greg Pitaro has been my Primary Care Physician (PCP) for over ten years. He's checked my blood pressure and cholesterol levels, taken my temperature and made me say "aaaaah" when I've caught strep throat from my daughters, and has always made me feel empowered with information. When I saw Dr. Pitaro to talk about my concerns about being fifty he was patient, informative, clear, and right to the point.

It's not about preventing death. It's all about preventing preventable death.

Certain deaths are preventable. Every year an estimated 900,000 Americans die from preventable illnesses, and millions more are disabled by them. It doesn't have to be this way. Take care of your body and it will take care of you. Do the right things (eat well, exercise, don't smoke, keep a good weight, listen to your body) and you will be doing everything that is in your control to keep preventable illnesses and disease out of your life. Here's what he told me.

Top Ten Causes of Preventable Death

1. Smoking
2. High blood pressure
3. Obesity
4. Inadequate physical activity
5. High blood glucose level
6. High LDL cholesterol
7. High salt intake
8. Too low intake of omega-3 fatty acids (from seafood)
9. High levels of trans fat in the diet
10. Alcoholism and alcohol abuse

The Usual Suspects

You don't need to get crazy imagining exotic illnesses. The biggest dangers are exactly what you'd guess. The leading causes of death for American women over fifty are, in order: heart disease, cancer, stroke, lung disease, and Alzheimer's disease. Heart disease is responsible for about 30 percent of those deaths and cancer for another 20 percent. The good news is that heart disease and some cancers can be prevented, especially if you keep your blood pressure in check and don't smoke.

I asked Dr. Pitaro for a primer on the major threats that might get between us and our long-term health goals, starting with the number one cause. I also consulted with Dr. James Underberg, a specialist in heart disease prevention and lipidology who is a key expert in *Chapter 2: Keep the Beat.*

Cause No. 1: Heart Disease

Since heart disease and stroke are responsible for killing one-third of older women, the entire next chapter is devoted to heart health. But here are the basics.

Cardiovascular disease, or CVD, is a group of problems related to the breakdown or blockage of the heart or blood vessels. Blood delivers oxygen and energy cells that make up our bodies. If the heart can't pump blood, or if blood doesn't move efficiently through your veins and arteries, you can develop CVD.

How to Prevent CVD

Most heart disease is related to the build-up of fatty substances—plaque and cholesterol—on the walls of the arteries that carry blood. Most heart disease can be prevented by eating healthy foods, not smoking, getting regular exercise to keep your heart strong and your arteries free from build-up, and minimizing stress and anxiety, which can put strain on your heart.

Cause No. 2: Cancer

Are you thinking "Good grief, why is she doing this? I thought this was going to be a fun book about great hairstyles and good sex! She's starting to freak me out!" No, no, no. You just have to face a few facts and make yourself more aware, informed, and tuned into your body, and then we'll get to the fun stuff.

We will survive.

About one in three women will be diagnosed with some form of cancer in her lifetime, so we can't ignore it. The majority of us will survive. The overall five-year relative survival rate is as high as 97 percent for the most common forms of cancer, when it is caught and treated early. The best way to catch cancer in the act is to know what you're looking for.

What is cancer?

All cancers begin in cells in the body. Cells make up tissues, which make up the organs of the body. In a healthy body, cells grow and divide to form new cells as needed. When cells grow old and die, new cells take their place, but sometimes things go wrong. New cells form when the body does not need them, and old cells do not die when they are supposed to. The extra cells in the body form a mass of tissue—a tumor, which can be either benign (not cancerous) or malignant (cancerous). Sometimes tumors stay put, but they can spread out and run amok in our bodies (metastatic cancer). If cancer spreads and cannot be controlled, the cancerous cells interfere with the ability of healthy cells to function properly, and that's when the real trouble begins.

How common is cancer?

- Cancer is the primary cause of 1 of every 4 deaths in the U.S. overall.
- More than 1,437,200 new cancer cases were diagnosed in 2008.
- There were about 565,000 cancer deaths in the U.S. in 2008.

Many cancers can be prevented.

About 5 percent of cancers are due to inherited gene mutations. Many of the other 95 percent can be avoided. Here are some recent facts from the American Cancer Society:

- 170,000 cancer deaths in 2008 were related to tobacco.
- One third of all cancer deaths were directly related to obesity, physical inactivity, and poor nutrition.
- Many of the more than 1,000,000 skin cancers diagnosed in 2008 could have been prevented by proper protection from the sun and avoiding indoor tanning.
- Regular screening by health professionals can prevent some cancers, such as cancer of the cervix, colon, and rectum.
- Screening tests may result in early detection and an increased cure rate of cancer of the breast, colon, rectum, cervix, skin, and oral cavity.

The best preventatives for most cancers are the same as for most of our other health concerns:

- **Avoid smoking.**
- **Keep weight in check.**
- **Get regular exercise.**
- **Control diabetes.**
- **Be aware of your family history.**
- **Eat a lot of fresh fruits and vegetables and not too much fat.**

What are the warning signs of cancer?

There are many kinds of cancers, but most cases occur in the same few places in the body: breasts, lungs, colon, uterus, lymph nodes, thyroid, and skin. Some cancers—like pancreatic cancer—develop with little warning and few well-known risks. There are regular screening tests that can help find a few cancers early which are covered later in this chapter and in *Chapter 3: Changes Down Under*. The sooner cancer is diagnosed, and the sooner treatment begins, the better the odds of survival. To give yourself the best chance of beating cancer, you need to rely on your own good sense and watch for signs, such as:

- **Chronic coughing or wheezing**
- **Feeling short of breath**

Vitamin D and Cancer Prevention

Vitamin D's importance in promoting bone health and reducing risk of osteoporosis is well established, but there's new evidence that the "sunshine vitamin" can reduce the risk of certain cancers and cardiovascular disease. Low vitamin D levels in the body (below 30 mg/ml) may predispose a woman to developing some cancers. Women over fifty should take in between 1,200 and 1,500 IU of vitamin D every day. To do this by diet alone would be impossible, so supplements are essential, in conjunction with eating foods that are good sources of vitamin D.

- **Coughing up blood or mucus with blood spots**
- **Sudden, unexplained weight loss or weight gain**
- **Difficulty swallowing**
- **Pain or discomfort in the pelvic area or abdomen or a persistent stomachache**
- **Feeling full but unable to eat**
- **A pale or jaundiced complexion**
- **Weakness and fatigue despite regular sleep**
- **Repeated infections**
- **Fever and night sweats**
- **Bruising or bleeding easily, including frequent nosebleeds**
- **Bone or joint pain**
- **Swollen lymph nodes in the armpit, neck, or groin**
- **Any persistent and inexplicable problem or pain**
- **Vaginal spotting if you are post-menopausal**

If you develop any of those symptoms—and especially if you develop two or more at the same time—report them to your doctor immediately. Keep in mind, many of these could be caused by problems other than cancer, so your doctor will conduct various tests (usually non-invasive ones, although biopsies may be necessary in some cases) to determine the cause and to help you decide on treatment.

Lung Cancer

Lung cancer is the #1 leading cause of cancer death for women. Although almost twice as many women are diagnosed with breast cancer compared to lung cancer, lung cancer deserves a special mention here because it kills many more of us. But it is avoidable.

What causes lung cancer?

Smoking. We are considered the smarter sex, and yet more women smoke than men. Lung cancer can also be caused by secondhand smoke or by toxins in the environment, but smoking is the biggest culprit. Once you quit, your lungs start to heal, stopping your risk from increasing.

I used to smoke.

During my discussion with Dr. Pitaro, I blurted out "I used to smoke!" Since I've been seeing him for over a decade, he already knew that. I suddenly needed to know if I should get a chest X-ray, a CT scan, anything and everything right then and there. He waited until I stopped hyperventilating (How could I have done that to myself? What about how my hair used to smell, and my breath, and my clothes? I started having terrible flashbacks of the little bits of tobacco that would be at the bottom of all my handbags . . .), and calmly explained how this would likely impact me. I started smoking when I was a teenager, and smoked on and off until my mid-thirties, never more than eight or so cigarettes a day. He said I was still considered low risk, because I hadn't smoked a pack or more a day, and I stopped almost twenty years ago. Relief. The statistical cancer risk didn't go down when I quit, but it isn't increasing either, because I no longer smoke. It just stopped where it was. What's more, our risk of developing cardiac disease lowers significantly after quitting (by over 50 percent starting the first year after you quit). Each year you don't smoke the risk gets lower. I'm breathing easier now.

What if you still smoke?

If you do, try your best to quit. You don't need to be told how dangerous it is to your health. Talk to your doctor about the best approach for you. Get a patch, get gum, get help, but you must quit—for your lungs, your heart, your skin, the people around you, your life.

Are there any screening tests for lung cancer?

There is no early test for lung cancer. There have been studies on the usefulness of chest X-rays, sputum cytologies, or CT Scans to screen for lung cancer in people who do not have symptoms, but so far the tests that doctors have now are only effective in confirming a diagnosis.

Cause No. 3: Emphysema

Lung disease is the fourth biggest cause of death in women in the U.S. While several chronic lower respiratory diseases, including asthma, are grouped together under the heading of lung disease, the most serious for people over fifty is emphysema. Emphysema used to be more common among men than women, but that is changing now that more women than men are smoking. It is usually caused by smoking or secondhand smoke, which makes emphysema, like lung cancer, a preventable disease.

What is emphysema?

Emphysema is a chronic, progressive lung disease in which the air sacs in the lungs are damaged severely enough to impair your ability to breathe and absorb oxygen. Because it develops gradually, it often goes undetected until it is quite advanced and is usually diagnosed in people between fifty and sixty years of age. Symptoms include:

- **Shortness of breath**
- **Fatigue and tiring easily during physical activity**
- **Chronic, mild cough**
- **Loss of appetite and weight loss**

How is emphysema diagnosed?

Since many of the symptoms of emphysema are similar to other lung diseases—including lung cancer—your doctor will perform a full physical exam and will also take a chest X-ray and conduct certain tests to measure your lung capacity and function and the amount of oxygen in your blood.

Cause No. 4: Alzheimer's Disease

I admit it. I forget things. Is this a sign that I'm getting Alzheimer's disease, or is it just normal, age-related memory loss? Our brains do slow down a bit as we age, but severe memory loss and seriously impaired reasoning skills are not "just part of aging" and should be addressed. Some Alzheimer's-like symptoms can be caused by treatable conditions like vitamin deficiencies, depression, thyroid problems, or excessive alcohol consumption.

What is Alzheimer's disease?

Alzheimer's disease is an irreversible and progressive brain disease that destroys brain cells, causing severe problems with memory, thinking, and behavior, and is the most common form of dementia. It ultimately leads to death. It can occur at almost any age, but is more likely once you're over sixty-five. Alzheimer's currently has no cure—but some symptoms can be treated and managed, especially in the early stages. Here are a few basic facts we should know:

- **One out of eight people age sixty-five or older has Alzheimer's.**
- **That number doubles for every five-year age interval beyond age sixty-five.**
- **5.3 million people have Alzheimer's in the U.S.**
- **Alzheimer's is the seventh leading cause of death for older adults, but the fourth for women.**

How is Alzheimer's diagnosed?

Because of the nature of Alzheimer's disease, the person may not know she has it. Diagnosis can be difficult, so a specialist is often required if family members or a PCP suspects Alzheimer's. There are a few tests (MRI, blood tests) that can be done to see if what's happening could be the onset of Alzheimer's—the earlier it is diagnosed, the better it can be managed.

Can Alzheimer's be prevented?

There is so much we don't know about Alzheimer's—including what causes it—but it seems to share some risks with more routine types of memory loss. Recommendations to both improve mental function and guard against Alzheimer's include:

- **Exercise your body.**
- **Exercise your brain: tackle cross word puzzles or Sudoku, learn a new language, knit a complicated pattern, have new experiences—anything to challenge your mind.**
- **Keep your blood pressure down.**
- **Don't smoke.**
- **Eat lots of fruits and vegetables.**
- **Keep a positive attitude and enjoy life—if we stay alert and engaged, we automatically keep our brains active.**
- **Have a busy social calendar—the more engaged we are socially, the healthier we remain.**

Quality of Life

We've covered the major causes of death, but what about diseases that affect quality of life? Heart disease, stroke, cancer (specifically lung, breast, and certain gynecological cancers), emphysema, and Alzheimer's disease are statistically the most deadly for women over fifty—and the threat from all of them can be reduced by the choices that we make—but there are a few diseases that put a big damper on our quality of life.

Arthritis? Already?

My hair is naturally wavy. I usually scrunch it up a bit and leave it to air dry (see *Chapter 9: No More Bad Hair Days*). Recently, I scrunched it so hard that my middle finger began to hurt. The pain lasted over a week. Convinced I had broken my finger in the name of beauty, I made an appointment with a hand surgeon who had once treated me for carpal tunnel syndrome. The X-ray showed a little bursitis that the doctor said would go away eventually. Then he casually said, "Oh, by the way, you have some arthritis in your thumb." What? Only a few things have made me feel old since I turned fifty. This was one of them. Arthritis? Me? I couldn't believe it. My grandmother had arthritis, and I remember how she suffered with it. But hadn't she been way older than fifty? "Look at the X-ray again," I told him. "You must be mistaken." It turns out you can get osteoarthritis (the most common form of arthritis) at any age, but once you are over fifty, the chances of getting it somewhere in your body increase dramatically. It's also more common for women than men. And, yes, when the doctor checked the X-ray again, there it was.

What is arthritis?

Arthritis is a general term that means inflammation of the joints. Osteoarthritis is a degenerative joint disease, and the most common type of arthritis. It can occur in any joint in the body when there is a breakdown of the cartilage. It is usually seen in weight-bearing joints of the hips, knees, and spine. Cartilage serves as a "shock absorber" that covers the ends of the bones in joints. Once it starts to deteriorate, the bones can rub against each other causing pain, inflammation, and swelling. I remember my grandmother's swollen fingers, and how she would complain about her "arthritic hands." It was distressing to her because she loved to knit and having arthritis made it very difficult (although it didn't stop her from knitting the most amazing mohair bikini for me when I was fifteen. For sunbathing, of course—not swimming.)

Why do some people get arthritis?

- **Heredity—You can inherit a defect in a gene responsible for making cartilage, which causes defective cartilage, and then rapid deterioration.**
- **Obesity—Carrying around extra weight puts stress on your body, including joints and cartilage.**
- **Injury—People who break bones near a joint are prone to developing osteoarthritis in that joint.**
- **Overuse of joints—Using certain joints repeatedly for work (bending at the knees or elbows, for example) can cause osteoarthritis in those areas.**

How is arthritis diagnosed?

If you suspect that you have arthritis, your PCP can do an X-ray, but usually your description of where the pain is, and what it feels like, is a good indication of arthritis.

What can you do to alleviate arthritis pain?

- **Physical therapy and muscle-strengthening exercises**
- **Hot and cold compresses**
- **Use of supportive devices such as canes and crutches**
- **Medications such as acetaminophen, anti-inflammatory drugs, and steroids**
- **Acupuncture**
- **In severe cases, surgery to replace joints (such as hips and knees)**

Can arthritis be prevented?

Maintain a healthy weight and exercise regularly, especially to strengthen your bones and muscles to better support the work that your joints have to do. There's no guarantee that you won't still get arthritis (what exercise is there for a thumb?), but it will help.

Rheumatoid Arthritis

Rheumatoid arthritis (RA) affects more women than men, and generally those over fifty. Rheumatoid arthritis is an unusual disease in that it is symmetrical. If you have it in one thumb, you'll have it in the other. This is one of its distinguishing features that differentiates it from other types of arthritis. While the exact cause of rheumatoid arthritis is unknown, doctors believe it's a combination of genetic, environmental, and hormonal factors. It's possible that a virus or bacteria invades the body, alters the immune system, and attacks the joints and sometimes other organs.

The Rheumatoid Arthritis-Periodontitis-Heart Connection

There seems to be a connection between joints, gums, and the heart. If a patient has RA, she often has periodontitis (gum disease) as well, or the reverse. It's a known fact now that if you have periodontitis, you are more prone to developing heart disease. It might all come down to a certain blood protein—C-reactive protein—that indicates inflammation in the body. Inflammation in the body can indicate a higher risk for heart disease. One way a doctor can assess whether a patient

has rheumatoid arthritis is to test for inflammation in the body. If you have one of these three, you should be screened for the other two, and have the C-RP test as well.

It's time for a plan to take control of our health to understand what the issues are and know what we need to do about them. With guidance from the experts, the comprehensive "Do—Don't Do—Listen" Plan was created specifically for women over fifty. Incorporate this plan with the information on heart and gynecological health, skin care, nutrition, and exercise found in other chapters and you will be in control of your health.

Here's the good news.

The odds of contracting the vast majority of major illnesses and diseases can be greatly reduced if we:

- **Do things that promote health.**
- **Don't do things that undermine health.**

- **Listen to our bodies for changes in our health.**

The Plan

Review and discuss this plan with your own physician. This is a general wellness program, but you are a specific woman. Genetics might put you at a higher risk for certain diseases, but there's no guarantee that you will contract any of them. Follow this program, and you will take charge of your health, improve your quality of life, and decrease your risk factors. You can't change your genes or your age, but you can change your lifestyle—what you do, what you don't do, and how well you listen to your body.

The "Do" List

The "Do" list is our essential guide to things we should do after fifty. There's no need to go crazy with "boutique" total body medical screenings that you may have seen on talk shows. We just don't have to go that far, or spend that kind of money, to keep tabs on our health. Stick with these basics of good health and you'll be doing plenty.

DO: Get medically organized.

Don't be in a position where a health crisis arises—or even just a routine check-up— and you're searching for your insurance card or your doctor's address. Start a Personal Medical Information file for each person in your home. Include the following:

- **Health care providers' names, addresses, phone and fax numbers.**
- **List of medicines that you take, including dosage, who prescribed it, when it was prescribed, and why.**
- **List of vitamins and herbal supplements that you take, with their daily or weekly dosage.**
- **Lists of all known allergies.**
- **Immunization record going back as far as possible.**
- **Conditions for which you are currently being treated.**
- **A copy of all medical test results and physical exam reports.**
- **Insurance policy and a copy of your insurance card.**

What's in your wallet?

Put a copy of important medical information in your wallet. Include the medications you take and the dosage, allergies you have, and your doctor's name, address, and phone number.

DO: Get a Primary Care Physician (PCP).

Get a doctor who will be your "health point person." Your primary care physician will be your go-to doctor for annual physical exams, yearly flu shot, and all those general aches, pains, and common illnesses that pop up. Your PCP will keep track of your medical reports, health concerns, will know when something isn't right, and should be able to pull up a flow chart showing your weight, cholesterol, and blood pressure for each year. She'll know what you do to exercise, what supplements you take, how you eat, what diets you've tried . . . in a word: everything. If you need a specialist she will recommend the best doctor to treat the condition that you have.

Choosing the right primary care physician.

If you don't have one, get one. If you don't know who to go to, start by asking your friends and family to recommend the best doctors in your area. You may have to spend a little time researching, but it's time well spent. If you meet one and don't feel like you're getting what you need, keep looking. Your insurance plan may limit your pool of possible doctors, so start with those that are in your network. Not all doctors take Medicare insurance, so it's best to get yourself associated with one who does. Then when you start to use Medicare benefits at age sixty-five, you won't need to find a new doctor.

Please listen when I speak to you.

Your primary care physician must have the ability to listen to your concerns, show empathy, and work with you to understand your symptoms and address the problem. If you are not getting this from your doctor, find another.

Judge your doctor by the doctors he keeps.

Your PCP should be well connected to other doctors and able to refer you to the best specialists. Ideally, your PCP will be "computer connected" to other specialists, allowing each doctor to pull up your information at the touch of a button. This kind of "network approach" to health care is available almost anywhere. Being connected by computer isn't an absolute must, but having a PCP who is connected with your local medical community is.

That doesn't mean you should ever let your guard down.

You may love your doctor, but this is your body, and your life. You can find the ideal primary care physician, who can, in turn, refer you to the best specialists in the country. That does not mean that you should just hand your life over. Pay attention to medical information, and ask questions about anything that you don't understand. Listen to your body—and make yourself heard—if you feel something isn't right. Never feel foolish about getting second, or even third, opinions. Ask your PCP if she is up on all the latest health research. Every year, new studies are published about women's health and your PCP should be aware of new screening tests, medications, or research that could have an impact on your life. You deserve to have a doctor who respects, encourages, and supports your desire to be vigilant about your own health.

The good patient.

We expect a lot from our doctors, but it's a two-way street. I asked a few doctors to tell me which behaviors they see in patients that impede their ability to provide the best care. These are the most common concerns:

- **The patient brings friends or family into the checkup room who then take over the conversation.**
- **The patient doesn't reveal the entire truth about her lifestyle.**
- **The patient stops taking medications without consulting the doctor because the symptoms disappear, or she just doesn't want to take them anymore.**
- **The patient thinks there's a magic pill for**

anything that ails her, and asks for medications instead of changing her habits.

- The patient is a "serial screener" who wants screening tests done even if she doesn't need them, which can cause complications and waste money and time.

DO: Get an annual physical exam.

Consider this a yearly get-together with your primary care physician. Your doctor should talk to you about your health, any special issues, your life in general, and will take several kinds of measurements, comparing the numbers to those from the previous year (or several years) to see patterns or changes in your body. Your doctor will discuss adjustments you might need to make in your life to get closer to the ideal numbers for you. In the screenings section below, the "Gold Standard" numbers are listed, and, while you should try to do everything you can to achieve those "Gold Standards," the closer you get to them, the healthier you are. Remember: you might be

doing everything right, and still need extra help from medication. That's okay. Don't beat yourself up about it. Many doctors prescribe medications to help alleviate certain symptoms while the patient is making lifestyle adjustments. Think of it this way: lifestyle changes first, meds as a backup, but sometimes they may have to go together.

DO: Tell the truth, the whole truth and nothing but the truth.

When you begin your annual exam, tell your doctor every little thing about yourself and your family health history. Don't hold anything back, and never lie about what you do, and don't do. Your doctor is not there to judge you but to help you (and if you feel judged, get a new doctor). Things in your genes or your past or present lifestyle can have major effects on your well-being and your doctor can't know about them if you don't tell. Be prepared to discuss everything you know about your parents' and siblings' health, too. For women, a key predictor of long-term health is your mother's health history, specifically her experiences with pregnancy and menopause.

DO: Get measured.

At your annual exam, your doctor will want to check what your body is doing, and how it's looking. Are you gaining weight? If so, is it in your belly area? What is your natural body shape? As we pass fifty, these questions mean more to us and our doctors than just how we fit in our new pair of jeans. Where your weight is distributed, and how much you gain or lose each year can be important early indicators of health concerns. Your doctor will check the following:

- **Height,** to make sure we're not losing inches, which could be a sign of osteoporosis or scoliosis of the spine.
- **Weight** because the risks for many illnesses can be lowered if we keep our weight at a good level. Rapid weight gain or loss can be a symptom of certain serious conditions.

- **Body Mass Index (BMI)**—weight in relation to height is considered to be more important than weight alone. A BMI of 18.5 to 24.9 is ideal.
- **Waist Circumference**—indicates where your fat is being distributed. For women, it's best to be under 35 inches, or less than half of your height.
- **General Shape,** to assess your proportions and general shape. Too many women are inappropriately concerned about their weight when, in fact, their weight may be just right for their build. A woman's shape is a better predictor of her cardiovascular health than her absolute weight.
- **Electrocardiogram (EKG),** to see what you look like inside. Wires will be taped to areas of your body, including your chest, and the machine will make a graph of your heart's electrical activity as it is actually beating. An EKG can pick up abnormal heartbeats, heart muscle damage, blood flow problems in the coronary heart arteries, and heart enlargement.

DO: Get your blood pressure checked.

Your blood pressure will be taken at every annual exam (or more often if there is a specific concern). This information is used to keep tabs on the health of your heart, and your risks for developing heart disease, stroke, diabetes, and metabolic syndrome.

What is blood pressure?

Blood pressure is the force of blood against artery walls when the heart beats and then rests. A blood pressure check results in two numbers. Systolic pressure (the top number) indicates the pressure the heart needs to pump blood through the body. The diastolic pressure (or bottom number) indicates the pressure that occurs when the heart relaxes between beats.

Ideal blood pressure for women: less than 120/70.

Blood pressure of 140/90 or higher indicates hypertension (high blood pressure).

Why is hypertension a problem?

Hypertension forces your heart to work harder than it should and can reduce the flow of oxygen in your body. It can cause heart disease, stroke, kidney damage, blindness, and many other medical problems.

What can you do about hypertension?

Hypertension becomes more of a challenge after fifty because your blood vessels get stiffer and narrower as you age, causing or exacerbating hypertension. Hypertension is also directly linked to lifestyle—obesity, smoking, not exercising, and eating too much processed food or salt. Often, if you change how you live your life, you can naturally bring your blood pressure level down without drugs. Genetics can contribute to high blood pressure, but medication can help. If you have made a realistic attempt to lower your blood pressure with lifestyle changes, but it's not going down, your doctor will probably consider medication. Buy a blood pressure monitor to check your blood pressure regularly.

DO: Get your blood screened

Your doctor will take blood samples during your annual physical exam to conduct several tests. A few are screenings specifically related to the health of your heart (cholesterol, triglyceride) while others are to give you and your PCP a sense of your general state of health. For best results, do not eat or drink anything (except water) for at least 9 hours prior to the test. (There are also a few very important heart-health screening tests that are covered in detail in the next chapter) Here are a few common blood tests.

1. Blood Cholesterol Check

Cholesterols are waxy substances that occur naturally in the body, and are necessary to build cell membranes and help with other important cell functions. Too much can clog arteries, leading to atherosclerosis. There are two main types of cholesterol: HDL (the "good" cholesterol) and LDL (the "bad" cholesterol). HDL are high-density lipoproteins that remove cholesterol from the blood; and LDL are low-density lipoproteins that build cholesterol deposits on the blood vessels.

Guideline total cholesterol counts for women:

Total: Optimal under 200

Borderline High 200–239

High 240 and over

LDL vs. HDL Counts

The LDL number should be low. If LDL is too high, it can lead to cholesterol buildup and blockage of the arteries, which can lead to heart disease.

LDL: Optimal under 100

Near Optimal 100–129

Borderline High 130–159

High 160–189

Very High 190 and over

HDL is the good cholesterol that helps remove the bad cholesterol (LDL) from the body. This number should be high, since it indicates how much heart protection you have.

HDL Optimal 60 and over

Ideal blood cholesterol levels for women:

Total: under 200

HDL: over 60

LDL: under 100

2. Triglyceride Check

The triglyceride level is another important number that is a strong indicator of potential cardiovascular disease. Triglycerides are another type of fat (similar to cholesterol) found in the blood. What's important for you and your doctor to know is that the acceptable levels are lower for women than for men. Even though the American Heart Association says that the acceptable level is under 150, recent studies conducted by the American Heart Association and the Women's Health Initiative suggest that an over-fifty woman's risk for cardiovascular disease increases after her level goes beyond 50. We are not just little men. Women have different biological makeups. Discuss triglycerides with your doctor because many PCPs aren't aware of the most recent information as it pertains to women. It's not uncommon for high triglyceride levels to go hand in hand with high LDL and low HDL numbers.

Ideal triglyceride level for women:

Total: under 150 (try to get it as low as possible)

If we control our weight, increase physical activity, quit smoking, and lower the intake of alcohol, saturated fats, trans fats, and cholesterol, you can help to lower this number. Medication may also be necessary.

3. The Complete Blood Count (CBC) and The Chemistry Screen

The CBC count will give your doctor a count of your white blood cells, red blood cells, hemoglobin, platelets, and anything in your blood, all of which helps to deter-mine the status of your general health. For instance, an elevated white blood cell count could indicate inflammation, or an infection, going on somewhere in your body. The Chemistry screen will check levels of several substances that are normally found in the blood such as Vitamin D, Vitamin B12, ferritin, homocysteine, uric acid, sodium, potassium and—very importantly—glucose, or blood sugar.

Blood Sugar (Glucose)

Your ability to regulate blood sugar is harder once you're over fifty. The ideal level is under 100. Blood sugar levels normally go up and down during the course of a day. If you're healthy, they rise and fall just a bit, but if you're not eating the right foods, don't eat often enough, or not moving your body, blood sugar levels can spike and crash, wreaking havoc in your body in many ways. Elevated blood sugar can take a toll on memory, even if the levels are only slightly elevated. More importantly, if it goes up and stays there, you could develop diabetes. This can happen to anyone, but is especially likely if you have a family history of diabetes, high blood pressure, and if your daily exercise is walking from the sofa to the fridge to the car and back again. The single most effective way to regulate blood sugar is—drum roll, please—the eating right and physical activity combo plan (see *Chapter 5: You = What you Eat* and *Chapter 6: Move That Body*). But first: get it checked.

Ideal Blood Sugar Level:

   Under 100

4. The Thyroid Blood Check

Thyroid-stimulating hormone (TSH) is secreted from the pituitary gland and it causes the thyroid gland to produce thyroid hormone. The level of TSH should be checked to see if your thyroid is healthy or if it is underactive or overactive, both of which are common and treatable, and occur more frequently in women than men.

What happens with an underactive thyroid?

Most women who have thyroid disease have an underactive thyroid. It is easily diagnosed and treatable, often with medication. Symptoms include fatigue, reduced libido, weight gain, high cholesterol, dry skin, and depression. Too frequently, women ignore these symptoms, believing this is how you feel once you're over fifty.

What happens with an overactive thyroid?

The symptoms of an overactive thyroid can mimic those of a heart condition or anxiety by creating a rapid heartbeat. Women can experience unexplained fatigue and weight loss. In addition, the thyroid gland may be swollen and tender, which is another sign that 1) it's not a heart problem and 2) it's not in your head. Medication is generally required.

A low level of TSH could also be an indicator of thyroid cancer, which is a highly detectable and treatable cancer. If caught early, it rarely moves to other parts of the body, but stays put in the thyroid and can almost always be cured.

The annual exam is a critical part of your plan for health.

Your blood pressure, body measurements, and EKG results will be available on the spot, but the blood work will have to be sent out to a lab. Review the results with your PCP, and get a copy of the test results sent to you so you have them for your Personal Medical Information file. Based on these numbers and your general health, your doctor will be able to determine if you should just keep on doing what you're doing, if you have to make some small changes, or if your health plan (including lifestyle) needs a complete overhaul.

Quick overview of what happens at the annual physical exam:

- **Talk with your doctor about everything that's going on with you.**
- **Weight/height/waist measurement**
- **Blood pressure check**
- **EKG**
- **Blood work**
- **Follow up and ask questions.**
- **Get a report of your exam, with all of your numbers for your Personal Medical Information file.**

DO: Know your numbers.

Know your weight, height, blood pressure, HDL/LDL cholesterol, triglycerides levels, and understand what they mean. If they're not ideal, think about them the next time you are waiting for a parking spot closer to the store so you won't have to walk so far, and the next time you're about to dunk a doughnut into that latte.

Is that all there is?

After fifty, there are simply more things that can happen to us. Not will. Can. That's just the way it is and ignoring them won't make them go away. There are a few other screening tests you should do to make sure that you find certain illnesses before they go too far. In conjunction with your annual physical exam, these extra tests will be highly effective at catching certain diseases in the early stages, while you can fix them. Some can save your life and others will improve the quality of it. Not everything can be screened. Some things only require screening if you have specific risk factors—family history of a certain disease, or symptoms. But there are some sensible tests that we can and should do regularly. Some of these involve doctors other than your PCP—regular trips to your gynecologist, optometrist/opthalmologist, and dentist, are essential to overall health.

DO: Essential Screening Tests:

1. Colonoscopy

A colonoscopy allows a doctor to see and closely inspect the inside of the rectum and entire colon for signs of cancer or small growths that might become cancerous. It's the third most commonly diagnosed cancer in the U.S. The risk of developing colon cancer increases with age and more than 90 percent of cases are diagnosed in people over fifty. It's preventable and treatable if caught early. The only way you can catch it early is by having a colonoscopy, but less than 40 percent of Americans have them. Let's face it: it's not everyone's favorite medical test. But it's still a very good idea.

The preferred means is still a traditional colonoscopy, not a virtual one (a noninvasive screening method which uses X-rays and computers to produce 3-D images of the colon.). Think about it this way: If the doctor who is performing a virtual colonoscopy sees something that must be removed, guess what? You will have to have a procedure to remove it. A virtual colonoscopy only detects growths, requiring another procedure to remove them. And whether you have a traditional colonoscopy or a virtual one, you must go through the whole yucky day-before prep (to completely clean out your colon area) anyway. On top of that, most health insurance companies (including Medicare) will pay for a traditional colonoscopy. Not so with a virtual one. If you're going to do it—and do it you must—do it the right way.

How often should you have a colonoscopy?

If your parents or siblings had colorectal cancer, you should have a colonoscopy ten years before the age your relative was diagnosed. For example, if your mother was diagnosed with colon cancer at age fifty-eight, get your first colonoscopy at forty-eight. If there's no family history of colon cancer, have your first one at age fifty, and then every five to seven years thereafter, depending upon what your doctor advises.

What about the "off" years when you're not getting a colonoscopy?

Women over fifty should get a Fecal Occult Blood Test every year they don't get a colonoscopy. This test, which is done by your PCP, is an easy way to be proactive about your health so that nothing will be allowed to slip through the cracks, so to speak.

2. Diabetes Screening

Diabetes is a major risk factor for heart disease and stroke. It is also the number one cause of kidney failure, blindness, and lower limb amputation in America. Diagnosing and controlling diabetes is especially important for women, because a diabetic woman's risk of developing cardiovascular disease is even greater than that of a man with diabetes.

What is Diabetes?

Diabetes is a metabolic disorder that affects the pancreas and disrupts the body's ability to process blood sugar, or glucose. It is usually described as either Type 1 or Type 2. Type 1 diabetes is caused by genetics and is usually diagnosed in children or younger adults. Type 2 diabetes may be influenced by genetics, but it is almost entirely caused by lifestyle and is usually diagnosed in people over fifty.

What are some of the risk factors of Type 2 Diabetes?

- **Over fifty**
- **Overweight**
- **Waist measurement is greater than 35**

inches, or half a person's height
- Physically inactive
- Family history of diabetes
- African American, Hispanic, American Indian or of Asian descent
- Women who delivered babies that weighed 9 lbs. or more

What are some of the symptoms of Type 2 Diabetes?

Sometimes there are no symptoms, but your doctor will check your blood sugar level as part of your annual exam. If detected early enough through this simple blood test, dietary and lifestyle changes can actually reverse diabetes. The first signs of diabetes can be detected at a stage called pre-diabetes, often signaled by an overproduction of insulin: before blood sugar levels go up, the insulin levels tend to go up. Some of the more common symptoms of diabetes include:

- Fatigue
- Nausea
- Frequent urination
- Unusual thirst
- Unexplained weight loss
- Blurred vision

- Frequent infections
- Sores that don't heal quickly

What are some of the signs that you're in the pre-diabetes stage?

- Insulin level goes up
- Weight gain (specifically around the abdomen)
- Increased appetite
- Elevated blood pressure

Even in the pre-diabetes stage it can be difficult to make effective lifestyle changes to reverse the trend. A doctor may start a patient on a medicine to help alleviate the symptoms of pre-diabetes while she is starting her lifestyle adjustments. This can give her a better chance for her lifestyle changes to work, so that she can eventually stop taking the medicine. This approach can help stop the cycle, before she becomes a full-scale diabetic.

How often should you get the blood sugar test for diabetes?

Every year during your Annual Physical Exam. Most doctors will consider you diabetic if your glucose level is over 126.

3. Pap Test Screen, Pelvic Exam, and HPV Test

These three important tests measure your gynecological health. The pap smear is performed by your gynecologist during your annual gynecological exam to screen for cervical cancer. It supplements the physical pelvic exam and detects abnormal changes in cervical cells that may turn into cervical cancer. Before the pap smear was developed, cervical cancer was the leading cause of cancer death among women. Now it ranks fifteenth and has a 92 percent cure rate when detected early. The human papilloma virus (HPV) test will also be given, especially if you've had an abnormal pap smear, been diagnosed with a sexually transmitted disease (STD), or are practicing unsafe sex or safe sex but with multiple partners. HPV is a common sexually transmitted infection that is the main cause of cervical cancer. (See *Chapter 3* for more information.) Get these tests every year during your annual gynecological exam.

4. Sexually Transmitted Disease (STD) Tests

Just because we're over fifty doesn't mean we shouldn't have some fun. But even older women need to have safe fun. Use condoms, don't engage in risky sex, and make sure you know the scoop on your partner before you proceed. No matter if you've been out of the game for a while, it's still wise to get tested. Discuss your risk factors with your gynecologist, and together decide if you should be tested for HIV, Hepatitis B and C, and syphilis while you're there for your annual gynecological exam. Certainly consider having these done if you're about to start a new sexual relationship, and insist that your new partner do the same. Other common types of STDs include genital warts, genital herpes, and trichomoniasis, all of which have obvious symptoms.

5. Breast Self-Exam and Mammogram (Breast X-Ray)

We've made great progress in diagnosing and treating breast cancer and, when it's detected early, the survival rate for breast cancer is up to 97 percent. The key is early detection. A monthly self-exam is one of the best ways to take care of your health, and according to the National Breast Cancer Foundation, 70 percent of all breast cancers are first found by women doing their own self-checks. Annual mammograms after fifty are recommended. Many women over fifty also get a sonogram of their breasts, either at the same time as the mammogram, or six months after the mammogram, so that their breasts are being checked by one or the other screening test twice a year, instead of once a year. Because my sister was diagnosed with atypical ductal hyperplasia (a form of pre-cancer) at age forty-seven, I now get an annual MRI of my breasts at the same time as my mammogram. This is an option that should be discussed with your doctor, to see if it makes sense for you, although not all insurance companies will cover it. (Please see *Chapter 3* for more information about breast cancer.)

6. Bone Density Test (DEXA)

You want to be strong enough to take care of yourself when you get older.

Your first baseline bone density test should be at age fifty, and then subsequent tests every two years thereafter. Bone density testing is a simple procedure. Early testing for bone loss is essential to make sure you're not heading toward osteoporosis, which can cause substantial bone loss and deterioration, making you more vulnerable to broken bones. Some bone loss is treatable with medications that can stop the progression of this disease, and even reverse some bone loss. The best defense is to increase your intake of calcium and Vitamin D through supplements and food, and start a strength-training program. (See *Chapters 5* and *6*.)

7. Skin Cancer Screening

One person dies of melanoma every hour in the U.S., and a diagnosis of skin cancer occurs more times per year in the U.S. than any other type of cancer. If skin cancers are found early, there is an excellent cure rate. Undetected, however, this can be a fast-moving cancer. At least once a month, look at your body to see if there are any changes. Do this monthly check in daylight and in front of a full-length mirror. (Helpful tip: do your monthly breast exam at the same time.) If you see any changes in existing moles or spot new ones, visit your dermatologist as soon as possible. While some people are more at risk than others (fair-skinned blondes and redheads, for example), everyone is at risk. See your dermatologist every year for a full-body check, including your scalp and between your toes. (Read *Chapter 7: Love the Skin You're In* for more tips on smart skin care.)

8. Vision Screening

For the last few years, I've had to keep a 6x magnifying mirror stuck to my regular bathroom mirror so that I don't end up putting mascara on my lips. Presbyopia (an age-related condition whereby the eyes have trouble focusing on objects that are close) is a natural byproduct of getting older. Though almost everyone is affected by presbyopia, there are several eye-related diseases that are more severe. All of these can be detected in their earliest stages during your annual vision screening.

- **Glaucoma**—This is a group of diseases that cause damage to the optic nerve. The most common occurs when the eye's drainage canals are partly clogged.
- **Cataracts**—Age-related cataracts are most often seen in people over sixty. A major cause is exposure to ultraviolet B radiation from the sun. With this disease the lens over the eye starts to cloud over, affecting vision. It's fixed surgically by removing the clouded lens and replacing it with a permanent, plastic lens.
- **Macular degeneration**—This is a leading cause of blindness in older people and is caused by hardening of the arteries in the macula, which is the light-sensitive tissue in the center of the retina. An annual screening is essential because it's very hard to detect on your own. Treatment is usually medication and sometimes laser surgery.

What can you do to preserve your vision?

Exercise and eat right. Carrots really do help, offering high levels of beta-carotene (no pun intended) which is converted into Vitamin A. Vitamins C and E and Omega-3 fatty acids can help reduce the risks of cataracts. Smoking and excessive sun exposure are the worst things you can do to your eyes.

The best things you can do for your eyes:

- Don't smoke.
- Don't overdo sun exposure.
- Always wear sunglasses to protect against the rays but also the against the environment in general. (Added bonus: sunglasses help protect the delicate skin around the eyes, reducing wrinkles.)
- Wear hats whenever possible. This protects your facial skin, too.
- Eat lots of fruits and vegetables (especially carrots and sweet potatoes) and take flax seed oil daily.
- For dry eyes, use over-the-counter moisturizing eye drops several times a day but skip any of the ones that claim to get the red out, because they work only temporarily and cause your eyes to get even more red in the long run.
- Reading glasses do not have to be prescription strength to be effective. Over-the-counter is fine, as long as you buy the correct magnification number. Your ophthalmologist or optometrist can tell you what that number is.
- While using the computer, wear reading glasses that are half the number of your normal reading glasses.
- If you do a lot of work (or even fun stuff) at the computer, make sure you take regular breaks, so your eyes can have a rest. Just a few minutes of looking away will help but, if you can, look out a window or go outside every twenty minutes so that you can focus on far away objects, countering the "up close" focus of computer work.
- While at the computer, keep your seat higher, rather than lower, so that you are looking down at the computer screen. This causes your eye lids to be more closed than open, giving air less room to circulate around your eyes, which will help with "dry eye."

9. Hearing Test

By age sixty-five, one-third of us are candidates for hearing aids. And I might be one of them soon, because my husband and kids sometimes have to repeat what they've said to me—and it's not because I haven't been paying attention.(Well, most of the time.)

How often should you get your ears checked?

Your PCP will check your ears during the annual exam for wax buildup and so on. After the age of fifty, you should see a specialist every three years to evaluate your ears, ear canals, and eardrums and to make sure there are no serious problems.

What can you do to keep your hearing intact?

- If you use earbuds or headphones, ask a friend standing near you if she can hear the music. If she can, it's too loud.
- If you still go to rock concerts (and I do!) then bring along the soft, foam earplugs. You'll still be able to hear everything, but the noise level won't hurt your eardrums.
- Earwax is a protective barrier and contains bacteria-fighting elements. But too much can sometimes build up. Doctors advise against using cotton swabs in favor of over-the-counter eardrops that soften the wax so it can be gently washed out in the shower.

10. Dental Exam and Cleaning

Seeing your dentist twice a year for a dental exam and cleaning isn't just important to keep your pearly whites looking good. You need to be screened for periodontal disease (gum disease) and oral cancer.

- **Periodontal disease**—This is a chronic bacterial infection of the gums that destroys the bone and tissues that hold the teeth, and is the leading cause of tooth loss in adults. Gum disease is associated with an increased risk for heart disease and rheumatoid arthritis. Oral bacteria can enter the bloodstream, attach to fatty plaques in the coronary arteries, and cause clots to form. Regular check-ups, cleanings, brushing, and flossing several times a day greatly reduce these risks.
- **Oral cancer**—Although relatively uncommon, oral cancer kills over 8,000 people a year—twice as many deaths as cervical cancer. You should be vigilant in looking for signs: white or red spots in the mouth. If you see them, let your dentist know immediately and she will most likely refer you to an oral oncologist. Tobacco and alcohol abuse are the main oral cancer-causing suspects, but there may also be a link between oral cancer and HPV (human papillomavirus),

the same virus that causes most cervical cancers.

DO: Get Vaccinated.

After fifty, getting vaccinated against common illnesses can save us from pain, misery, and worse—influenza and pneumonia rank right behind diabetes as a leading cause of death.

Here are the vaccinations you should get and how often:

- Flu shot every year
- Pneumococcal (for pneumonia) every year after age 65
- DTP (for diptheria, tetanus, pertussis) booster every 10 years
- Zostavax (for shingles) once after age 60
- Hepatitis B before traveling to a third world country

The Master "DO" List

The most important and effective "Do" items are under your control—and most are common sense. Here is a summary of specific proactive things you can do to take charge of your health and wellness.

Right now:

- Organize medical information in one place.
- Put essential health information in your wallet.
- Find a primary care physician (PCP).

Once a year:
Annual physical exam for the following:

- Blood pressure
- Blood work
- Body measurements
- Bone density test
- Fecal occult blood test (or a colonoscopy, recommended every 4–7 years per your PCP)
- Diabetes screening
- Mammogram

Annual gynecological exam for the following:

- Pap smear
- Pelvic exam
- HPV test

Other Tests:

- Skin cancer screening
- Vaccines: flu shot, plus any others that are due

- Annual vision Screening
- Annual hearing Screening (every three years if you're doing fine)

Twice a year:
- Dental exam and cleaning

Every month:
- Skin self-check in full light in front of a full-length mirror
- Breast self-exam

Every day:
- Sleep seven to eight hours.
- Floss and brush teeth several times a day.
- Eat healthy foods that are low in saturated fats.
- Take supplements (multivitamin, calcium, Vitamin D and Omega-3 Oils).
- Exercise—including cardio and strength training.
- Keep waist size under 35" or less than half your height.
- Maintain a healthy weight.
- Wear sunscreen (at least 30 SPF), sunglasses, and a hat when outside.
- Listen to your body and look for changes in how you feel.

The Master "Don't" List

There are things you can do and choices you make—every day—to prevent some of the really nasty stuff from happening. Over 80 percent of all cancers, for example, are directly related to the use of tobacco products, to what you eat (or don't eat) and drink, and to how much you move your body. Take control and remove these "Don'ts" from your life.

Don't:
- Smoke
- Eat lots of saturated fats, processed foods, or too much salt.
- Drink more than one alcoholic drink a day or seven drinks total in a week.
- Use a tanning booth or spend time in the sun without sunscreen or a hat.
- Keep excess weight on your body—especially around your belly.
- Be sedentary.
- Have unsafe sex.
- Ignore changes in your body or assume that poor health, aches and pains, memory loss, and so on are "normal".

Most of all: Learn to listen. (To yourself.)

We're very lucky to be living in a time when many diseases and illnesses can be prevented, and some can be caught earlier than ever due to screenings. However, even without a screening, your body will almost always give you a sign when something is wrong: a nagging cough that won't go away; vaginal bleeding when you haven't had your period in four years; a chronic stomachache no matter what you eat. If you pay attention, your body will tell you a lot. So take time to listen to what it says.

Get on board.

In addition to what has been recommended in this chapter, other components of a healthy lifestyle are detailed in *Chapter 5* and *6*. Stay with the recommended programs, and review the results when you go for your next physical exam. If you make a huge effort with lifestyle changes (or even a small one, to get started) and your health numbers don't really change much, don't give up. Genetics can be a very powerful influence on our bodies. You may need a medication or two to help get you where you need to be, and that's okay. Your good lifestyle habits will still reward you, even if it seems challenging and even if it takes a long time. Every little step you take toward your goals will take you that much closer to better health. It's in your power—and it is your right—to be fit, healthy, productive, and happy for the rest of your life.

Don't worry. Be healthy.

Get more information.

To learn more, check out the following organizations and websites recommended by our experts:

- **Alzheimer's Association, www.alz.org, for information on diagnosing and treating Alzheimer's and other memory loss issues.**
- **The Alzheimer's Project, www.alzheimers project.org, is a fascinating HBO series that features the best researchers and scientists studying Alzheimer's Disease.**
- **The American Heart Association, www.americanheart.org, for information about heart health, heart disease, stroke, and diabetes.**

- **Mayo Clinic Health Information, www. mayoclinic.com,** a general health resource with helpful descriptions of specific diseases and conditions.
- **The National Cancer Institute, www. cancer.gov,** for information about cancer types, prevention, diagnostics, and treatments.
- **The National Lipid Association, www. learnyourlipids.com,** for information on cholesterol and triglycerides.

- **smokefree.gov** for tools and information to help quit smoking, including an online guide and expert counseling by phone, instant messaging, or in person.

And the following web resources:

- **www.webmd.com**
- **www.everydayhealth.com**
- **www.4women.gov**
- **www.healthcentral.com**

Chapter 2

Keep the Beat

Love Your Heart

My grandmother once told me, "Heart attacks don't run in our family. Cancer does." Thanks, Grandma, very comforting thought. But she was right. Having a family history of heart disease is a risk factor for developing it. Knowing that no one in my family had died of a heart attack offered little comfort, because I remembered reading somewhere that just being a woman over fifty automatically puts you at risk. Could this be true? I must have misread it. Maybe I didn't have my reading glasses on?

The Heart of the Matter

It was disconcerting when I realized how little I really knew about the heart, and the risks associated with heart disease. Where am I in the spectrum? Am I doing everything right to keep my heart beating for a long time? Am I really at risk just because I'm a woman over fifty? I had no idea.

This is what I wanted to know:

- **The basics of cardiovascular disease**
- **The risks for women over fifty**
- **Screenings and tests that we should consider**

- **Ways to prevent heart disease**
- **The warning signs of heart attack and stroke**

I'm not alone.

Most women are as confused about heart disease as I am. We still think it's a "man's disease" even though it kills more women than men every year. This lack of understanding means that many women tend to ignore the physical symptoms of heart disease, and doctors often suggest that stress is the culprit. Fortunately, the focus is starting to shift toward post-menopausal women, with more studies highlighting our own unique health risks. The more we learn, the healthier we will be.

What do we need to know?

Dr. Jennifer Mieres is one of the country's best and most respected "healthy heart experts." She is the Director of Nuclear Cardiology at NYU Medical Center, and a national spokesperson for the American Heart Association's "Go Red for Women" campaign. A champion of patient advocacy and community outreach on heart disease in women, Dr. Mieres started my education with this very important statistic:

Cardiovascular disease is the number one killer of women.

Just to drive the point home, she added a few more disconcerting facts:

- Heart disease accounts for one in three deaths per year for women—and more than all cancers combined.
- Stroke is the number three killer of women, right behind heart disease and cancer, but the number one cause of disability.
- One in eight women between the ages of forty-five and sixty-five already have some kind of heart disease.
- More women than men die from heart disease.

Women need to be better informed about heart disease:

- More than 95 percent of women who die from cardiovascular disease have at least one major risk factor.
- 95 percent of women who have heart attacks start to feel their symptoms a month or more before the actual heart attack occurs.
- Women tend to wait longer than men before going to the hospital.
- Two-thirds of women who have heart attacks never make it to the hospital.
- For women, age becomes a risk factor after fifty.

We can change these statistics.

- Women can lower their risk of cardiovascular disease by over 82 percent by making simple healthy lifestyle changes.
- Over 80 percent of heart disease is preventable.

What do these facts tell us?

First (if it isn't obvious by now), heart disease is a woman's single greatest health threat, especially as we age. Just being over fifty and a woman puts you at risk. Second, women tend to ignore the symptoms. But here's the kicker: most heart disease can be prevented.

But to understand the risks and the best prevention strategies, there is some basic information you need to know about the workings of the heart and arteries, and what all of the medical terminology means.

What is Cardiovascular Disease (CVD)?

Cardiovascular disease, also known as CVD, is a label used for the main group of heart-related diseases and abnormalities, including heart attacks, stroke, congestive heart failure, peripheral vascular disease, and congenital heart disease. CVD is the term used throughout this chapter to refer to heart-related diseases in general.

What are Coronary Artery Disease (CAD) and Coronary Heart Disease (CHD)?

These two are common terms for the same condition. They are used interchangeably to describe a disease caused by the narrowing and hardening of your arteries (atherosclerosis) which decreases the supply of blood to the heart. It is a type of CVD.

What is atherosclerosis?

Arteries are the vessels that carry blood from your heart to the rest of your body, and they can stiffen and thicken as you age. That process is called arteriosclerosis—meaning "hard arteries"—and it can make your heart pump like crazy to push blood through the arteries. When the arteries narrow and harden due to the buildup of fatty substances— the usual cause—it is called atherosclerosis. (I remember growing up, hearing about elderly family members and neighbors who had "hardening of the arteries"—much easier to say, don't you think?) This whole process is silent and slow. It happens over a period of years and is the usual cause of heart attacks, strokes, and other cardiovascular diseases. It is preventable and treatable and, because atherosclerosis is so important in understanding CVD, you need to know more about it.

Basic facts about "hardening of the arteries":

- Atherosclerosis starts when the inside of the arteries is injured due to smoking, high blood pressure, high cholesterol, diabetes or a combination of these.
- Inflammation in the injured areas creates bumps along the artery walls, and cholesterol plaque can form along those bumps.
- As atherosclerosis progresses, bumps

get bigger and can create a blockage in the artery.

- When arteries are clogged, blood flow to muscles and organs is reduced, which can cause other problems.
- Once arteries narrow as a result of the build up of plaque, they may temporarily stop blood from flowing, which can cause pain.
- Sometimes a section of plaque can suddenly break off or rupture, which can form a clot that sticks in the artery and blocks the flow of blood.
- If a clot occurs in the heart, it can cause a heart attack.
- If a clot occurs in the brain, it can cause a stroke. If a clot occurs in the legs, it can cause peripheral artery disease (PAD).

Atherosclerosis occurs in different areas of the body—the heart, brain and legs—causing different kinds of CVD:

- **Coronary Artery Disease (CAD):** When plaque starts to build up in arteries of the heart it is called coronary artery disease (CAD). CAD can cause angina (chest pain). A sudden rupture which creates a clot can cause a heart attack. CAD is the number one single killer of women.
- **Cerebrovascular disease:** When plaque builds up in arteries of the brain, it is known as cerebrovascular disease. If that plaque ruptures and blocks blood flow to the brain, it will cause a stroke. Stroke has the potential for permanent brain damage or death and is the number three killer of women, but it is the number one cause of disability. Temporary blockages in brain arteries can cause transient ischemic attacks (TIAs), which are mini-strokes that warn you that a real stroke might be coming down the pike.
- **Peripheral Artery Disease (PAD):** When arteries in your legs harden and narrow due to plaque buildup, this can cause poor circulation, pain while walking, and wounds and sores that don't heal. PAD is a common condition that occurs in people over fifty and is a leading cause of disability in people with diabetes. Sometimes people think that the pain they feel in their legs while walking is a normal part of aging, which can often lead to non-diagnosis and non-treatment.

How do you know if you have atherosclerosis?

If you have any of the specific symptoms of CVD—chest pain, chest pressure, unexplained fatigue, decrease in exercise capacity, shortness of breath, poor circulation, or leg pain—you should see your doctor, who may refer you to a cardiologist. Your regular primary care physician (PCP) will also be looking for signs of atherosclerosis during your annual check-up. When the doctor takes your pulse, checks your blood pressure, or listens to your heart with the stethoscope, she is checking that your arteries are clear.

If your doctor suspects atherosclerosis, some of these additional tests may be used to help check for blockages in your arteries:

- **Blood tests to measure cholesterol and blood sugar.**
- **Ultrasound tests to measure blood flow and blood pressure in different parts of your body.**
- **Electrocardiogram (ECG or EKG) to measure the electrical impulses from your heart. Sometimes an EKG is combined with exercise known as a stress test where you walk or run on a treadmill or ride a stationary bike.**
- **Angiogram is a kind of X-ray that uses a special dye that is injected into your arteries to see how well blood is moving through your body and to spot any blockages.**

What can you do to prevent atherosclerosis?

Whether you need a procedure or a medication, adopting a healthy lifestyle is the real key to prevention. No matter where you are in the spectrum of heart disease, and what your personal risk factors are, you can reduce your risk by over 82 percent if you eat right, exercise, don't smoke, keep your blood pressure in check, and maintain a good weight.

What can be done if you've been diagnosed with atherosclerosis?

For women who already have serious atherosclerosis, certain drugs can slow or prevent the progression of plaque buildup and slow the damage to the arteries. Depending on the degree, location, and cause of the buildup, doctors might prescribe cholesterol-lowering drugs like statins or fibrates, or anticoagulants like Coumadin, or antiplatelet medications like aspirin. Sometimes medications that treat risk factors like high blood pressure or diabetes are also helpful.

In severe cases of atherosclerosis, clot-dissolving drugs, an invasive procedure such as angioplasty, stent placement, or other surgical procedures may be necessary. Angioplasty is a fairly common procedure in which doctors open a clogged artery with a laser or use a thin catheter to inflate a tiny balloon that compresses the plaque against the artery walls. Sometimes a mesh tube (called a stent) is then placed in the artery to keep it open. Endarterectomy is a surgical process that actually removes the plaque and fats from a clogged artery and it is often used in the neck to help prevent stroke. In the most drastic cases, surgeons will actually graft a bypass—made from synthetic tubing or a blood vessel from another part of the body—to go around a blocked artery.

What is Hidden Heart Disease?

Although millions of women have been diagnosed with CVD, there are a few million more who have a very hard-to-diagnose form of heart disease known as "Coronary Microvascular Syndrome." Also known as "Hidden Heart Disease," in this condition plaque builds up on the walls of extremely small arteries, rather than in the larger arteries, as is typical in atherosclerosis. What does this mean? If you have symptoms of heart disease such as chest pressure or shortness of breath, but your angiogram (a test to pick up on blockages in larger arteries) shows that everything is normal, don't stop there. Make sure your doctor knows that you have these symptoms. There are several highly sensitive screening tests that you may need that are specifically geared to picking up coronary microvascular syndrome. Having coronary microvascular syndrome is a risk factor for CVD, so be on the alert.

Three tests you should be aware of are:
- **Carotid Doppler ultrasound**—sound waves that pick up blockages in the neck

- **Cardiac CT scan**—super fast CT scan that sees calcium buildup in the coronary arteries, as well as possible blockages
- **Magnetic resonance imaging (MRI)**—can detect severe blockages in coronary arteries

These tests would only be used if you are having symptoms and there is no other explanation for those symptoms.

How do you know if you're at risk for cardiovascular disease?

In the past, women's heart health was assessed by the same standards as men's. We were placed in the high, medium, or low risk categories using the same set of criteria as men, and then we were treated accordingly. That is no longer the case. We now have our own set of criteria for determining our lifetime risks for CVD. They are:

- High Risk, if you have already been diagnosed with CVD, and/or have multiple risk factors
- At Risk, if you have even ONE risk factor (see list below)

What are the risk factors for CVD?

I've listed them with a quick look at "the numbers" (See *Chapter 1: Feelin' Alright*.) Being a woman over fifty is a risk factor, so guess what? We are all in the "at risk" category for CVD. If you add one or more of the following risk factors to "being a woman over fifty," you will be putting yourself into the "high risk" category. So, our goal is to keep ourselves—for the rest of our lives—in the "at risk" category, to the best of our abilities. Almost 90 percent of all heart attacks are caused by the following risk factors.

- **High Blood Pressure**—It should be 120/70 or under.
- **High Blood Sugar Level**—It should be under 100.
- **High Total and LDL Cholesterol**—LDL must be under 100 (but aim for under 70) and the total should not be higher than 200.
- **High Triglycerides**—Aim for under 150.
- **Visceral fat**—This is the fat around your abdomen, indicated by a waist

measurement of over 35 inches or more than half your height.

- **Inactivity**—Even if you're thin but you don't exercise.
- **If you smoke**—It's hard, but try to quit if you're still smoking.
- **A strong family history of CVD**—Learn what you can about family members who have been affected.
- **Too much stress**—Get it out of your life. Reading this list probably just stressed you out, but think about it this way: you *can* control most of these risk factors.

Two of these factors you cannot control: having a strong family history of cardiovascular disease and being a woman over fifty. But, don't go crazy about this. If you're really doing everything you can to minimize your risks, including taking medication if necessary, you'll be fine. Many of these risk factors are in your control: smoking, weight control, stress, and exercising. If you're in the "high risk" category, look at the risk factors list, and work on managing the ones you can.

Did you have pre-eclampsia during pregnancy?

There might be a connection between women who have pre-eclampsia (a condition that results in high blood pressure and leaky blood vessels) during pregnancy and future risk for cardiovascular disease. While the condition itself goes away soon after the pregnancy is over, women who develop pre-eclampsia could have a greater risk of a heart attack or stroke in later years. Let your PCP know if you had this condition during your pregnancy. Addressing this will help women and their doctors focus on preventing future CVD events by making the necessary lifestyle adjustments even earlier.

Metabolic Syndrome: Three or more of these risk factors, and you have it.

Metabolic Syndrome is a term used to describe a cluster of independent risk factors that increase the risk of developing diabetes, heart disease, and stroke. These are the same as the American Heart Association's Risk Factor list, and each one, on its own, puts a woman at risk for heart disease. But women are said to have metabolic syndrome if they have three or more of the following:

- **Waist measurement of more than 35″**
- **HDL (good cholesterol) of less than 50**
- **Triglycerides of more than 150**
- **Blood pressure higher than 130/85**
- **Blood sugar of more than 100**

This group of risk factors is usually caused by being overweight or obese, having poor nutrition, and by not getting enough physical activity.

Can metabolic syndrome be prevented?

Absolutely. Metabolic Syndrome isn't exactly a disease, but is more like a simultaneous measurement of several inter-related aspects of our health. We can control most of them. The most effective and safest way is to make changes in our lifestyle. We have to control our weight, reduce the fat around our waists, move our bodies every day, and eat a heart-healthy diet. Even if you do everything right, it's possible that you may need medication to improve some of the risk factors such as hypertension and high cholesterol—and those decisions should always be made with your doctor.

Another expert to help explain the workings of the heart.

In addition to the excellent information and advice I got from Dr. Mieres, I asked Dr. James Underberg to give me a more detailed understanding of how cholesterol affects the heart. Dr. Underberg specializes in preventive cardiovascular medicine, lipidology, and hypertension. His passion is researching the latest findings about the connection between lipids and heart disease in women and he graciously gave me the opportunity to pick his brain. With the combined input and experience of Dr. Mieres and

Dr. Underberg, we can better understand the complexities of the heart.

Besides the general risk factors for heart disease and stroke, are there other ways to gauge your heart health?

An annual check-up with your primary care physician (PCP) as discussed in *Chapter 1* is a critical part of your heart disease prevention strategy. In addition to helping your doctor assess your weight and general fitness, your annual exam will include checks on heart health basics like blood pressure, blood counts, and measurements of cholesterol, triglycerides, and blood sugar. Get those numbers checked every year—and adjust your lifestyle to keep them at the recommended levels.

Are there any special tests you should know about?

Over 85 percent of all sudden cardiac deaths are seen in people who are considered to be at low risk for CVD. Several tests were created which go beyond the traditional testing for CVD, to try to understand why people who are

seemingly healthy, in great shape, and have normal cholesterol levels still develop heart disease. These tests are not for everyone, but they are useful diagnostic tools for people who are healthy, with relatively low risk for heart disease, but have a strong family history of heart disease. They are also useful if your numbers from the regular tests (cholesterol, HDL/LDL, etc.) are borderline and your doctor is sitting on the fence with regards to putting you on medication. The usefulness of some of these tests is still debated within the medical community, but some experts feel very strongly about considering one or more of these tests, depending upon the risk profile of the person. Dr. Underberg described some of the special screening tests that you should know about:

- **LipoProfile ApoB test—ApoB, short for apolipoprotein B, is a component of LDL cholesterol. Several important clinical studies have shown that high ApoB levels may be more closely linked to heart disease risk factors than the LDL cholesterol for which millions of Americans are screened each year. ApoB proteins are particles that serve as little** vehicles that carry the LDL around our bloodstream. The particles bang into the artery wall, get in, and then release their passengers—LDL cholesterol—which then sticks to the artery walls, causing plaque build-up and eventually athero-sclerosis. According to the American Diabetes Association and the American College of Cardiologists, the ApoB test should be used in assessing the risk of anyone with low HDL, high LDL, high triglycerides, high blood pressure, or high waist circumference. The test is easy, and can be tacked onto your normal blood test at your annual exam.

- **High Sensitive C-Reactive Protein (hs-CRP) test**—C-reactive protein is a substance that is released into our blood if there is inflammation anywhere inside the body. Atherosclerosis is an inflamma-tory process, and so it causes CRP to be released into the blood, but only in a very small amount. The high-sensitivity CRP test is done to see if there is an increased level of the protein, indicating possible atherosclerosis. The ideal hs-CRP level for women is less then 1.0. Elevated levels of hs-CRP do not necessarily mean that you have heart disease, but they have been associated with a much higher risk of heart attack in women, even when the LDL number is low. Statin medication (Crestor or Lipitor, for example) can help to lower the levels of CRP in women without heart disease as a preventive measure. Women who are known to have heart disease will probably be put on statin medication to lower both the CRP and the cholesterol levels. Have a talk with your doctor about having this test, and then, once you see the results, you can decide together if you should start statin medication. The best way to lower CRP levels—hello, broken record—is to low-er and then maintain your weight. CRP is released whenever there is inflammation in the body, so it's possible that elevated levels could be caused by an unrelated infection such as arthritis, the flu, or even a sprained ankle. This is why if it's ele-vated, it's usually best to be tested at least twice, sometimes three times, before a conclusion is reached.

- **Ankle Brachial Index**—Peripheral Artery Disease, or PAD, is caused by the accumulation of plaque in the arteries of your arms or, more often, the legs. Do you get a cramp in your legs when you walk?

Is it hard to walk a short distance due to the cramping and because you're feeling tired? Don't think it's just because you're getting on in years. It could be due to PAD, which usually happens after menopause. Not everyone has symptoms, though, so it might be a good idea to talk to your PCP about having the PAD test, also called the ankle brachial index test, which entails measuring the ratio of blood pressure in your arm to that in your ankle. If it's different, it could show that a blockage is happening in the leg. If you are over fifty and have ever smoked or have diabetes, consider the PAD test as a precaution.

How can you prevent heart disease?

Keep your weight down, keep your waist under 35 inches, keep blood pressure and cholesterol at recommended levels, move your body every day, and don't smoke. Dr. Underberg also shared some highlights of the American Heart Association's recent report to doctors on preventing cardiovascular disease in women:

- **Women who already have CVD and/or multiple risk factors are at a significantly increased risk for future heart attacks or stroke and should have more aggressive preventive therapies.**

- **Lifestyle changes like weight control, blood pressure management, exercise, healthy eating, and quitting smoking—should be more aggressively encouraged by doctors to prevent CVD in women.**

- **Women should walk briskly for a minimum of 30 minutes most days of the week (or engage in some other moderate-intensity exercise), even if it is in 10-minute increments throughout the day. Longer walks of 60 to 90 minutes are ideal. Studies have shown that women who have several risk factors or have CVD already would benefit most from walking far and walking often, as opposed to engaging in high intensity or short workouts.**

- **All women should reduce saturated fats, processed, salty foods in their diets, and work to increase "good fats" like olive oil.**

- **Women should consider eating oily fish (salmon, for example) twice a week, and/or take a fish oil supplement (at least 1 gram) every day.**

- **Antioxidant supplements (such as Vita-**

mins C, E and beta-carotene) have not been proven to prevent CVD (or much else for that matter) and should not be used for this purpose.

- Folic acid, while once thought to help prevent CVD in women, should no longer be recommended for this purpose.
- Hormone Therapy (HT), while a good idea for some women to help alleviate severe menopausal symptoms, should never be prescribed for women to prevent CVD.
- Low dose aspirin (a baby aspirin, for example) has been shown to be beneficial for women over 65 in lowering the risk of stroke (not necessarily heart disease), but this should be discussed with your doctor.

The Warning Signs—Just in Case

All of us have at least one risk factor for heart disease—our age—and since heart disease can sneak up on us, we need to know the symptoms of heart attack and stroke. I asked Dr. Alexandra Stern, a cardiologist at NYU, to review

To salt or not to salt?

High-blood pressure can be related to high levels of salt intake, but Dr. Underberg explained that while only half of hypertensive patients are salt-sensitive, almost all of us consume more salt than we need. The average person eats more than twice the recommended limit of one teaspoon per day, and too much salt can raise blood pressure, which can increase the risk of heart attack and stroke. Salt is still a necessary nutrient, though, and lowering your intake of salt too much can increase your lipoprotein and cholesterol levels. You don't want to eliminate it, just reduce it to the right level. Salt is a major ingredient in processed and fast foods. If you cut back on those, you automatically cut back on the amount of salt you eat. Try sea salt—it's more intense so you'll use less. (See *Chapter 5: You=What You Eat* for more on healthful eating.)

the classic symptoms of heart attack and stroke, as well as those that seem to be more common in women. She's one of the smartest and most straight-to-the-point doctors I've encountered. Here's what she told me:

Heart Attack

Most women who have heart attacks feel symptoms weeks before they strike, but they often ignore the signs. They don't want to bother anyone; they think they can handle it on their own; they don't believe it could happen to them. More women would survive heart attacks if they acted on the signs. It's a common, but incorrect belief that people always feel chest pain if they're having a heart attack, like in the movies. Women are less likely than men to feel chest pain during a heart attack and often experience "atypical" symptoms.

Classic symptoms of a heart attack:

- Chest pain (this is usually with an acute heart attack)
- Pressure or tightness in the chest (like someone is sitting on you)
- Shortness of breath
- Sweating
- Pain or pressure in one or both arms that seems to start from the chest area

Symptoms more common in women:

- Pressure that radiates from the chest to the back, neck, or jaw
- Strange sensation often described as the bra straps being too tight
- Nausea and/or vomiting
- Indigestion or abdominal pain
- Weakness
- Unexplained fatigue
- Decrease in exercise tolerance
- Dizziness
- Lightheadedness
- Unexplained anxiety
- Heart palpitations (racing heart)
- Cold sweats
- Paleness

Whatever your risk level, always be prepared in the event of a heart attack.

- Keep a Personal Medical Information File in an accessible location (see *Chapter 1: Feelin' Alright*) including insurance information, a list of all your medications, a copy of any EKG reports, and a list of your risk factors.

- Make your heart attack action plan known to everyone in your household so they're as prepared as you.

If you are experiencing symptoms of a heart attack:

- **Call 911.** Do not delay more than 5 minutes. Do not call your doctor. Do not call a family member. Call 9-1-1 first, then call your doctor.
- **Do not drive yourself to the hospital.** Women who arrive by ambulance are treated more quickly.
- **Chew an uncoated aspirin** while you are waiting for the ambulance to help prevent further clots from developing. A chewed aspirin gets into the bloodstream more quickly than one that is swallowed.
- **Take a nitroglycerin tablet.** If you've already had a heart attack, your doctor should give you a supply. If you have chest pains or any symptoms that do not go away five minutes after taking one tablet, take another one every five minutes while waiting for the ambulance to arrive.

- **Grab your Medical Organization File** or ask someone from your household to get it.

A heart attack can lead to heart failure.

Once you have a heart attack, you are more prone to having chronic heart failure, which is a very serious condition. Heart failure is when the heart is no longer effective at pumping blood. Symptoms include shortness of breath, fatigue, swelling of the limbs, and fluid collecting in the lungs. Heart failure does not mean that your heart has stopped, as its name might imply, it means that your heart has become an inefficient pump. And people who have had a heart attack are at a high risk of developing heart failure. Early detection of heart disease is key to the prevention of heart failure.

Stroke

Stroke is the number three cause of death in the U.S., behind heart disease and cancer, and it's the number one cause of serious, life-changing, long-term disability. Through hard work and physical therapy, many stroke survivors can retrieve all or most of their physical and mental abilities.

Mark McEwen: Stroke survivor and cautionary tale.

Mark McEwen is a lucky man. He suffered a major stroke in 2005 but today he walks, talks, eats, drives, and does all those other things that we take for granted. It took him years of grueling physical therapy, special exercises, and lots of love and care from his family and friends to get him to where he is now.

My husband, Howard, has been one of Mark's closest friends since college and I've known Mark and his family for over seventeen years. We love him dearly, and it still hurts me to think about all the agony he went through.

But what happened to Mark is a cautionary tale for anyone, whether you're a man or a woman. Here's his story:

One night, Mark was in the airport, returning home to his family after a short trip. As he waited to board, he suddenly felt nauseous, weak, and just "off." Wisely, he didn't board the plane, but instead asked the airline personnel to call for help, and was taken to the local emergency room.

A misdiagnosis if ever there was one.

An experienced ER doctor and a nurse in a hospital in a major U.S. city checked Mark out thoroughly, took note of his symptoms (nausea, severe dizziness, not lucid), his blood pressure (high), his age (over fifty), and pronounced that he had . . . the stomach flu.

Stroke? It never even entered Mark's mind.

After a few hours, the ER staff told Mark that he could go home with a friend, and should drink plenty of fluids. No one at the hospital had mentioned the word "stroke." It hadn't even entered Mark's mind because he knew nothing about stroke, what it meant, or what the signs were. No one else had mentioned it and he felt that he was in the hands of professionals. Why would he doubt their diagnosis?

Although he still felt sick, Mark decided to fly back home. While on the plane, Mark had what turned out to be a massive stroke—and nobody noticed. He couldn't move or talk for a while but was finally able to stand up and get himself off the plane and onto a waiting wheelchair. Astoundingly, the skycap never asked if he was okay, but just wheeled Mark toward the exit, doing his job. From the chair, Mark tried to call his wife but after he pressed speed dial and heard her voice, he couldn't say anything. He pressed the speed-dial button nine or ten times and heard her answer but no words came out of his mouth. The wheelchair attendant had no clue about the drama that was unfolding in front of him, as Mark was facing forward and couldn't talk—he simply wheeled Mark to the baggage claim area and left him there. Mark continued to press the speed dial button on his phone, desperate to get someone, anyone, to help him. A stranger glanced over at him and as soon as their eyes met, the stranger saw that something definitely wasn't right. The man walked over, took the phone from Mark's hand, got his wife on the phone and together they pieced together enough information to realize that Mark was in very serious condition. The stranger called 911, and then once he knew that an ambulance was on its way, simply walked into the terminal, and disappeared, seemingly unaware that he had just saved a life.

The moral to the story? The early signs of a stroke can be misconstrued as the flu.

You need to know more about stroke.

A stroke occurs when the blood flow and oxygen to the brain are stopped due to a clot. When this happens, it literally starves the brain of oxygen and can quickly—and permanently— kill parts of the brain.

There are two types of stroke:
- **Ischemic stroke** is the most common kind of stroke (about nine out of every ten). It occurs when there is a sudden lack of blood flow to some part of the brain because of a blood clot. This is usually caused by atherosclerosis.
- **Hemorrhagic stroke** is caused by

bleeding in the brain, often due to an aneurysm in an artery. An aneurysm is a weak part of an artery that bursts, filling the brain with blood.

What are the signs that you may be having a stroke?

It's important to remember that for a stroke, the symptoms are SUDDEN. You may be having a stroke if you experience the following symptoms:

- **numbness or weakness in your face, arm, or leg, especially on one side of your body**
- **confusion, trouble speaking, or trouble understanding what is being said**
- **trouble seeing with one or both eyes**
- **trouble walking, loss of balance, or dizziness**
- **severe headache**

Some less common symptoms are:

- **pain in your face, leg, or arm**
- **hiccups**
- **nausea**
- **exhaustion**
- **chest pain**
- **shortness of breath**
- **pounding or racing heartbeat**

Many of the signs of stroke are flu-like—nausea, exhaustion, shortness of breath. But in a stroke, it comes on . . . suddenly.

If you think you are having a stroke, act quickly. A stroke needs to be treated within three hours after the symptoms start, and preferably within one hour, to maximize chances of survival and recovery.

What if you're with someone who might be having a stroke?

The National Stroke Association has developed the "Think FAST" program to help identify the signs of a stroke:

- **Face:** **Smile. Does one side of the face droop?**
- **Arms:** **Raise both arms. Does one arm drift down?**
- **Speech:** **Repeat a sentence. Are the words slurred?**
- **Time:** **Stroke is a major emergency. Call 9-1-1 ASAP.**

If you or someone you know experiences stroke symptoms, even for a few minutes, don't ignore them. Brief stroke signs that disappear within twenty-four hours may mean that you've had a mini-stroke.

A "mini-stroke" is a warning that a big one could be imminent.

A mini-stroke—transient ischemic attack (TIA)—occurs when there is a temporary reduction of blood flow to the brain. Symptoms may last a few minutes or even a day. TIAs are incredibly important warning signs because they indicate that a full-fledged stroke may happen. One in ten people who have a TIA will have a stroke within ninety days, half within the first forty-eight hours. This is likely what my friend Mark experienced.

There may be some symptoms of a mini-stroke, but not always. Most common are:

- **weakness or tingling in an arm or leg**
- **sudden temporary loss of vision in one eye**
- **sudden dizziness**

Mark's life was changed forever.

Recently, Mark was visiting us in New York, and during a heart-healthy dinner of whole wheat pasta, fresh tomato sauce, green beans, salad, and a glass of Pinot Noir, he told us about what he's doing differently now. "I made a vow to myself and to my family after my rehabilitation," he said. "For the rest of my life, I will do everything in my power to stay on top of this by watching my weight, eating healthy food, exercising regularly, and by keeping my blood pressure and cholesterol in check with my healthy lifestyle and my meds. Nothing is going to stop me." Mark is determined not to let stroke come his way again. His mother-in-law gave him a sign that says: "Never, ever, ever give up." For Mark, that says it all.

What does Mark want us to learn from his story of survival?

Mark is very lucky to be one of the 500,000 stroke survivors of 2005, and he will be the first to say so. But he also knows that having had a stroke is the number one risk factor for having another stroke. This has made him want to help us really understand our risks and to do everything we can to keep a stroke from ever happening to us.

The changes Mark made, and the things he urges us to do:

- Know your risk factors.
- Do something about all the "modifiable risk factors" such as: high blood pressure, high cholesterol, smoking, obesity, drinking to excess, type 2 diabetes.
- Learn the signs of stroke.
- Never ignore your body.
- Don't let them tell you it's the flu.
- Learn CPR.

Why learn CPR?

People who know CPR can administer first aid to heart attack and stroke victims before the ambulance arrives. The American Heart Association is on a mission to make sure that everyone in the U.S. can properly administer CPR. They offer free classes (and even a down-loadable First Aid and CPR guide for the Apple iphone). Check their website for a listing of Family & Friends CPR classes near you (www. americanheart.org) or call them at 877-AHA-4CPR to get trained as soon as you can.

Get on board.

To stay heart healthy for the rest of your life, our experts recommend this plan:

- Exercise every day (see *Chapter 6: Move That Body*).
- Eat right (see *Chapter 5: You=What You Eat*).
- Take 1 gram of fish oil supplements a day.
- Take 1,500 mg of Vitamin D a day.
- Drink in moderation (heart-healthy red wine is a good choice).
- Never smoke again.
- Keep your waist under 35" or less than half your height.
- Keep your blood pressure below 120/70.
- Know your family's heart history.
- Get an annual physical exam to check cholesterol and triglyceride levels.
- Ask your doctor if any of the special screening tests are recommended, including: ApoB test or LDL Particle Number test, High Sensitivity CRP test, Ankle Brachial Index test
- Listen to your body and never ignore the symptoms of CVD.
- Get trained in CPR.
- Advocate for your own health and never

- hesitate to get a second opinion.
- Share everything you've learned with every woman you know, regardless of age.
- Stay in touch with the latest research by periodically reviewing the information sources listed below.

Get More Information

Review these websites and books for more information on having a healthy heart.

Your Heart

- American Heart Association, www.AmericanHeartAssociation.org
- American Lipid Association, www.lipid.org
- "The Healthy Heart Handbook for Women" 2007, www.NHLBI.org

- www.hearthealthywomen.org
- *Heart Smart for Black Women and Latinas*, by Dr. Jennifer H. Mieres, MD, FAHA, St. Martin's Press 2008
- www.womenheart.org
- Women's Health Initiative (WHI), www.whi.org

Stroke

- American Society of Hypertension, www.ash-us.org
- American Stroke Association, www.strokeassociation.org
- www.markmcewen.com
- National Stroke Association, www.stroke.org
- *After the Stroke: My Journey Back to Life*, by Mark McEwen, Gotham Books, 2009

Chapter 3

Changes Down Under

Getting through Menopause (and Other Stuff)

A Fond Farewell to an Old Friend

When we talk about being a woman and over fifty, there is one big, unavoidable topic: menopause.

I went through transitional menopause, also called perimenopause, without a great deal of fanfare, or so it seemed to me. A few years ago, my period started to become less frequent, until one day in November 2003 I saw that particular "friend" (I still can't believe we grew up calling it that) for the last time.

There were a few months leading up to the big event, during which I tossed and turned, woke up at 4 a.m., kept a fan blowing on me all night, and (according to my kids and husband) acted grumpy. It wasn't horrible, just uncomfortable, and it didn't last that long. Many women experience more torturous aspects of menopause—hot flashes, mood swings, uncomfortable sex—and there are different schools of thought on how best to address them. The doctors I spoke with agree that the optimal plan of action depends upon a woman's individual physical health, family history, and the degree to which she is suffering from the symptoms.

Ch-ch-ch-changes

I was confused about what was happening to my body (flashback to when I was going through that other change: puberty), and increasingly unnerved by information I heard in the news and from friends about certain treatments. Some questions I had were:

- **Would the symptoms get worse?**
- **Should I be doing something special for it?**
- **Were replacement hormones (HT) dangerous?**
- **What about bio-identical hormones?**
- **Would my bones get thin and break?**
- **Was I more likely to get cancer?**
- **Was I now more at risk for a heart attack or stroke?**
- **Would I ever have sex again?**

I went to see Dr. Clarel Antoine, ob-gyn at New York University's Langone Medical Center in Manhattan. Dr. Antoine brought both of my daughters into the world, and we credit him for saving the life of our oldest, Sarah, who made a shocking and unexpected entry into the world at 27 weeks, weighing just over 2 pounds. She remained in the hospital for two and a half months. It was quite an experience for all of us, but today she is a healthy and happy teenager. Dr. Antoine has earned a special—and especially trustworthy—place in my heart.

Cut through the noise; look at the patient.

While Sarah spent those months in the Neonatology Intensive Care Unit, there were moments when we were not sure if she was going to make it. She was hooked up to monitors to check her heart, breathing, and oxygen intake. The monitors beeped constantly. It was terrifying. Whenever Dr. Antoine came to visit Sarah, he did not appear to focus on the monitors. He looked at Sarah. He could tell if she was distressed or not just by looking at her.

That's how Dr. Antoine suggested I deal with the new challenges that come with being fifty: don't get overwhelmed by all the noise. Understand your body, and look at it carefully. You can read

every book, review all the websites, and have all the information you could ever want about the challenges of menopause, the benefits and problems associated with Hormone Therapy, the potential of developing osteoporosis, and the risks of certain cancers as we age. But when all is said and done, Dr. Antoine—who has dedicated his life to improving women's health and bringing compassion to medicine—believes it all comes down to one thing: you are an individual with a unique story, family history, and experience of menopause. Be informed, read the books, and Google everything, but most of all, make your doctor look at you, listen to you, and help you investigate your symptoms. Only then can you decide what's best for you.

The Invasion of the Body Snatchers

This was reassuring, but I still wanted to know: what's happening to my body, and why?

Dr. Antoine recommended that I meet with Dr. Margaret Nachtigall, a leading NYU reproductive endocrinologist and an authority on women's health issues and menopause. Dr. Nachtigall who is one of the most compassionate and lovely people I've ever met, held my hand and explained it all in easy-to-understand language.

It starts with estrogen.

From puberty to menopause our bodies make estrogen—one of three primary female hormones—from our ovaries. (The other two are progesterone and androgens.) Estrogen stimulates the development of adult sex organs during puberty, helps retain calcium in the bones, regulates the balance of good and bad cholesterol, and aids in other body functions. During perimenopause (the transition phase to full menopause which can last up to six years or more, but usually less) the production of estrogen slows down. After menopause (or if a woman has her ovaries removed), it stops. When a woman has gone twelve months without a menstrual period, she has officially reached menopause, which many women experience by the age of fifty-one.

What happens when the estrogen stops?

The gradual slowdown—and then end—of estrogen production marks the natural end of your ability to conceive. But it also causes a series of changes in your body that can wreak havoc on your quality of life.

Because of estrogen's multiple functions, every organ can be affected as you adjust to life without it. Over 75 percent of women have some symptoms of perimenopause, which can include:

- **Mood swings**
- **Migraines**
- **Hot flashes**
- **Dizziness**
- **Weight gain**
- **Lack of libido**
- **Vaginal dryness**
- **Dry eyes**
- **Dry skin**
- **Increased sleep latency (the time from when we put our heads on the pillow until the time we actually fall asleep)**
- **Sleep disturbances (waking up during the night and not being able to fall back to sleep)**
- **Osteoporosis (loss of calcium from the**

bones, which leaves them brittle and prone to fractures)

You don't have to suffer through this.

- **You can take steps to counter all or most of these symptoms.**

What can you do right now?

- **Stay healthy.** Maintain a common-sense "smart lifestyle" approach: eating well, keeping a good weight, getting plenty of sleep, and exercising regularly. A healthy body is more adaptable and resilient.
- **Eat well.** Dark green vegetables and whole grains and foods rich in calcium and Vitamin D can mitigate some of the symptoms of menopause and prevent weight gain. Natural phytoestrogens in soy-based foods (like soymilk, tofu, and tempeh) can help to reduce hot flashes and other effects of estrogen loss. (Detailed nutrition information is in Chapter 5: *You=What You Eat.*)
- **Exercise.** Regular exercise helps avoid weight gain, evens out moods, and makes it easier to get to sleep and stay asleep. Strength training helps preserve bone density and muscle mass against the dangers of osteoporosis. (Specific exercises and workouts are in *Chapter 6: Move That Body.*)

For more persistent or uncomfortable symptoms, there are other possibilities:

Hormone therapy (HT)

HT is a form of drug therapy in which you are given estrogen to replace the estrogen that you are no longer producing. If you have not had a hysterectomy and still have your uterus (which is most of us) you will be given progesterone with the estrogen, which will reduce the risk of uterine cancer. Estrogen and progesterone therapy together = HT.

The benefits of estrogen include:

- Diminished hot flashes
- Improved sleep patterns
- Decreased depression and mood swings
- Vaginal walls kept from thinning or becoming too dry
- Strengthened bones

Estrogen alone? No.

It's not recommended. Years ago, doctors

prescribed "unopposed estrogen replacement" but that treatment is no longer advised. Estrogen alone can contribute to the development of endometrial cancer. If a woman has had a hysterectomy, however, there is no longer a worry about this form of cancer, and so ET (Estrogen Therapy) can be used.

Estrogen with progesterone? Yes.

Levels of progesterone, which is produced by your ovaries during the ovulation process, drop dramatically once you stop ovulating. Progesterone helps to prepare your body for pregnancy, but it also acts as an "estrogen-balancing agent" and can protect against the dangers of excess estrogen, like an increased risk of uterine cancer. Progesterone is almost always prescribed with estrogen.

Benefits of HT (estrogen/ progesterone combination):

All the benefits of using estrogen (see above list), plus the following:

- **Skin can look better and younger**

- **Can reduce risk of hip fractures**
- **Can lower the risk of colorectal cancer**
- **Can possibly lower the risk of heart disease (if HT is started shortly after menopause begins)**

HT: Is it safe?

Studies indicate that HT is the most effective tool to diminish severe symptoms of menopause, but it should never be used to prevent disease. Yes, it could be safe for the right person, but this is a decision that must be considered very carefully with your doctor, because so much depends upon your:

- **family history**
- **personal medical history**
- **age when menopause begins (that's when you should start HT, not 20 years after)**

HT: Here's what we know right now.

There have been several studies to examine the efficacy and safety of HT. The most well-known was the Women's Health Initiative (WHI) study—a seminal fifteen-year study that began in 1993 and involved over 161,000 relatively healthy, postmenopausal women between the ages of fifty and seventy-nine. The study reviewed several treatments to determine which would be most effective in preventing heart disease, osteoporosis, and cancer in post-menopausal women. The three treatments were: HT, diet modification, and calcium/vitamin D supplementation. (Interestingly, the WHI study did not address how HT affected women's symptoms during men-opause, which is why women consider HT in the first place, not to combat disease.)

Those women in the HT group were given either HT or a placebo. In 2002 the study was stopped because there appeared to be a slight increase in heart disease and breast cancer among women who were using HT. Confusion ensued—among doctors and patients alike—and the resulting media coverage confused the issue further, creating a state of near hysteria.

In 2006, when the data was revisited, correctly analyzed, and published, it showed that for women who are suffering from severe symptoms of menopause, HT, given at the lowest dose, for the shortest period of time,

and very close to when menopause begins, is the most effective treatment. There will be more to the HT story because it is continuously being studied. Be on the lookout for new research as it develops, by checking out the resources listed at the end of this chapter.

Some of the risks involved in HT include:

- **Possible increase in risk of developing breast cancer, ovarian cancer, stroke, and other health problems. The link to these diseases is still being studied. Women who have had any of these illnesses, or have a strong family history of them, are advised against using HT.**
- **Possible blood clots in the deep veins of the legs and lungs, specifically in women who have a history of blood clots.**

Is Hormone Therapy right for you?

- **HT should be given in the lowest dosage possible to relieve symptoms. The progesterone dose, especially, should be low because of a possible connection between progesterone and breast cancer.**
- **Timing is everything—HT must start as close to the onset of menopause as**

possible. With each passing year, the impact is diminished, and the risk of cancers and heart disease increases. In fact, when the WHI study was revisited, it found that women who started close to menopause had an 11 percent decrease in heart disease.

- HT is the most effective treatment for quality of life symptoms—reducing hot flashes, vaginal dryness, and sleep disruptions by over 90 percent.
- HT should be considered a short-term treatment—severe symptoms stop within three to five years in 80 percent of women.

What about bioidentical hormones?

There's been a lot of talk recently about preserving our "youthful glow" through bio-identical hormones. These are hormones from plants that are combined to simulate the effects of estrogen. What's rarely mentioned, however, is that bio-identical hormone therapy is not FDA-approved, has the same risks at HT, and possibly a few other risks as well. Don't go down this road unless you've discussed it with your doctor, are aware of the appropriate doses, and understand the risks.

Is that all there is?

No, there are other options to consider in addition to lifestyle and HT. These options treat the symptoms individually, not systemically, and most have minimal side effects or risks. They include:

- Localized vaginal estrogen in cream,

The Safest and Most Effective Use of Hormone Therapy

- Start when menopause symptoms first begin.
- Keep doses as low as possible.
- Re-evaluate every year.

tablet, or ring form (such as VagiFem), which combat vaginal dryness. These require a prescription, and don't carry the same risks as estrogen used in HT.

- Non-estrogen, over-the-counter vaginal treatments such as Replens.

- Over-the-counter vaginal lubricants which are usually applied prior to sex (such as KY-Jelly and AstroGlide) are highly effective for women who experience uncomfortable sex due to dryness.

- Certain antidepressant medications often help relieve mood swings, night sweats, and hot flashes, but these are still being studied.

- Red clover, aloe vera, soya plant, and other herbal products may help with hot flashes. Talk to your doctor about these options.

Facing up to cancer.

Now that menopause seems more manageable, I'm ready to confront something bigger, something I haven't wanted to think about.

Cancer—especially the gynecological cancers—is very high up on the "fear factor" list. When I was in my twenties, thirties, and even forties, I thought it could never happen to me. As I approached fifty, however, I became acutely aware of the possibilities. I wasn't obsessed with contracting a severe disease, but I became more conscious of my fears. I wanted to do something about them but I didn't have the information I needed to understand my risk and what I could do about it. The experts reviewed the most current research.

A few facts about breast and gynecological cancers:

- Breast cancer is the most frequently diagnosed cancer among women.

- Breast cancer ranks second as a cause of cancer death in women, after lung cancer.

- 77 percent of breast cancer occurs in women over fifty.

- Women are six times more likely to die from heart disease than from breast cancer.

- The five-year survival rate for women with breast cancer is 98 percent.

- We have more than a 90 percent chance of beating cervical or uterine cancer if it's detected early.

We can be screened for some of these cancers, but not all.

You may already know the preventive measures we can take; you may have been told about them over and over again; you may already be doing them. Still, read this section carefully, and make sure you're informed and doing everything you can.

Breast Cancer

This is the most commonly diagnosed cancer for women and the second leading cause of cancer death for women. The average age of the woman who contracts it is 61. If detected and treated early, there is a 98 percent survival rate (if the cancer has not spread to other parts of the body).

What is breast cancer?

Breast cancer begins as a lump or small formation of abnormal cells in the breast, usually in the glands or ducts. It's important to catch it at this stage, before the cancer spreads to the lymphatic system or to other parts of the body.

You are more likely to contract breast cancer if you:

- have a strong family history (mother, sister, daughter).
- went through early puberty (before twelve) or late menopause (after fifty-five), or both.
- have never been pregnant, or if you had your first child after thirty.
- are over fifty.
- are obese.
- have very dense tissue in your breasts.
- had atypical ductal hyperplasia (a precancerous condition).
- used HT to combat menopause (depending upon how closely HT was started after menopause began).
- have inherited genetic mutations (BRCA1 or BRCA2).

You can help to reduce your risks of getting breast cancer if you:

- Get annual mammograms—and, if you are considered high risk, sonograms and MRIs.
- Examine your breasts every month for any lumps.
- Exercise.
- Keep your weight under control.
- Follow a healthy diet, low in fats.
- Limit your intake of alcohol.

- Discuss the use of chemoprevention medications (such as tamoxifen and raloxifene), and oral contraceptives with your doctor.
- Get genetic testing if you have a strong family history of breast cancer.

You might have breast cancer developing if you:

- see or feel a lump in your breasts.
- see a change in the skin on the breast—thickening, swelling, distortion, tenderness, redness, or scaliness.
- have discharge from the nipple (which could also be due to a hormonal abnormality).
- see dimpling of the breast.

What are the available treatments for breast cancer?

Alone, or in combination:

- Lumpectomy—surgical removal of the tumor
- Mastectomy—surgical removal of the breast
- Chemotherapy
- Radiation
- Drug or Hormone Therapy

Because my sister was diagnosed and treated for atypical ductal hyperplasia (a form of pre-cancer when too many cells line the wall of the milk ducts) a few years ago, I am now considered at-risk. So I started getting MRIs annually, along with my mammograms. A few years ago, I got both screening tests as usual. The mammogram showed that everything was perfect, but on the MRI, there was a tiny little dot that looked like it could be something. I had a biopsy done, which showed that it was one of those scary "false positives." That (and the fact that my insurance doesn't pay for it) is the only negative aspect of getting a breast MRI every year if you and your doctor determine that this is necessary for you.

Uterine Cancer

This is the most common gynecologic cancer in the United States. About one in forty-one women will develop endometrial cancer, and most are over fifty years old. It is crucial to pay attention to your body, and tell your doctor immediately if there are any changes, because it is highly treatable if detected early and there is a 95 percent survival rate.

What is uterine cancer?

The uterus is the organ where a fetus can develop. The wall of the uterus has two layers of tissues. The inner layer is the endometrium, where most malignant tumors start, which is why this cancer is often referred to as endometrial cancer.

You are more at risk for uterine cancer if you:

- have passed menopause and are over fifty.
- are obese, hypertensive, or diabetic.
- had fertility issues or menstrual problems.
- have a family history of uterine cancer.
- have never given birth.
- have had other forms of cancer, such as of the breast, ovary or colon.
- have taken "unopposed estrogen" (without progesterone).
- have taken tamoxifen (a drug therapy to prevent breast cancer) and are postmenopausal.
- went through puberty before age twelve and/or through menopause after age fifty-five.

You can reduce the risk of getting uterine cancer if you:

- immediately report irregular bleeding and spotting to your doctor.
- get a yearly pelvic exam and vaginal ultrasound.
- don't take "unopposed estrogen" (without progesterone).
- maintain a healthy weight.
- consider the use of oral contraceptives as a preventive measure (discuss with your doctor).

You might have uterine cancer developing if you:

- have postmenopausal bleeding or spotting, which can come and go.

What are the available treatments for uterine cancer?

- Surgery (hysterectomy)
- Radiation
- Chemotherapy
- Drug therapy

The warning signs of uterine cancer are clear. Don't ignore them.

Irregular bleeding or spotting is an

early warning sign for uterine cancer, and it should never be ignored. If you've gone through menopause and you are bleeding or spotting, call your doctor. If it occurs, a pelvic sonogram should be scheduled immediately. The only way to diagnose this disease is for the uterine tissue to be examined through biopsy, ultrasound, hysteroscopy, or a D&C.

Ovarian Cancer

Ovarian cancer is the second most often diagnosed gynecological cancer, but it causes the most deaths. Often called "the silent killer," it is difficult to detect and is usually diagnosed only after it has spread. One in sixty-eight of us could develop this cancer. It is frequently presented as a gastrointestinal problem. If ovarian cancer is treated before it spreads, there is a 92 percent survival rate. But only 19 percent of women are diagnosed at this stage. You must be vigilant about checking on how you're feeling, and report any changes to your doctor immediately.

What is ovarian cancer?

The most common form of ovarian cancer starts in the tissue that covers the ovaries, which during our reproductive lives, produce estrogen and progesterone.

You are more at risk for ovarian cancer if you:

- have never been pregnant or had your first pregnancy after age thirty.
- never used birth control pills.
- used Hormone Therapy to combat menopause symptoms.
- have women in your family who have had cancer.
- started puberty before age twelve, and went through menopause after fifty-five.
- are over fifty.
- have a diet that is high in fats.
- are obese.

Is there a link between ovarian cancer and obesity?

This connection has been studied for many years, with conflicting results. However, it seems as though a surplus of estrogen produced by fat cells in the body may be driving an increase in ovarian cancer in women who are considered obese (BMI of 30 or more).

You can reduce your risks of getting ovarian cancer if you:

- **are extremely alert to changes in your body.**
- **immediately report any changes to your doctor, who will conduct a pelvic exam and an ultrasound for evaluation.**
- **use oral contraceptives, especially if you are at risk for developing hereditary breast or ovarian cancer.**
- **choose to take preventative measures such as a hysterectomy or surgery to remove the ovaries (after considering the risks of having your ovaries removed).**
- **maintain a good weight, and eat a diet high in vegetables and grains and low in fats.**

You might have ovarian cancer developing if you:

- **feel bloated for no reason.**
- **have pelvic or abdominal pain.**
- **have back pain.**
- **abdomen has increased in size.**
- **have difficulty eating.**
- **are losing weight without reason.**
- **have frequent and regular indigestion.**
- **are experiencing urinary incontinence or need to urinate frequently.**
- **are constipated.**
- **are extremely tired without cause.**

These symptoms often appear together and are frequently mistaken for digestive problems, so if you are having one or more, get to your doctor for a check-up as quickly as possible.

Are there any screenings for ovarian cancer?

There are ongoing studies to try to find the best way to detect this cancer as early as possible. A pelvic exam only occasionally detects ovarian cancer, generally when the disease is advanced. If you are considered at risk for the disease (see list above) or have specific symptoms, then the following three tests might be used in combination:

- **Pelvic exam**—an exam of the vagina, fallopian tubes, ovaries, and rectum
- **Transvaginal ultrasound**—a procedure used to examine the vagina, uterus, and fallopian tubes via a sonogram
- **Blood test for the tumor marker**

CA-125—a test that measures the level of CA-125 in the blood, which might be a sign of certain cancers

Many doctors routinely perform these screening tests on women over fifty during annual gynecological exams. Discuss these tests with your gynecologist.

What are the available treatments for ovarian cancer?
Usually, a combination of all three:

- Surgery, usually to remove one or both ovaries
- Chemotherapy
- Radiation

Cervical Cancer

Death rates have gone down steadily over the past few decades due to prevention and early detection. One in one hundred thirty-eight women in the United States will develop cervical cancer, but the cure rate is over 92 percent when detected early. Treating pre-cancerous lesions can prevent almost all of them from turning into cancer, which is why the cure rate is so high.

What is cervical cancer?
Almost all cervical cancers are linked to a common infection in the cervix called human papillomavirus, or HPV. (A new vaccine can protect against HPV if administered before a woman starts having sex, but it's too late for most of us now.) Most women who have HPV do not get cervical cancer. Cervical cancer always begins with pre-cancerous lesions, but only some of the lesions turn into cancer.

You are more at risk for cervical cancer if you:

- have certain strains of HPV.
- are infected with HIV.
- are over thirty.
- smoke.
- have problems with your immune systems.
- were exposed to diethylstilbestrol (DES) before birth.
- previously had precancerous lesions of the cervix.
- engage in unsafe sex and have a history of multiple partners.

You can reduce the risks of getting cervical cancer if you:

- get a Pap smear every year.
- have precancerous lesions that were detected early, removed by cryotherapy, laser, or surgery.
- get tested for HIV and HPV, depending on your sexual lifestyle.
- practice safe sex.

You might have cervical cancer developing if you:
- experience abnormal vaginal bleeding.
- have spotting or discharge.
- bleed after sex.
- have pain and problems with urinating.
- have swollen legs in conjunction with any of the other possible warning signs.

Are there any screenings for cervical cancer?

Yes, and that's the biggest reason why the incidence of death has been declining—early detection through these screening tests, both of which are often used together:

- **Pap smear**—should be done annually.
- **HPV test**—this is now often used in conjunction with the Pap smear, but has been performing so well as a screening that it might replace the Pap as the standard protocol someday.

What are the available treatments for cervical cancer?

- **Surgery**—pre-cancerous lesions may be removed in various ways. Invasive cervical cancer is treated with surgery.
- **Radiation**
- **Chemotherapy**

But prevention is the best way to keep it out of your life. It's your body. You need to take care of it, look at it, listen to it, and talk to your doctor about it. Over 90 percent of women who get cancer do so even

Early detection + early treatment = a successful strategy for cancer survival.

though there is no family history. Sometimes, you just get it, and sometimes you get it because you haven't taken all the steps to prevent it. Now that you know the facts, make sure you do everything you can to catch cancer early.

Are you considering a hysterectomy?

A hysterectomy may not always be necessary. Over 90 percent of hysterectomies are performed for reasons other than getting rid of cancer. Consider the latest thinking about the ovaries and uterus before you make a final decision. Often when a woman is having a hysterectomy to treat uterine cancer, her ovaries are also removed to keep her from contracting the relatively rare—but deadly—ovarian cancer. However, your ovaries are much more important to your post-menopausal health than doctors once thought. It's been found that women who have their ovaries removed can have a higher risk of heart disease, osteoporosis, and certain cancers, specifically lung cancer.

And yet, they are routinely removed when they are still healthy. A full hysterectomy is often prescribed by doctors in order to deal with heavy bleeding, a prolapsed womb, or painful fibroids. There might be a safer way to treat the problem, and the hysterectomy itself may cause new problems. There are a few reasons why a hysterectomy might be in order—for instance, a diagnosis of uterine, cervical, ovarian, or some other gynecological cancer. It may also be recommended for adenomyosis—a severe form of endometriosis, if the uterus has prolapsed to the point where it's actually exiting your body—but even then, there are other options, such as corrective surgery or using a pessary (which helps to literally hold the uterus in). Listen to your body, and listen to your good common sense. Don't agree to major surgery that you may not need until you have all the facts and have exhausted all other options. And always get a second or third opinion. It's your body.

Get on board.

For menopause:

* **Take a multivitamin to supplement your healthy diet with the right amount of**

vitamins and minerals.

- Take calcium (1,500 mg per day).
- Take Vitamin D (1,500 IU a day).
- Add flaxseed oil (1000 mg once a day) and soy (in foods such as tofu) to diet to reduce minor symptoms of menopause, such as occasional hot flashes and dry eyes.
- Do strength training four or more times a week
- Use a vaginal estrogen tablet or ring to restore moisture and suppleness to the vaginal area. It is a localized treatment and is only absorbed into the walls of the vagina, without going into other organs of the body.
- Consider HT as way to alleviate (severe) symptoms.
- Get a bone density test every two years.

For preventing cancer:

- Get annual screening
    - —Pap smear and HPV DNA test
    - —Breast mammogram and MRI
    - —Pelvic exam and ultrasound
- Keep weight in check.
- Limit intake of alcohol.
- Do a monthly breast self-exam.
- Listen to your body and notice any change in how it looks and feels.
- Immediately call your doctor if you feel

something is different, especially:

- —unusual bloating and symptoms of gastrointestinal ailments
- —bleeding or spotting
- —lumps in breasts or anywhere around the breast area, including under arms, or changes in the skin on breasts or nipples

Be your own health advocate. Don't let anyone convince you that you are "just fine" if something seems wrong. Insist that your doctor looks at you, listens to you, and investigates your symptoms.

Get more information.

Know your facts and take control. Review the information presented by the following organizations:

- The American College of Obstetricians and Gynecologist (ACOG), www.acog.org
- The North American Menopause Society, www.menopause.org
- The Women's Health Initiative (WHI), www.whi.org
- American Cancer Society, www.cancer.org
- The Mayo Clinic, www.mayoclinic.com

Chapter 4

Sex

Wanting What We Have and Getting More of It

Sex? Remember that?

When I met Howard in the sweltering summer of 1992, we started rocking and rolling immediately. In our late thirties, we knew what we were doing—and we liked doing it. But, from the moment we got married a year later, we were thinking about getting pregnant, actually pregnant, recovering from pregnancy, or enjoying (and coping with) the results of the pregnancy: babies, toddlers, and now, two teenagers. It wasn't exactly conducive to swinging from chandeliers.

Parenthood

One year to the day after Howard and I got married, Sarah was born, almost three months early. For the first year or so, I spent more time checking to make sure she was still breathing than I did kissing my husband. And, really, how hot and heavy can you get with the sounds of a baby monitor next to the bed? On top of that, we had demanding jobs and were mentally and physically drained. I spent the next few years obsessively trying to get pregnant again. I took my temperature every morning and alerted Howard whenever my trusty ovulation kit told me that I was in the two-to-three day conception window. What had once been pleasure had turned into a second job—for which we might or might not ever get paid.

Welcome to Jamaica, Mon.

When Sarah was two years old, we took a much-needed vacation to Jamaica. We were starting to get snippy with each other and stressed out from work, Sarah's birth, trying to get pregnant again, and still getting to know each other as a couple. Before leaving for Jamaica, I had an appointment with Dr. Antoine, my ob/gyn and the wisest man I know. He said: "Barbara, do not take your thermometer, your ovulation kit, or your mindset that you must get pregnant. Go, relax, enjoy, have fun, have sex, have wine, and what will be, will be." You probably know the punch line to this story. Our second daughter, Elizabeth, used to tell people she was Jamaican.

Fast-Forward to Fifty

In the years that followed, our love life perked up again and was as normal as it could be, given our work loads and the two young children who managed to crawl into our beds nearly every night. While it had been a very stressful beginning, we took a long, deep breath, and got back to the business of life. Since we were no longer having sex to procreate, it became easier, more fun, and relaxed. We went out, saw friends, traveled a bit, and took advantage of every opportunity to be alone. Our friends thought we were smart for carving out time for each other, and our kids made fun of my husband whenever he called me his girlfriend.

Now that our daughters are teenagers, we have even more opportunities to be alone, if you catch my drift, but . . .

Are we doing it enough?

For many women, once we're over fifty things can start to change. I read some statistics about how many times per week married Americans made love (with each other), and it's hard not to compare. I brought this topic up with my friends, hoping to get insights into how other committed couples handle their love lives. The specifics were different, but the basic question was the same: I love my husband and he loves me, so why aren't we having more hot sex? At this point it's not like anyone has to tell us what to do in the bedroom. We've been doing it for decades, even if it feels like we haven't done it in decades. I hated thinking that maybe things were slowing down, and that they might slow down even more. It's true that menopause can make sex less comfortable for some women, and our libido can drop off. But just because a woman is postmenopausal, does she automatically lose interest? Forever? Was that the future? I had to talk to someone who had the answers.

The Sex Expert

Esther Perel is an internationally respected therapist and the author of the best-selling book *Mating in Captivity: Unlocking Erotic Intelligence*, which has been translated into twenty-four languages. At our first meeting, Esther explained (in her very sexy French/Israeli accent) that in over twenty years of working as a relationship therapist, she sees the same scenario over and over: long-married couples who love each other, but are no longer interested in making love (at least not with each other). She wanted to know why, and so she devoted herself to getting the answer. Esther is a couples therapist, not an expert on sexual health. However, gynecologists and other physicians frequently call on her to help them better understand their patients' sexual psychology. Most doctors don't know what to do with a woman who asks about sexual issues. They may be able to deal with her genitals, but not with her sexuality. If a woman has a problem she'd like to discuss with her doctor, she might be too embarrassed to bring it up. Esther is helping the medical community to help their patients who have questions about their sexuality. Maybe now doctors won't tell us that our problems are in our heads, or change the subject, or tell us that this is what happens after menopause. Because, guess what? According to Esther, sex after fifty may very well be the best sex you'll ever have.

Group Therapy with Esther

Since sexuality is very personal—and since we're all different—with different sexual orientations (gay, straight, bi-), or circumstances (married, dating, looking), I invited several brave and curious women over fifty to join me in interviewing Esther to make sure that we covered a range of concerns. We spent many hours together sipping coffee, nibbling on mini-muffins, sometimes blushing, and revealing stuff about our sexual lives that was, well, revealing. Most important, our questions were answered. We left the session contemplating our erotic selves in new, fresh ways. Some of what Esther told us was counter-intuitive, but all of it made sense. We couldn't wait to get home.

An Inconvenient Truth

After fifty, you can lose touch with your randy younger self. Maybe you've been in a relationship for a while and the edge has worn off; or, you're bored with your partner or yourself; you may have body image issues; you're not as energetic as you used to be or feel like you're too busy for romance. Combine these with the physical changes that can come with menopause, and sex can slide down the priority list pretty fast. Most of us still crave intimacy and enjoy sex—when we have it. But many of us also say that we aren't having it enough. What to do?

The new reality: After fifty, you have sex because you want to, not because you have to.

When Esther wrote her book, she posed a simple question: Why does sex slow down between two people who love each other? For the first time in history, people are living long enough to have sex for many years after they are done having children. Women over fifty can now have sex because we want to, not because we have to. A very liberating thought, no? But often, we stop wanting it. So how can we want it again?

You can do it! America's strange relationship with sex.

Esther, who was raised in Belgium and Israel, views America from an outsider's perspective. According to Esther, Amer-

icans are exceptionally goal-oriented people. Even when it comes to sex, we believe that with hard work, anything is possible; there's no obstacle that you can't overcome. Conversely, we think that if you fail at something, it's because you're unmotivated, self-indulgent, and lacking in spunk. This makes us believe that loss of desire is an operational problem, and that if we slap the right plan in place, it can be fixed. That's why there is a huge market for self-help books like *Seven Weeks to Better Sex* and *Five Minutes to Orgasm Every Time You Make Love*, and for products like Viagra. Women's magazines burst with stories about how to do this, how to do that, how to do it more, and how to do it better. Most of the discourse is about the mechanical and the operational, not about the desire or the motivation. We talk about sexual functioning rather than sexual feeling. If it is about functioning—like when a man takes a Viagra pill—then all is well with the world. Or is it? Most definitely not, says Esther. She made some other points about how cultural ideas about sex can put a damper on the joy of having it.

Understanding these attitudes will help to put them into context and get them out of your head. They are:

- **The Puritan work ethic.** Sex in our society is often viewed as either smutty or saintly. Our generation was raised to think that if a woman enjoyed sex too much, she was a slut, but that she was supposed to have sex with her husband as her wifely duty. It's an issue of " pleasure." Wanting pleasure can cause us to feel guilty, and we tend to speak of having to "earn" or "deserve" it—much like the Puritan work ethic. It seems that the only thing we allow ourselves to be totally passionate about is our work and over-consumption.

- **Everything is "work."** "I'm working on it" is an often-used phrase, whether it's about the food that's still on your plate or a sexual relationship. To use the word "work" about something that is meant to be a pleasure, whether it's eating or sex, is crazy to Esther. Why do you always have to be a productive citizen?

- **We are youth-centric.** Check any magazine, advertising campaign, TV show, movie, or clothing store, and you'll see that America is in love with youth. We've convinced ourselves that being young is more important than being wise or experienced. How can women over fifty feel good about ourselves if we're aspiring to some imaginary ideal that is impossible for us to attain?

- **We measure everything.** We love to compare and keep score. How long, how many times, how often. Sexual activity is measured, comparisons are made, but the important stuff of sexual expression like desire, willingness, and love are not easily measured, and so, not discussed nearly as much.

- **We talk too much.** Talk shows, reality shows and celebrity tell-all books go on endlessly about things that used to be dealt with as a matter of course (and in private). All of the talk can make us worry more.

- **We don't believe in secrets.** Popular marital advice tells us that lack of sex means lack of intimacy means lack of closeness, therefore you need more talk, more communication, and more transparency with your partner. On the contrary, excess information and over-sharing can put a damper on desire, while a little mystery can feed attraction.

- **We want our partner to be our everything.** Many people put too much of a burden on their partner to be the one and only meaningful person in their life—best friend, lover, confidante, advisor, co-parent—and it's just way too big a role for any one person to fill. It takes a village to meet all of your emotional needs.
- **Do it for your health.** Articles talk about how sex is good for your heart and your skin; it burns calories, relieves stress, and helps slow the aging process. Those are great bonus benefits, but will you do it just because it's good for you?

Sexual Healing

While the self-help and medical industries are busy promoting cures for all of our ills, Esther's research tells her that the majority of women who are in good relationships and aren't having much sex are, in fact, sexually healthy. Most of the sexual problems associated with menopause can be addressed with simple solutions, like lubricants or small doses of estrogen (see *Chapter 3*). A minority of women are suffering through true sexual dysfunction. In reaction to this group, an entire industry has popped up with experts and books—which has caused the rest of us to believe that sex is over after fifty. And that, says Esther, is a total shame because we have the potential to have even better sex lives now than when we were younger, because we:

- are more confident.
- are more experienced.
- are liberated from menstruation.
- are free from possible pregnancies.
- can be more "me-focused" instead of "other-focused."
- are not doing it because we have to, but because we want to.

We're at a crossroads.

There's a moment in our erotic lives that we all eventually get to at least once—a crossroads where our sexuality changes for one reason or another. Esther sees it all the time. A woman going through menopause could realize that her experience of sex is changing and decide that she is done with it. She can shut down that part of herself, lock the door, and throw away the key. She could decide to focus on the dryness, the discomfort, and the slowing down of her sex drive. Or she could solve the physical problems and embrace this new life with a sense of freedom—no more periods, no more worries about getting pregnant, no more doing it because there has to be a result. She can view sex as a form of play, fun, and pleasure. It's a choice.

Let's get on with it!

Having been prepped for the session with Esther, we were ready, and had a lot of questions.

How do you become sexually confident?

Developing your sexuality is a process of learning to view yourself as a "sexual being." View yourself as a sexual person and take charge of your sexual life. Then you will project desirability and sexual confidence. Your attractiveness as a sexual being is completely self-determined. If you don't feel desirable, then it doesn't matter what you look like or how much your partner says he desires you. If you don't feel sexual yourself, then sex won't be pleasurable for you. Many of us learned to judge sexual experience, based on how good it was for the man. If it was good for him, then it had to automatically be good for you, right? No, not right. To be a true sexual being, a woman must take responsibility for her own pleasure, wants, and satisfaction. A sexually confident woman cares about her partner's experience, of course, but it isn't the determining factor for her own sexual experience.

What if you look in the mirror and don't feel sexy anymore?

Many women over fifty can become sexually inhibited because they think they are no longer attractive and sexy, and as a consequence they shut down. But that's not reality. A sexy woman is a woman who is into sex, who wants it, and who is into her partner. What's really sexy isn't your body shape or age. It's that you want sex. In all her years of being a therapist, Esther has rarely encountered a man who has said that his low sexual drive is related to how his wife looks. But he will be turned off if she has stopped being interested in sex. No one wants a partner who does "pity sex" or who just goes through the motions.

What about those women who have fabulous bodies and who still view themselves as being undesirable?

How you feel about sex is often a reflection of how you feel about yourself—your body, your entitlement to pleasure, and how deserving you think you are—not how you look. In American society, body image gets intertwined with permission to feel desire and to feel attractive. But most of us have been indoctrinated to never feel good enough about ourselves. There are huge industries out there eager to make us feel insecure about how we look so that we will buy whatever they are selling. Name the body part, and it could be better. They tell us we will be sexy only if we get rid of the fat, smooth the wrinkles, bleach the freckles, whiten our teeth, and dye our hair. Recognize the sales pitches for what they are and ignore anything that tells you to be or do something different in order to "deserve" love, happiness, and good sex.

Does parenthood have to squash the sex?

No, but the transition from two to three (or more) is a profound challenge for every couple. Everything changes—our relationships with our spouses, our friends, our parents, and even ourselves. Priorities shift, and most of our resources go into building a family. For the couple, there's less of everything—less money, time, freedom, privacy, intimacy, and sex. Eventually, we come out of it with redefined roles in the context of a whole new entity: the family. But successful family life needs constancy, predictability, and stability—the very things that can undermine eroticism. It's very hard for some women to return to the selfishness of desire after becoming mothers. Desire is inherently selfish, but much of family life is about self-denial and selflessness. Staying connected to your sexuality is even more challenging, but it's something you have to do. Immersed in your roles as parents, it's hard to see yourselves as a sexual pair anymore. What to do? View yourself first as an individual—separate from your partner and children—and then, with your partner, build an erotic space to be lovers and not parents.

What about couples who say that they are "best friends," but rarely have sex?

Some couples who come in to see Esther say they are "best friends," but never have sex. It is an existential problem: how do you reconcile having both comfort and excitement at the same time in the same place with the same person? It's hard to have sexual desire for your best friend, because there's no tension in friendship and desire thrives on tension and mystery and the unknown. Did you start out with more friction but evolved into a less sexual kind of friendship? Has your relationship become familial where one of you takes the role of father, mother, or sibling? This kind of complacency is probably the most important factor in squashing sex— more than stress, children, being tired, or having no time. But, this is all fixable. Figure out what your roles are with each other, and try to make ad-

justments. Sometimes guidance through counseling is necessary.

Why don't you have wild, spontaneous sex anymore?

Spontaneous sex is a myth. Why, you ask yourself, are you not having wild, spontaneous sex now that you've been married for over fifteen years? The answer is that it was never spontaneous. When you were just dating, you had sex on your mind for hours, maybe even for days, leading up to the experience. In many cases you set the date, thought about it, decided what to wear, where to eat, and many other details. Now the planning seems more deliberate. But that in itself can be sexy. It's about having a willingness to engage, which can lead to desire, which can lead to arousal, which can lead to the experience. Couples who have a good sex thing going take time to figure out what they need to do to make it happen. Whatever it is, they know what it takes to make the transition from the work or domestic life to the erotic life, and they make planning part of the erotic journey.

What if he's the one who doesn't want it?

News flash: if you're having less sex, chances are it's him, not you. The reason probably has nothing to do with you, either—not your weight, age, hair, or clothes. With men, very often it's related to a health problem or a medication he may be on for cholesterol, diabetes, or blood pressure, many of which are known to create some sexual problems. He should discuss it with his doctor. Your partner's probably over fifty, too, and things might not work the same way they used to for him either as his hormones start to shift and maybe his fitness levels decline. Here's how it often plays out: for much of their lives, men initiate because they already have an erection or feel one coming on. But with age, that doesn't happen automatically anymore, and for many men, this can squash their interest in having sex. Your partner's not used to needing stimulation, and it can be troubling when this happens. He doesn't know what to do, except avoid it. The woman thinks it's her fault and that he's no longer attracted to her. She's gotten so used to him having a hard on without her help, that when she needs to do something to get him to want sex, she can feel threatened. It's a situation rife with disappointment, suspicion, and frustration. Some common reactions include affairs, avoidance, or a prescription for Viagra. (The majority of Viagra users stop after a few months because it gets the man to function, but it does not give him desire.)

This creates a need for a more relationship-based approach to sex, which women already understand. The man then needs to get used to something that women are comfortable with—cultivating a relationship to build desire and arousal—and the woman has to get used to the fact that this is something the man now needs, too. Once they can both do that, couples can have a great sexual life together. This is one of those times when that crossroads comes into play: will you as a woman choose the path that will allow you to work with your partner on overcoming this obstacle—which will likely include some shifting of previously held feelings—or will you choose to close up shop?

Being over fifty presents more stressful and scary situations—illness, death, job loss, aging parents. What used to be occasional, now seems like the norm. It's heavy, sometimes depressing, stuff that can put a real damper on your interest in sex. It's true. There will be periods in your life when you are dealing with external distractions and you could become less active sexually, but that doesn't mean that you should stop thinking of yourself as a sexual being. Cultivate the erotic space with your partner so that when the opportunity presents itself, you'll see that your sexual energy is alive and well, and you'll be ready.

How do you make an erotic space?

Whether you have kids or not, an erotic space is essential to having an erotic life with your partner. It's not a physical place, necessarily, but an emotional spot where the two of you go to get physical. The erotic space is where you come together—not as responsible and productive citizens, adults, parents, or caregivers—but as lovers. It's a space where sex can happen, if that's what you both want, and a space where you are not busy taking care of anyone else. Esther offered a few great ideas on how to create an erotic space:

- **Use that BlackBerry. Texting and emailing to connect in that erotic space—nothing about Johnny's report card or getting the tires changed—is very sexy. It's a way of flirting with each other, and building the anticipation of physically entering that erotic space when it becomes possible. Send him a playful text or email during the day, to start an erotic thread with each other. When you get home, you won't have to make such a huge transition from your roles as mother/father/CEO to lovers.**

- **You mean we're not the same person? Respect your partner's "otherness," his separateness, the stuff he's interested in that you may not be. Don't go overboard feigning enthusiasm for his hobbies, but give him time to pursue them. When individuality and differences are accentuated, you actually see the other person as a separate being from yourself.**

Eroticism requires separateness, and it thrives in that erotic space between you and your partner.

- **Can you introduce me to that cute guy over there?** Watch your partner while he's playing a sport, chatting at a party, giving a speech, or wrestling with the kids. Look at him as a man, not as your husband or the father of your children. Look at him with fresh eyes. If you see that he is attractive to others, you could be more sexually attracted to him. This creates a sense of risk, mystery, and desire, which makes you interested in entering the erotic space.

- **What? Me worry?** It's not sexy to have to worry about your partner. He feels the same way. The damsel in distress thing just doesn't work in the bedroom. While you don't have to be a dominatrix, being fragile or needy can be a turn off. You want a partner who can handle himself, who isn't dependent on you or insecure. Good sex requires you to be selfish. You can't be worried about the other person, because you need to be entirely focused on yourself. If your partner is needy, it's difficult to let go and have a really good time.

- **Learn to flirt.** Social flirting is acceptable in many parts of the world, but in our goal-oriented society people (usually men) often feel that you flirt in order to score—that there must be a result. Mild flirting with others can build your sexual confidence and make you feel sexy. Flirt for fun, not to make your partner feel jealous or insecure—and you need to let your partner flirt, too.

> Build it, and he will come: once you have the erotic space, how do you enter it?

The list of excuses for not having sex is endless, and saying no can be habit-forming. We wanted to know Esther's magic formula for—poof!—getting into the mood. She described three main ways—entry points—through which women can get there:

- **Arousal.** Women are aroused by more things than men. Your path to arousal might be fueled by a movie, book, fantasy, lingerie, or any number of things. When you are aroused, and you encounter your partner, one thing can lead to another. Arousal leads to desire, and desire leads to sex. Figure out what gets you going, and use it when you need it.

- **Desire.** Desire is wanting to be turned on. With this entry point, you want to get aroused, and you want to actively engage in getting turned on with your partner. Desire can be stoked when you see your partner in a new way. For instance, when you see him dressed up in a new shirt, or doing something that he enjoys, even when you see him flirting with the bank teller, you may feel desire for him as a man. You then have to act on that desire by using some of the tools that kickstart your arousal, which will get you to the experience.

- **Willingness.** The most important entry point for women over fifty may be the willingness to be engaged in desire. If you've been ignoring, neglecting, or denying your sexual self for a while, then you must consciously decide that you want sex in order to even let yourself feel desire. Willingness should never be confused with pity sex or sex you feel you have to do. Simply acknowledge that you are ready, able, and willing, and let your partner know that he has to help a little, too.

There will be days when one entry point works better than another, but what it really all comes down to is—the willingness to be sexual. You just need to figure out which entry point you were going to use. You may need to nudge yourself sometimes, and that's okay. We talk ourselves into doing things all the time—going out, attending an event, cooking dinner—but people think we shouldn't have to talk ourselves into having sex. Talking yourself into sex can actually be a turn on, and we usually end up being happy that we did it.

You can have several marriages in your life.

Wow. That one piqued our interest, and made us a little worried. Are our marriages doomed? Must we get divorced and move on to a new person for excitement? No, that's not it at all, Esther explained. Of course there will be those of us who do get divorced or become widowed and enter into another committed relationship. But there's an alternative: by reinventing yourself and your sexual relationship with your partner, you can have a new marriage with the same person. Esther estimates she's had three already. It's a lovely, romantic, and exciting thought. You had the newlywed marriage and the young parent marriage and now you can have the older, wiser marriage—and so on. If we follow Esther's advice, and take our partners along for the ride, we could start over, with each other. Get married to Howard again? I do.

And if you're not married?

Married, dating, single, looking, men and women, women and women, men and men—the concept is the same. You've got to make your erotic space together, and find your entry points. It's up to you, and it's all about you.

You own your sex life.

Our sex lives can be as hot as we want, for as long as we want. It's up to us. Engaging in sex is wonderful, but it doesn't always have to be the end result. Keeping in touch with yourself as a sexual being and being intimate with your partner in the erotic space will sustain your erotic life, and that's really the point. People often ask Esther to recommend oil or lotions or bedroom tricks to make their sex lives more interesting. Her response is always the same: don't even think about new lingerie or some acrobatic position until you've developed your sexual confidence and created an erotic space. You'll both end up feeling ridiculous because those things won't allow you to address the underlying issues. Once you've built—or rebuilt—a solid sexual foundation with your partner, then the real fun can begin. Because, after fifty, that's what it's all about, isn't it? Fun and pleasure. Stop being so serious about it, relax, and have a great time! If you're not sure where to start, I recommend Jamaica.

Get on board.

We all learned a great deal from Esther. We explored many questions that we had about keeping our erotic selves going strong after fifty—and reigniting the fire, regardless of the particular circumstances. Some of our favorite tips are:

- **Consider the entry point you might want to use.**
- **Accept that sometimes you're simply not in the mood.**

- Understand that sometimes he may not be in the mood, and that's also okay.
- Think less about how you look.
- Make a point of building (and visiting) that erotic space—because you can't always be on vacation, right?
- Create a separate email account which no one else can check, and try texting one another throughout the day.
- Think about him a little more during the day, not as a father, husband, or business executive, but as a man.
- Create an environment in your home which is calm, happy, accepting, loving and (appropriately) sensual.
- Let your children see that you and your partner are connected on many levels, through handholding, hugging and smiling. You are their role models, after all.
- Use a lubricant when you need it.
- Use a prescription estrogen product, if needed (discuss with your doctor).
- Do twenty Kegel exercises twice a day to keep that part of your body in shape. (It's simple—just squeeze that muscle, hold it, and let it go. There's nothing to it.)
- Stay healthy and stay active so that you have enough energy for anything.
- Stay connected to other people, as well

as to your own interests.
- Ask friends for new ideas—you're never too old to learn.
- Check out some of the fun toys that are out there
- Stop reading studies about how often other people have sex. Who cares?

Get more information.

- *Chapter 3* discusses the physical aspects of menopause, and steps you can take to alleviate discomfort associated with it. Other good resources are:
- www.more.com
- www.mypleasure.com
- *Hot Monogamy: Essential Steps to More Passionate, Intimate Lovemaking* by Patricia Love and Jo Robinson, Plume, 1995
- *Mating in Captivity: Unlocking Erotic Intelligence* by Esther Perel, Harper, 2006
- *The Sex-Starved Marriage: A Couple's Guide to Boosting their Marriage Libido* by Michele Weiner Davis, Simon and Schuster, 2003
- The good old-fashioned bodice-ripping novels are custom-made for getting women in the mood. I know, I know, I couldn't believe it either.

Chapter 5

You=What You Eat

No More Mindless Eating

Growing up, I didn't think much about food, unless it had something to do with peanut butter, especially when it was slathered on a piece of soft, white Wonder Bread. I remember going to the Brooklyn Wonder Bread plant on a school field trip, and we all got a miniature loaf—in a fabulous polka-dotted wrapper—to take home. Each spongy white slice was "enriched," so mothers everywhere were satisfied.

One potato, two potato. . .

My German grandmother was from the "made-from-scratch" school of cooking, and reveled in her post-war ability to put meat and potatoes (and gravy and potatoes—and more potatoes) on the table every night, except Friday nights when the menu was fish. Cooking was a source of pride for her and she was very concerned about making sure that my sister and I got the right foods and vitamins every day, as specified in the food pyramid. Each morning, waiting for us at the kitchen table was a glass of freshly squeezed orange juice, which always had a cover on it so that "the vitamins won't escape." She tried to get us to take a spoonful of cod liver oil, too, but we ran out the door with our book bags before she could pour it.

TV Dinners, Anyone?

Her "old country" notion of good health wasn't far off from what nutritionists are telling us to eat today: fresh foods, yogurt, whole grain bread, fish oil (although her menus were sometimes a little heavy on the meat and potatoes). All of these things were a part of Grandma's own daily eating regime. It was my mother's generation that preferred the processed, easy-to-make foods. TV dinners, our generation's fast food, was a Saturday night staple for my sister and me. Included with the fried chicken and mashed potatoes in the cleverly-designed aluminum foil "plate" were loads of sodium, and lots of fat. But who cared? They were the perfect meal when watching *The Addams Family* or *Get Smart*.

They just don't make those fat cells like they used to.

Looking back now, I cringe, but at the time, we thought it was delicious. No doubt this "fine dining" helped fatten up my fat cells. We're all born with a certain number of fat cells, and then we gain more during puberty, when the sex hormones kick in. (Fat cells are generally not created after puberty.) When we gain weight, our bodies store fat, but the number of fat cells remains the same; each one just gets fatter. (An exception to this rule is if an adult gains an extraordinary amount of weight.) The size of fat cells in adult bodies has its beginning in early childhood and adolescence, when fat cells are being formed. The more fat cells we had as children—and the fatter they got—the harder they are to get rid of as adults.

When I was in my twenties and thirties, my weight was pretty constant. Once in a while—after too many Twinkies or peanut butter and jelly sandwiches (on Wonder Bread, of course) eaten during those all-nighters I used to pull at work—an extra few pounds would creep on until my Jordache jeans wouldn't zip. I'd cut back on eating, or try some new diet fad, and in a couple weeks, it would be back to normal.

No more.

Those days of quick and easy weight loss are long gone. Things started to change slowly—but steadily—until at fifty-one, I weighed fifteen pounds more than I did in my thirties. Not terrible, it's true. But those pounds seemed to be slowly working their way onto my body—in what felt like a permanent way. Maybe it was all those TV dinners finally catching up with me. Suddenly, I saw a vision of me five years hence. It wasn't very pretty, and definitely not healthy. Being overweight can cause many illnesses (see *Chapter 1: Feelin' Alright* and *Chapter 2: Keep the Beat*). Surplus estrogen is produced in fat cells, and too much estrogen can cause certain cancers. Not good at all.

How does it happen?

Easy—eat more, exercise less, and go through menopause. A little weight gain (up to five pounds) is normal after menopause, but gaining more than ten is not. The first five years after menopause is a critical time for re-evaluating your nutrition and exercise program, since this is when we tend to gain weight and lose bone mass.

What are you going to do about it?

Like many women, the first thing that I thought of to get rid of my sneaky new pounds was to go on a diet. Health experts may disagree on how people should lose weight, but there's one thing that they do agree on: when people "go on a diet," they have a 10 percent chance of succeeding. That's only a 10 percent chance of either losing the weight and keeping it off, or losing the weight at all. Why?

Diets don't work.

Many of us view the word "diet" as a synonym for "lose weight," not "get healthy and stay healthy." There are hundreds of "lose weight diets." All of them promise drastic and quick reductions in pounds and fat, but there's one simple question you have to ask yourself before you start on one: "Can I eat this way for the rest of my life?"

Many weight-loss diets overemphasize one particular food or type of food (like grapefruit or protein), and ignore the first principle of good nutrition: a balanced diet that includes a variety of foods. Taking a vitamin pill won't make up the difference. As soon as we come off the boring, rule-bound diets and revert back to "real-life eating," the weight pops right back on. Worse, very often ex-dieters have lost the ability to naturally regulate their eating, so we pack on an additional ten pounds. Then, to take off the weight again, we try another diet. This is the yo-yo dieting syndrome, and it wreaks havoc with your metabolism. Remember those fat cells? Every time you lose weight/gain weight/lose weight/gain weight, you make it harder and harder for them to lose fat, and for your body to lose weight. It's a vicious cycle that guarantees failure. Time to get off.

Woman cannot live by protein alone.

One of the most popular and enduring diets of recent decades has been the Atkins diet— and I know it well. I went on the diet specifically to lose the very stubborn last ten pounds I carried after the birth of my second daughter. (I had gained fifty pounds, but we don't need to talk about that.) I gave up pasta and bread—even whole wheat—believing that all carbs were bad. I felt deprived, and my common sense told me that I wasn't getting all the nutrients I needed, and that this way of eating couldn't be sustained (it can't). As I got closer to fifty, the weight started to creep up again, and I began to feel unwell and lethargic, which caused me to slow down my exercise. My body was sending me a message.

What kind of role model am I?

I was failing miserably as a role model for my daughters. I insisted that they eat their broccoli, but I never touched the stuff. Too many carbs, Dr. Atkins whispered in my ear. It was definitely time for a sensible, grown up, life-long solution.

Dr. Fischer Feels Our Gain

After all my experience on the Atkins plan, it made sense to meet with Dr. Stuart Fischer who, for over eight years, ran the Atkins Center with the founder, Dr. Robert Atkins. Dr. Fischer agrees that the low or no-carb way of eating just isn't sustainable long term. He now runs the Park Avenue Diet Center in New York and is a strong proponent of choosing a wide variety of foods—including olive oil, whole grains, vegetables, and fruits—along with a certain amount of healthy protein every day.

Even though Dr. Fischer has the word "diet" in the name of his clinic and title of his book (*The Park Avenue Diet*), he embraces the "anti-diet" way to lose weight. He believes the path to better health and appearance needs to include physical, psychological, and behavioral changes that reinforce one another. All "diets" treat the symptoms, not the cause. It's like giving an aspirin to reduce a fever without curing the source of the fever. The answer, he believes, lies in totally reevaluating yourself—down to your clothes, hair, and your attitudes.

It's a whole body experience.

The principle behind Dr. Fischer's plan is to address the different components of image simultaneously. If you focus only on losing weight, but still wear the same shlubby clothes, or have a hairstyle that makes you feel unattractive, you are more likely to fail. For women it must be a whole body and mind experience.

Plain and simple truth: overweight = health problems.

Dr. Fischer gave me the State of the Union Address on obesity in this country. It is not good. Over two-thirds of American adults are overweight. While none of us wants to be overweight, we often don't realize that we are helping to make ourselves sick by carrying around more weight than we should. Many diseases are directly related to being overweight (see *Chapters 1* and *2* for more details), so it's in our best interest to shed as many extra pounds as we can, especially if the weight is around our waist area. This, Dr. Fishcher said, is the worst kind of fat—visceral fat.

What is visceral fat?

I'd never heard of "visceral fat" before, but I didn't like the sound of it from the minute I heard Dr. Fischer mention it. Visceral fat. It sounded sneaky and mean. Sure enough, it is sneaky and very mean. It's fat that you can't see. It's fat that can surround your heart and internal organs. Not good.

Good news—it's easy to get rid of visceral fat.

It's easier to get rid of visceral fat than that extra padding on your tush. You simply need to eat better, move your body more with regular exercise, and lower your intake of saturated fats (found in meat and even poultry), and away it will go. Visceral fat is like a checking account—easy in and easy out.

We all have subcutaneous fat, which is the noticeable layer of fat that lies just below the skin. Visceral fat is deeper, beneath the muscles, and can be dangerous fat because it surrounds vital organs and is metabolized by the liver, which turns it into cholesterol in the blood. Post-menopausal women who have excess abdominal fat have a greater risk of metabolic syndrome which can precede diabetes and heart disease. (See *Chapters 1* and *2* for more information).

How do you know you have visceral fat?

If you are overweight, chances are quite good that you have visceral fat. However, even normal weight women can have excess belly fat. Measure your waistline, because visceral fat tends to be right around your abdominal area.

Pinch the inch: your waist size should be less than half your height.

The goal should be a waist measurement that is less than thirty-five inches, or less than half your height. Put away your scale and bring out the tape measure.

Simple, but not always easy.

Someone said that to me once. I didn't quite get it at the time, but now it makes so much sense. We've established our goal: a waistline of less than thirty-five inches (simple), so now let's get to how we get there (not always so easy). But first, know that every little step you make toward your goal is a huge step toward a better life. With every fraction of an inch, you are healthier.

How do you do it? Stop dieting, start eating.

Dieting does not work, but eating does. So many diets don't take into account the behavioral and emotional relationships that people have with food. You use food to bond with your friends and families, soothe yourself, help with stress, and celebrate your successes. This is why diets that restrict you are not sustainable. With entire food groups or too many calories cut out, the body compensates and either slows down the metabolism or it creates such intense cravings that we can overeat.

Who are you?

Commit yourself to being a healthy woman—a woman who deserves good health. We're getting older, but we can be healthy, too. Envision how you want to look, feel, and be, and what you need to change to get there. Look at what you eat. Look at your hair, makeup, skin, how you work out, how you spend your time, and how you present yourself to the world (see all the chapters that follow this one for good ideas). What does the "ideal" you look like?

How does she dress? Converse? Carry herself? The truth is, once you start eating better and losing weight, you'll look and feel better, and will be motivated to do everything better. The dots get connected and one action begets another. Before you know it, you're the hottest fiftysomething in your 'hood.

The Doctor's Doctor of Nutrition.

Nutrition is complicated and complex, so I sought expert advice from Dr. Laura Lefkowitz. Dr. Lefkowitz is a physician—she is trained in radiation oncology and psychiatry, but decided that instead of treating people after they had already developed a disease, she would help patients prevent it in the first place. She went back to school and now specializes in health and nutrition counseling. Dr. Lefkowitz works closely with her patients' primary care physicians and is considered the "Doctor's Doctor of Nutrition and Health."

Lose the pyramid.

I knew very little about nutrition (beyond that infamous food pyramid) before my first meeting with Dr. Lefkowitz but she made one thing clear: eating the wrong foods will have a long-term impact on our health, but eating the right foods—consistently, not as a fad—will offer a good fighting chance to stay healthy as we age. She laid out a sensible, comprehensive plan for women over fifty.

First, an explanation of "low blood sugar" and "metabolism."

These two terms are used a lot with regard to food and weight loss and understanding how to control them will help you to lose weight, and keep it off.

- **Low blood sugar**—Sugary foods and those that are highly refined (meaning far from "whole") such as white bread and white flour pasta turn into sugar in the blood. Eating such foods creates a temporary surge in blood sugar followed by an overproduction of insulin (to try to process all the sugar), which causes a blood sugar crash within hours. The technical term for this is hypoglycemia, or low blood sugar. You've probably experienced it. You can feel awful from this and then are tempted to eat to overcome how you feel, and usually you'll crave something sweet because of all that excess insulin. If this happens repeatedly and frequently, the body thinks it's supposed to be storing excess sugar as fat, for future use. So, more fat is stored, and it becomes a big, vicious cycle.

- **Metabolism** is the measure of how efficiently our body burns fuel (food). This metabolic rate varies between individuals, but also with our body composition over our lives. After menopause, the percentage of muscle tissue decreases relative to the percentage of fat tissue, so we burn fewer calories because muscle burns more calories at rest than does fat. If you consume the same amount of calories now as you did when you were younger, and you're not burning more calories, you will gain weight.

The Plan is Simple: Whole Foods in Sensible Portions

Eating for health and enjoyment are not mutually exclusive. For me, this was a revelation and a relief. Dr. Lefkowitz does not believe in diets. She believes in eating whole, unprocessed, pure, clean foods, and keeping a close eye on portion sizes (i.e. not over-consuming). Do this and you will succeed.

The foundation of your new lifelong eating plan:

- Eat whole foods.
- Eat more vegetables.
- Eat more whole grains.
- Eat throughout the day (every two to three hours).
- Eat breakfast every day.
- Drink lots of water.
- Stay away from processed foods.
- Keep an eye on portion sizes, especially if you're in the weight-loss stage.
- Aim for organic when possible.
- If you just have to have something that makes you happy, that's okay, just continue with your healthy eating afterwards.

What is a whole food?

"Whole foods" are foods that are unprocessed (or processed very little) and very close to their natural state. Some examples are fresh or frozen vegetables, whole grains (whole wheat, brown rice, quinoa), fruits, nuts, seeds, legumes (beans), eggs, and milk. Fish, poultry, and meats that are prepared without any additives or modifications are also considered "whole foods." A serving of grilled salmon steaks would be considered a whole food, but Mrs. Paul's Fish Sticks are not.

These are guidelines, not rules.

This isn't all or nothing. Don't think of this as a one-shot diet and give up and go back to your old ways if you have that occasional piece of strawberry shortcake. It's okay if you do! There's no need to get ridiculous about this. This is a suggested framework, and you should follow it according to how it makes you feel, and how well it works (it will work, though).

Can you live without these? Try.

Try your best to remove these foods from your kitchen and your body. None of them have any real nutritional value, and all of them can wreak havoc with your metabolism and blood sugar level, possibly causing you to gain weight, or at the very least, stop you from losing any:

Sugar and high fructose corn syrup

Both can make you fat, offer empty calories, mess up your blood sugar level and metabolism, ruin your teeth, affect your mood, and offer zero health benefits. They're in a shocking percentage of foods so check the labels. This includes drinks such as soda.

Artificial sweeteners

Splenda (Sucralose), Nutrasweet (Aspartame), Equal (Aspartame), Sweet' N Low (Saccharin), and any "diet" foods that list these as ingredients are trouble. People who are overweight are the largest consumers of foods that contain these chemicals. These sweeteners fool the brain into thinking that real sugar is being eaten. The blood sugar level drops, and the cycle continues.

White flour

This includes white bread, regular pizza and pasta, cookies, cakes, pies, donuts, and anything that is made with white flour. Years ago, companies stripped away the important and healthy parts of the wheat kernel—the bran and the germ (as in wheat germ)—because factory bakers found that this "refined flour" (the stuff of wonder bread) was easier to work with and prolonged the shelf life of the flour and the products made with it. To offer any health benefits at all, flour must include both the bran and the germ.

White rice

Like white flour, white rice has all the nutrients stripped away. Asians historically have one of the lowest incidences of heart disease and cancer. It's not because of the white rice, but from the vegetables and soy-based plant proteins they eat. (And probably because of all the meat they don't.)

Instead, start buying and eating these foods:

Organic foods

Most produce is sprayed with pesticides and chemicals, which can enter our bodies when we eat the food. Organic produce is easily available in every supermarket, no matter where you live. You can also find it at your local farmer's market. Start out with some organic produce, and then expand your organic horizons and buy organic breads, grains, meats, and dairy. Organic can cost a bit more, but hopefully that will change as demand increases.

Whole grain products

Whole grains are those that haven't had their nutrients "refined" out of them: the list includes oatmeal, whole wheat, brown rice, whole wheat pasta, barley, buckwheat (kasha), millet, and quinoa. They contain essential enzymes, iron, dietary fiber, vitamin E and the B-complex vitamins. Because the body absorbs these grains slowly, they provide sustained energy, keep you feeling fuller, longer, and will help keep blood sugar levels stable.

Brown Rice

Brown rice is incredibly nutritious, has all the bran layers and nutrients intact, has the highest amount of B vitamins out of all grains, and contains iron, vitamin E, amino acids, and linoleic acid. It's high in fiber, extremely low in sodium, and is made of eighty percent complex carbohydrates. It is an amazing food that can be used in many different ways—alone, mixed with veggies and beans, in casseroles, in sushi rolls, pilafs, and puddings.

Beans

Beans—black, chickpeas, lentils, split peas, pinto, and navy—are one of the best ways to add plant-based protein (as opposed to animal protein) to your diet. They are high in iron, B vitamins and fiber, and there are so many different kinds of beans, and ways to prepare them, that you'll never get tired of eating them. They are great in soups, chilies, and burritos, or the classic red beans and rice, but a simple dish of brown rice, black beans and some steamed or sautéed vegetables, with a pinch of sea salt and olive oil mixed in is a perfect meal.

Vegetables

They're are loaded with vitamins, minerals, and antioxidants and should be eaten in unlimited quantities every day (except corn and sweet potatoes).

Dark green leafy vegetables

Bok choy, kale, swiss chard, and spinach are the foods most missing in modern diets, but eating dark greens is essential to good health. There are dark, leafy greens you can use in salads—arugula, mache, lettuce. Greens are very high in calcium, magnesium, iron, potassium, phosphorous, zinc and Vitamins A, C, E and K. They are loaded with fiber, folic acid, chlorophyll.

Nuts and seeds

Eating almonds, walnuts, cashews, pecans, sunflower seeds, and other nuts is an easy and simple way to add healthy fats to your diet. The data on the benefits are overwhelming. Eating just a handful of nuts five times a week can reduce the risk of coronary artery disease between 25 and 40 percent. Seeds and nuts are a great, portable snack, and are terrific used in the preparation of many meals. Avoid the oil-roasted, salted ones and stick with raw or dry-roasted.

Calcium

It's best to get calcium from low- or non-fat sources, but even better to get it from non-dairy sources, such as leafy greens, broccoli, kale, almonds, sardines, canned salmon, tofu, and sesame tahini. Calcium from these other foods is easier for our bodies to absorb than from dairy products. (Most of us don't realize this because the dairy industry and their great ad campaigns work hard to convince us that milk is the best source of calcium.) One or two servings of dairy a day is fine, but focus on other sources. We still need supplements, since in order to get the full amount from food, we would have to eat more than we can.

Fruit

Apples, melons, oranges, and plums are all naturally sweet, juicy, and make great desserts. Many fruits are loaded with antioxidants (especially berries), fiber, vitamins, and minerals. They are low in calories, high in nutrients, portable, easy to eat, and mix well with other foods, such as yogurt or cereal.

Protein

There is protein in so many of the things we eat during the course of a normal day that this country would be hard-pressed to ever be considered "protein-deprived." Protein consumption varies according to individual need—usually between 40 and 60 grams per day. Your portion of animal protein should be no larger than the palm of your hand. Aim for grass-fed or organic beef and chicken, so you won't be eating the artificial hormones and antibiotics.

Eggs

Eggs are easy to digest and our bodies are able to absorb the majority of the protein found in them. They really are a near-perfect food. Try to eat several a week. If you are concerned about the yolks, you can have just the egg whites, for example, in an omelet. If you are eating the way this chapter suggests, eating an egg or two—yolk and all—will be okay. There is no nutritional difference between brown eggs and white eggs, but try to find those that are enriched with Omega-3 fatty acids when available.

Natural sweeteners

Natural sweeteners like maple syrup (not the artificial kind with high fructose corn syrup), honey, and agave nectar. Honey is one of the oldest natural sweeteners, and is also sweeter than sugar. It's the best thing to take for a cold or a cough. Agave nectar is a natural liquid sweetener made from the juice of the agave cactus. It is sweeter than sugar but has much less impact on your blood sugar levels. Use agave nectar in place of sugar in most recipes. There are others, and most can be bought in regular supermarkets, or health food stores.

Dark chocolate

Not just any dark chocolate, but really fabulous, delicious, dark chocolate, with at least 75% cacao (it's often listed right on the front). Have a little piece every day. Dark chocolate (more so than milk chocolate) is filled with cancer-fighting antioxidants and offers some fun benefits, too. Italian researchers found that women who eat dark chocolate have a higher sex drive than those who don't.

Red wine

There are anti-aging antioxidants found in red wine—resveratrol and polyphe-nols—that may neutralize disease-causing free radicals. Red wine is a natural blood thinner, helping to maintain a healthy heart. A recent study showed that a moderate amount of red wine consumed on a regular basis is the single biggest contributor to the Mediterranean Diet's longevity benefit. A glass (or two on occasion) with a healthy dinner is great, but limit yourself to no more than seven glasses a week. Studies have shown that women who consume more than the recommended amount of alcohol face a greater risk of developing breast cancer, countering all the health gains for your heart offered by red wine.

What about supplements?

We can't get everything we need from food. We'd eat too much, and consume too many calories, so taking a few supplements makes sense. Before you begin taking any supplements, have a complete physical exam—including blood work to check your nutrient levels—to make sure that you are not lacking in any specific nutrients. If you follow this eating plan, these supplements will help cover the basics.

Multivitamin/multimineral

Preferably one without iron, since after menstruation stops, we no longer need as much iron in our bodies. It should have sufficient amounts of minerals and vitamins that are essential for women over fifty—including Vitamin D and magnesium (both of which are necessary for proper calcium absorption).

Calcium—1,500 mg per day.

Calcium is a key component to maintaining good health, preventing bone loss and osteoporosis.

Vitamin D—1,500 IUs per day.

Vitamin D, known as the "Sunshine Vitamin" because our bodies manufacture it from sunlight, is essential for helping to regulate the levels of calcium that we absorb in our bodies. But Vitamin D itself may also be important in reducing the risk of cancer, cardiovascular disease, glucose intolerance, high blood pressure, asthma, some infectious diseases, certain cancers, and diabetes. While most milk has Vitamin D added to it, we would have to drink at least twenty glasses a day to get the minimum levels, so supplements are essential.

Fish oil—1,000 mg (1 gram) per day.

Fish oil is the best source of the Omega-3 fatty acids, DHA and EPA. There are so many benefits to adding a daily dose of fish oil to your diet: it helps prevent heart disease, improves blood circulation, builds immunity, reduces inflammation and clotting in blood and tissues, is useful in treating arthritis and rheumatism, helps dry skin, helps maintain a good luster to hair, and helps to prevent hair loss. I even give it to my dog.

Flaxseed oil—1,000 mg (1 gram) per day.

Unlike fish oil, flaxseed oil is rich in the third fatty acid—ALA. ALA is a short chain fatty acid, which is also found in walnuts, pumpkin seeds, and a few other plant sources, but not in fish oil. It helps mitigate some of the symptoms of menopause such as dry eyes, helps lower cholesterol and blood pressure, helps reduce the risk of certain cancers, improves the absorption of calcium, helps to burn fat, and treats some forms of depression.

The Easy, No-More-Mindless-Eating Plan

We can choose to eat unwisely, or we can choose to eat well. More than anything, we should choose to eat what we really need, and what makes us feel good and strong.

Do this healthy eating plan in conjunction with the fitness program outlined in *Chapter 6: Move That Body* for maximum success.

Keep track of your food with a food journal.

The best way to start this program is to keep a food journal. Get a special notebook and write down everything that you eat or drink for each meal and snack—including the amounts. Do this every day and all day, for a few weeks, if not longer. It really works. Women who keep journals while they are changing their eating habits are more successful than those who don't.

The following is a starting place for your own plan. An important component is to "front load" your eating: never skip breakfast. You need a healthy (no refined flour or sugar) breakfast to give you energy, stabilize your blood sugar level, and get your metabolism working to burn fat and calories throughout the day.

Drink this every day.

- **Water:** drink throughout the day. Getting enough water helps your organs function, and you won't drink any (or not as much) of the "other stuff" like soda or high calorie juices. Aim for eight glasses a day. Check your urine periodically. Is it dark? You're not drinking enough, and you could be dehydrated. It should be very pale yellow.

- **Coffee or Black Tea:** but no more than two cups, and the earlier in the day, the better. Try to have it early in the day, so that it doesn't interfere with your sleep, and always eat something with it. If you don't, the caffeine could act like sugar: your blood sugar level will surge, which will cause a blood sugar crash within hours. Too much caffeine can make you feel overly anxious, stressed, and moody. Regular black tea (like English Breakfast or Earl Grey) has the same effect. A few cups of coffee can slow down the aging process, fight off Alzheimer's, enhance short-term memory, lower your risk for stroke, and give you a better workout.

- **Green Tea:** several cups a day, hot or cold. The most beneficial liquid (after water) is green tea. Drink it hot, iced, however you like, but drink it. Women who drink green tea every day have significantly lower body mass indexes (BMI) and smaller waist measurements than those who do not. Green tea has antioxidants, and can help prohibit the growth of cancer cells.

- **Red Wine:** one small glass every day, or several times a week. If you enjoy wine, having one glass of red wine every day can have a positive impact on the health of your heart, and fight Alzheimer's, but allow yourself no more than seven glasses a week, max.

Eat this every day.

- **Nuts and Seeds:** 2 servings per day. Eating nuts up to one half hour before meals can fill you up, preventing you from overeating. They are high in protein, fiber, and heart healthy fats. Spread nut butter on other foods (get the kind with no sugar added, but salt is fine unless you're on a low-salt diet), add nuts and seeds to salads, mix them with fruit and vegetables, or eat as a snack. Aim for dry roasted or raw, unsalted.

One serving is:

12 Almonds

 4 Brazil nuts

10 Cashews

10 Hazelnuts

 6 Macadamia nuts

15 Peanuts

25 Pistachios

¼ cup Pumpkin seeds

¼ cup Soy nuts

1 tablespoon Sunflower seeds

¼ cup Walnuts

1 tablespoon Nut butter

- **Whole Grains:** Eat 2–3 servings per day. Steer clear of white bread and any other processed carbohydrates, white potatoes, white rice, and regular pasta.

One serving is:
1 slice whole wheat or some other whole grain bread

½ whole grain English muffin or bagel

½ cup cooked whole wheat pasta

½ cup cooked oatmeal

½ cup cooked brown rice

½ cup cooked millet

½ cup cooked bulgur

½ cup cooked barley

½ cup cooked quinoa

- **Vegetables:** As many and as much of most vegetables as you want, every day. Try to include a wide variety of color in your vegetable diet (it's a good indication that you're getting a balance of nutrients). Have at least one serving of a dark green leafy vegetable every day.

Serving Size: Unlimited

Limit your servings of these:
Eat 1–2 servings of the following vegetables (which are NOT unlimited because they're starchy and have a higher caloric count), in lieu of a whole grain at a meal, if you wish:

Corn (1 ear or ½ cup of kernels)

Peas

Sweet potato or yam

White potato

Squash (all varieties)

- **Calcium Rich Foods:** 2 servings every day. Whether dairy or plant-based, calcium is a key component of good health, especially for maintaining strong bones.

One serving is:
8 ounces skim or lowfat milk

8 ounces plain, lowfat, or no fat yogurt (preferably the strained Greek Style)

½ cup low fat cottage cheese, pot cheese, or farmers cheese

Canned sardines (3–4 ounces, with bones)

Canned salmon (3–4 ounces, with bones)

1 cup leafy green vegetable (spinach, kale, dark green lettuce, etc.)

1 cup broccoli

2 tablespoon sesame seeds

- **Fruit:** 2–3 servings every day. Eat fruit that's fresh, in season, and organic. Make one or more of your servings each day be a berry, since berries are highest in nutrients and antioxidants.

One serving is:

1 apple

2 fresh apricots

1 small banana (or ½ large)

½ cup blackberries

½ cup blueberries

½ cantaloupe

12 cherries

2 fresh figs

1 grapefruit

15 grapes

¼ honeydew

2 kiwi

½ mango

1 orange

1 peach

2 plums

½ cup raspberries

1 pear

1 cup strawberries

2 tangerines

1 cup watermelon

- **Protein:** 3 servings every day (animal or plant). We get protein in so many of the foods we eat, we are rarely at risk for being protein deprived.

Some foods that contain high levels of protein
One serving is:

½ brick tofu

1 tbsp. nut butter (peanut, almond, cashew, or sunflower)

½ cup low fat cottage cheese

½ cup low-fat or non-fat yogurt

½ cup pot cheese

⅓ cup ricotta cheese

⅓ cup feta cheese

- **Non-Animal Protein:** Varies. Foods that deliver high levels of protein that come from plants are lower in calories, saturated fat, and have more nutrients than animal-based proteins. Some grains are particularly high in protein, such as quinoa, kamut, millet and kasha. Also look for the new pastas that are high in protein. And of course, nuts and seeds are good sources as well.

- **Animal Protein:** For animal protein, try to buy organic, free-range, grass-fed, hormone- and antibiotic-free when possible, which will decrease your overall exposure to chemicals in your food. If possible, animal protein should not be eaten every day. Prepare it in a simple way to keep it as close to being a whole food as possible. Rule of thumb: don't overprocess.

Use your hand to measure animal protein portions:

- The portion size for beef, chicken, and pork is the size of your palm (not your whole hand), about 4 ounces.
- The portion size for fish is your whole hand, about 6 ounces.

Healthy animal protein choices are:

- Skinless chicken or turkey breast
- Beef with fat trimmed
- Fish and seafood (oily fish like wild salmon and arctic char are best)
- Eggs: 1–2 per day, or an unlimited amount of egg whites

Get on board.

Once you start keeping a food journal, you'll be surprised to see what you are really eating—and not eating—every day. It will help you stop mindless eating and make good choices. Here's a sample of my new way of eating, based on my food journal. Keep tabs on portion sizes and amounts.

5:30–5:45am—Jump start

Mix two tablespoons of lemon juice with a tall glass of warm or hot water and drink first thing every morning to cleanse, hydrate and jumpstart your system. Wait thirty minutes before eating or drinking anything else.

6:15am—Coffee

One or two normal-sized cups, and try not to use sugar or artificial sweeteners. Steer clear of the sweetened Starbucks venti anything, except on occasion.

6:30am—Breakfast part I

Break breakfast up into two parts, if you can. If you like eating a hearty breakfast first thing, then eat Breakfast Parts I and II together. Part I is usually a slice of whole wheat toast with nut butter and Part II is two eggs, a bowl of oatmeal (or other whole grain cereal) with fruit and toasted nuts, or yogurt with fruit.

7:00am

Get ready for work or work out. If you do exercise at this time, you'll be well-fueled from breakfast and coffee. You'll perform better, raise your metabolism, and burn more calories by eating some healthy carbs and proteins prior to working out—and coffee helps, too.

8:30–9:00—Breakfast part II (if you haven't already had your full breakfast earlier)

Have one or two scrambled eggs or an egg white omelet mixed with cooked kale from the night before, or some yogurt (my favorite is the Greek style, which is strained so it's thick like sour cream) mixed with blueberries and two tablespoons of flaxseeds or leftover grains from the night before. Drink water or green tea.

10:30–11:00am

Mid-morning snack. It stops your blood sugar level from dipping—cottage cheese, carrots, an apple, banana or a handful of berries or almonds. Drink water, sparkling water, or green tea (hot or cold).

12:30–1:30pm—Lunch

Try to get a lot of vegetables, a little protein, and a small amount of good carbs into this meal. Good options include a salad made with beans, tofu, fish, or chicken, together with an assortment of vegetables, or a green salad with soup (split pea, lentil, or vegetable). If you had a light breakfast, have an omelet, frittata, or two hard boiled eggs with some vegetables on the side. Brown rice and broccoli with chicken or tofu is another option. Whole wheat pasta with tomatoes, mozzarella cheese, and basil (uncooked) is a fabulous meal for lunch or dinner. All of these are easily made at home, and can be ordered in most restaurants. You might also put together a lunch from leftovers: mix together $1/2$ cup each of kale (sautéed the night before with dried cranberries and sliced almonds), garbanzo beans, and quinoa, or open a can of wild salmon, and mix it with a tablespoon of Greek strained yogurt and dill. Have water or sparkling water or green tea.

4:00pm—Afternoon snack

This keeps you from crashing. Have a piece of fruit or a few nuts. Or some sliced veggies with hummus or a black bean dip. If you didn't finish lunch, finish it now. Refresh yourself with more water or sparkling water or green tea.

6:30–7:30pm—Dinner

Start every dinner—whether eating in or out—with a green salad (the darker the leaves the healthier the salad), but with only a little oil and vinegar. Eat a small amount of protein and mostly vegetables (make one a dark green vegetable). Have a small portion of a grain or starch, but no more than $1/2$ cup. If your dinner does not include an animal protein, double up the size of the grain. As always, vegetables are unlimited in quantity. A few times a week, enjoy a glass of red wine.

Dessert

Try not to have dessert every day, but if you have a hankering for something once in a while (maybe twice a week), respect that need and enjoy it. Pay attention to the portion size and don't feel guilty. If you're in a restaurant, share a dessert with someone, or eat half and bring the other half home. As an alternative, have a little fruit and a small piece of dark chocolate.

Before 11 p.m.—Go to Bed!

The later you stay up, the hungrier you will be. If you wake up at 5:30 or 6:00, you need to be asleep by 10:30 or 11:00 anyway. We need at least seven hours of sleep to be healthy. Keep water next to your bed.

Recommended Products

Since most of the foods you are now eating are whole foods (organic fruits, vegetables, nuts, whole grains, and animal proteins) there are relatively few branded items. For those items that are packaged, a lot of different brands were tried to see which ones were the best, and the following are the winners. Most were recommended by Dr. Lefkowitz, and all had to pass muster not just with me, but with my family as well. Stock your pantry with these and you'll always have a meal close at hand.

Whole wheat pastas

- **Bionaturae (our favorite by far, especially the spaghettini)**
- **DiGiorgio**
- **Barilla (not organic)**

Canned beans

- **Westbrae Natural (my favorite)**
- **Amy's Organic**
- **Eden Organic**

Soups (making your own is best, but these are good in a pinch)

- **Amy's Organic**
- **Pacific Organics**

Bread (for your morning toast and sandwiches)

- **French Meadow Bakery "Women's Bread" (I eat a slice every morning, toasted)**
- **Food for Life Ezekiel 4:9 Sprouted Whole Grain Bread (there are many other flavors, as well as tortillas and other products)**
- **Arnold's Whole Wheat bread (my kids' favorite)**

Peanut butter and other nut butters

- **MaraNatha Organic**
- **ShopRite Organic (this brand, which comes in both chunky and smooth was voted "best peanut butter" by my daughters and me).**
- **Blue Diamond**

Brown rice

- **Lundberg's**

Other Grains and Cereals

- **Bob's Red Mill**
- **Kashi**
- **Arrowhead Mills**
- **Food for Life**
- **Nature's Path**
- **Cascadian Farms**
- **Healthy Valley**

Yogurt

- **Fage Total 0% or 2% Greek Style yogurt (plain)**
- **Oikos 0% Greek Style Yogurt (plain)**

Green tea

- **There are many green teas on the market, but the one that is often cited as having the most antioxidants is Tetley Green Tea. Try putting a few slices of fresh ginger in your tea. Make a whole pot and put in the fridge, with the sliced ginger, so you can have it ready to heat any time.**

Supplements

- **Multi-Vitamin: NatureMade Multi For Her 50+ No Iron (one per day)**
- **Calcium: Schiff Bone-Care Super Calcium-Magnesium with Vitamin D and Boron (three per day)**
- **Fish Oil: Nordic Naturals "Ultimate Omega" (one per day)**
- **Flaxseed Oil: Nature's Bounty Organic Flaxseed Oil (one per day)**

Does it work?

The day I walked into Dr. Lefkowitz's office I weighed fifteen pounds more than I wanted to, felt tired a lot of the time, and had slowed down my exercising. Six months later, the extra pounds were gone, and they're still gone. I feel great, exercising is a regular part of my life (see *Chapter 6*), and my annual physical showed an im-

provement in almost all of my health check numbers. The best part is I'm eating, not dieting. I have no interest in looking like I did when I was twenty-five, but I do want to be fit, healthy, and yes, I'll admit it . . . proud of myself.

Get more information.

There's a lot of information in this chapter about how to eat well, thanks to Dr. Lefkowitz and Dr. Fischer. If you are interested in digging even deeper into healthy eating, and want to experiment with recipes, start with these books and websites, many of which were recommended by our experts, and which I find very useful, informative, current, and to-the-point. For maximum success, read *Chapter 6* to really help you lose weight, get fit, and look fab.

Websites

- **American Heart Association, www.americanheart.org**
- **www.integrativenutrition.com**
- **www.lauralefkowitzmd.com**
- **National Cancer Institute, www.cancer.gov**
- **www.www.organicfacts.net**

- www.parkavenuediet.com
- www.womenfitness.net

Books

- *The Eat Clean Diet: Fast Fat-Loss That Lasts Forever!* by Tosca Reno, Robert Kennedy Publishing, 2006
- *Eat, Drink and Weigh Less: A Flexible and Delicious Way to Shrink Your Waist Without Going Hungry* by M. Katzen and Dr. W. Willet, Hyperion, 2006
- *Eating Well for Optimum Health: The Essential Guide to Food, Diet, and Nutrition,* by Dr. Andrew Weil, Alfred A. Knopf, Inc., 2000
- *Feeding your Hunger for Health and Happiness,* by Joshua Rosenthal, Integrative Nutrition Publishing, 2008
- *The Park Avenue Diet: The Complete 7-Point Plan for a Lifetime of Beauty and Health,* by Dr. Stanley Fischer, Hatherleigh, 2008
- *What To Eat,* by Dr. Marion Nestle, North Point Press 2006

Chapter 6

Move that Body

Exercise You Will Like to Do

No Pain, No Gain?
No Way!

As a kid, I got plenty of exercise by roller-skating—with a key hung around my neck—and bike riding around my Brooklyn neighborhood. My sister and I would get home from school, have Oreos and milk, do our homework as fast as we could, and speed outside to run wild with the other kids. On our bikes, we pretended to travel to places we were sure we'd never actually go. Crossing over 52nd Street would be Italy. The other side of Avenue N was London where we imagined we were standing outside of the house where the Beatles all lived together, like in the movie *Help*. But we had our boundaries—and they were strict. We couldn't cross over Utica Avenue and we couldn't travel further than seven blocks in any direction. We didn't, because we knew that there were many sets of parental eyes watching us. But how many miles we covered in that area, I can't begin to say.

So many bagels, so little time.

Once I got to high school, I focused more on books and boys than on exer-cise. By the time I got to college, I was living in Queens, going to St. John's University, and working nights and Saturdays at Bloomingdale's selling shoes (I've always had a thing for shoes, so this was a little bit of heaven) and not thinking about exercise. My greatest pleasure during college wasn't zooming around town on a bike, but going out with friends on Saturday night and coming home so late that I could pick up the Sunday *Times* and freshly made bagels on the way. I'd stay up eating the bagels and reading the paper, and then sleep until noon on Sunday, my one day off. Fabulous. Being barely twenty, I could live this lifestyle and still look fit.

In my late twenties, I not only returned to exercise, I became the quintessential Gym Bunny. I had the stretchy headband, the leg warmers, the one-piece leotard over tights. My role models were "Feel the Burn" Jane Fonda, and "Let's Get Physical" Olivia Newton-John. I worked all day, and then went straight to the gym with my (huge) Sony Walkman strapped to my arm.

I even allowed myself to be tortured by the famous Radu, who was—and still is—Cindy Crawford's exercise guru. His classes were viewed as the most difficult in the city and I remember huffing and puffing my way through each expensive hour wondering if my face looked as pained and tortured as my body felt. This wasn't fun. Did it really have to be this hard to be in shape? Did I really have to live by the "No Pain, No Gain" credo? I stopped. Cold Turkey.

Bye-bye, workout. Hello, middle-aged spread.

When I had my second daughter at the age of forty-one, I was overwhelmed, time-deprived, and burnt out on all of the exercise programs. Working out was the easiest thing to drop. Always in the back of my mind was the nagging feeling that someday, yes "someday," reality was going to come from behind and kick me in my out-of-shape tuckus. And so "someday" I was going to pick up those free weights I had in my closet and spend a few minutes with them, but "someday" never came. Until . . .

Go, mommy, go!

The New York City Marathon goes past our apartment building on First Avenue. Each year, we know someone in the race, and my kids and I get out our markers and make signs to help cheer everybody on. A few years ago, we were standing in our usual spot on the corner when Sarah turned to me and said, "I want to hold a sign that says 'Go, Mommy, Go!'" Elizabeth, then five years old, immediately turned to our neighbors and said, "My mommy is going to run in the marathon!" Everyone looked at me, and all I could think of to say was: "Yes. Yes, I am."

I had never willingly run in my life. I could do a passable plié and even march up a StairMaster pretty well. But run? Not since the dreaded annual "Field Day" at P.S. 203.

The *Wall Street Journal* to the rescue!

A few days later, when I was hoping that everyone had forgotten about my impulsive promise, I saw an article in the *Wall Street Journal*. It was an interview with former Olympian and marathoner Jeff Galloway. He talked about how anyone can run a marathon by following his simple program. The more I read, the more excited I became. Yes, I thought. Yes, I can do this. But first I had to talk to Jeff.

You can do it!

Jeff is a regular contributor to *Runner's World* magazine and wrote the best-selling book, *Galloway's Book on Running*. His book, *Marathon: You Can Do It!*, made so much sense to me that I couldn't wait to get started. Jeff spent time with me, explaining his philosophy and his passion for this program, and I was convinced. Yes, I could do it.

I did it!

I completed the New York City Marathon by sticking with Jeff's training program, which involved liberal walk breaks while running at a steady pace. It took me six hours to complete, but I did it. My kids were very proud of their mom.

I'm still doing it!

Learning to run the correct way has helped me have a renewed sense of how much fun exercise can be. I plug in my earbuds, tune in to Tom Petty, sometimes grab Gunther, our dog, and . . . run (with walk breaks). It keeps the weight off and my health check numbers where they should be. It's good for clearing my head, too. Before you take out your old running shoes (or buy new ones), keep reading because there are steps we need to take before we start running. 10,000 steps, to be exact (we'll get to that later in the chapter).

Why we should all do it.

As we get older, we lose muscle strength, flexibility, sense of balance, and our bones start to thin. It's part of the natural aging process. During the first five years after menopause—unless we actively do something about it—we'll lose 1 to 2 percent or more of our bone mass every year because we're losing estrogen, inching our way toward osteoporosis.

What is Osteoporosis?

Osteoporosis is a degenerative bone disease that causes our bones to get thinner and weaker, significantly increasing the chance that a bone will fracture. According to the National Osteoporosis

Foundation, over ten million American women have osteoporosis and millions more have low bone density (osteopenia), which means they're heading toward osteoporosis. Most don't know it. Too often, it's only after a woman has a fall and breaks a bone that it's discovered she has severe bone loss.

Who is most at risk for Osteoporosis?

The most important factors that contribute to osteoporosis are:

- **Age and menopause**—The older you are, the greater the risk.
- **Gender**—Women are much more at risk of developing osteoporosis because women have less bone tissue than men and lose it more quickly due to menopause.
- **Lifestyle**—If you don't get enough calcium or Vitamin D, do little to no weight-bearing exercise, or smoke and drink too much, you're more prone.
- **Medications and certain diseases**—Osteoporosis has been linked to the use of some cortisone drugs as well as to certain diseases such as hyperthyroidism, rheumatoid arthritis, and chronic illnesses that limit mobility.

- **Family history**—Bone loss and fracture might be hereditary, but this connection is still being studied.

Osteopenia: The first stop before osteoporosis.

When I was forty-seven, Dr. Antoine sent me for my first DEXA test—an important diagnostic tool to measure bone mineral density. In this test, low-dose X-ray beams scan your lower spine (lumbar), hips, and forearms for ten to twenty minutes, analyzes bone density at multiple sites, identifying problems and giving a benchmark or baseline against which future studies can be measured. The primary purpose of the test is so your doctor can determine whether you are at risk of having fractures.

At the time of the test, I was just a few months past the marathon and was still doing some running but it had dwindled down to two times a week at best. I was also menopausal and still an Atkins-style eater—low carbs, few vegetables or fruit, lots of meat protein, and very little calcium. To top it off, I hadn't been taking vitamins.

When Dr. Antoine sat me down to review the results of my first bone density test, he had a very stern look on his face. He told me that my numbers were closer to the borderline than he was comfortable with, and I needed to take specific actions—immediately—if I was going to keep them from sliding downward. He gave me very strict instructions: more calcium-rich foods, 1,500 mg of calcium supplements and 1,500 IU of Vitamin D supplements each day, and more strength training for my entire body. Uh-huh, I said. Will do. But didn't. I stayed with my own program, because I was convinced that I knew better. I wasn't yet fifty, and had been so used to excellent health my entire life that I couldn't imagine that my bones would actually start to work against me. Big mistake.

Four years later, just after I turned fifty-one, Dr. Antoine convinced me to do a second bone density test after I put him off for two years. And what did it say? I have osteopenia. Yes, there it was. Right on the report, in black and white.

Osteopenia is like the first stop on a train. In a few more stops, you're at osteoporosis. In the four years since my last bone density test, I had done nothing at all to prevent this train from chugging down the tracks. The numbers were just slightly below the "normal" line, but the facts were clear—in four years I had lost a measurable amount of bone density. A trend had been established, and now I needed to do everything I could to stop it. But how?

Get moving!

With my new resolve to get strong and fit for life, I wanted the best experts to tell me what to do and how to do it. My goal was to create a program that included cardio to strengthen my heart, lungs, and lower body, burn fat, and maintain weight; weight-training to build muscle mass and strengthen my bones; and more activity throughout the week to keep my energy up and everything feeling (and looking) good.

Here's the first lesson I learned: when you start something new, you need to walk before you run.

10,000 Steps

That's how many steps we should take every single day. I had heard about the "10,000 Step Plan" introduced by former U.S. Surgeon General C. Everett Koop, but never really paid attention to it until it kept coming up in conversations with my nutrition and fitness experts. I started to wonder how many steps I took in a typical day and whether I would be considered physically active.

Then my thoughts turned to my husband Howard. I was sure Dr. Koop had Howard in mind when he was formulating the 10,000 Step Plan. If I could find a way to convince Howard to take more steps, then anyone could do it. Plus, it would put him on the road to better health.

Happy birthday, Howard. You have your very own . . . pedometer!

I had a brilliant idea (well, I thought so anyway). For Howard's birthday, I bought two basic pedometers—one for him and one for me. The first day we wore them, we were shocked at how little we walked in a normal day. After all,

we're in New York City, where walking is a part of our lives. On days when I didn't go for a run, I took less than 4,000 steps. Howard was tracking even fewer. Drastic action was required.

Figure out a way to get to 10,000 steps, every day.

We quickly realized that for most of us, our daily routine doesn't include 10,000 steps. We have to make choices to get out there and walk. Howard walks around his office or our apartment until he's hit his number. He walks while he's talking on the phone, chatting with our daughters or me, walks home from his office, and walks our dog.

Need a reason to walk? Get a dog.

Our girls have been asking for a dog since they could speak but we held out until this year. Not interested in training a puppy, I convinced the family that the only way to go would be to get an adult "rescue dog." We adopted Gunther through the American Brittany Rescue Network. He's handsome and goofy and he's also turned out to be a great motivation for walking. Living in the city, we can't just open our back door and let him out. It's a pretty big drop from the eighteenth floor, so we have to take him on long, intentional, fast walks four times a day. Every night, Howard and Gunther take a long walk all around the neighborhood, for at least forty-five minutes (about 3,000 steps) and I take Gunther on his morning and mid-day walks or sometimes on a run through Central Park. Howard and I are well past our 10,000 steps every day now . . . thanks to Gunther.

Tips for getting to 10,000 steps every day.

- **Get a pedometer.** A simple, inexpensive one is all you need to count every step. If you have an iPhone, there's an "app" for a pedometer.
- **Build up to 10,000.** Every step you take is one step closer to better health. Add 200 or 500 steps a day until you hit your goal of 10,000. Go at your pace, but keep going.
- **Find reasons to walk.** Walk to the store, or work, or out to lunch instead of taking the car or bus or taxi. When you drive somewhere, park at the far end of the street or the parking lot—there's usually more room there, too. Take the stairs instead of the elevator.
- **Walk your dog.** Even if you have a huge yard, your dog can use the extra exercise, too.
- **Explore your town.** Most cities have municipal trails, multi-use paths, and interesting downtown areas that make for beautiful walking routes.
- **Wear good shoes.** These are the shoes you should be wearing whenever you are engaged in an "intentional walk." But make sure that all (okay, almost all) of your shoes are comfortable enough to walk some distance—it will encourage you to add a few steps throughout your day.
- **Walk around the house (or your workplace).** If you're on the phone, walk, don't sit. Take advantage of every opportunity to move, and look for new ones.
- **Follow the running program outlined in this chapter.** By doing so, you will eventually hit your 10,000 steps mark very easily on your running days

and have more energy for long walks on your non-running days.

- **Give it six months to stick.** It takes most people at least that long to change old habits and lock in new behavior.

Walk before you run.

The 10,000 step idea is an effective way to get into the habit of moving every single day. To make a new routine stick, you have to make it regular. Once you've got momentum, you'll give yourself even better health benefits by adding in some cardiovascular exercise (or just "cardio" to the Gym Bunnies).

I decided that running would be a part of my cardio exercise plan, and went back to the man who got me started in the first place: Jeff Galloway.

Why running?

This is a valid question. Why run? Why not some other form of exercise? There are many ways to get your heart pumping: circuit-training, aerobics classes, spinning on a stationary bike. But running is the most streamlined, basic, get-to-the-point form of exercise there is, and is very efficient when it comes to health benefits per hour. You can do it anywhere, anytime, and (once you've got your shoes) for free. You can do it alone, with a friend, or like me, with Tom Petty (on my iPhone) and a dog. It feels good if you do it right.

Think you're too Old? Think again.

Many people over fifty are afraid to run, because they think running or even strenuous walking will hurt their joints. It won't if it's done right. After thirty years of doing his run/walk program, Jeff has never had an injury. Running—at any age—offers many positive benefits: reduced risk of heart disease, cancer, diabetes, depression, and dementia. Contrary to what many people believe, running does not predispose joints to arthritis. The reverse is true. Without exercise, those at risk of osteoarthritis can be crippled by stiff, deteriorated joints. Exercise that increases strength and aerobic capacity can reduce pain, depression, anxiety, and improve quality of life.

What if you have a disease or condition that makes running difficult?

Arthritis, heart disease, and other serious conditions can actually be helped by running and other forms of exercise. Most people who have chronic health problems can improve their health by exercising. Walking or running can help counter the effects of disease and will make you feel better, stronger, happier, and more confident. Consult with your doctor to make a few adaptations for your specific situation.

If it feels so good, why do runners have that pained look on their faces?

Do you ever see a runner who looks happy? I rarely do. Now I know why. They're in pain. Their legs are aching. Their lungs are burning. They're tired. This worried me before I started running, but I learned from Jeff that running doesn't have to be that way. It can even put a little smile on your face.

So, what's the trick?

There's no trick. What makes this program work is that you won't be sprinting madly down the street and you won't be running the whole time. You'll be alternating light, gentle running with regular walk breaks—and plenty of them.

Before you start your new life as a runner, take the time to prepare.

1. See your primary care provider.

Get the necessary health checks and get her green light before starting.

2. Visit a podiatrist.

If you've never seen a podiatrist, now is the time. You may have issues with your feet which could impede your running progress, and cause unnecessary discomfort. If left unattended, this can cause aches in your feet, legs, and hips, and possible injury. The stress of fifty-plus years of pounding those feet—sometimes in very high heeled or pointy-toed shoes—can cause problems as we get older. When your feet hurt, so does everything else. A good podiatrist can recommend specific running shoe brands that are best for you, and where to go to get the best service.

3. Go to a running shoe store.

Your podiatrist will recommend the best running shoe store in your area, but also get recommendations from your local runner's group. Good running shoes that fit you and are designed to support your particular needs are critical. A good store will have well-trained salespersons who will measure your feet and check your running gait (by having you run several yards). Break in new running shoes by walking around in them as much as possible before you take them for a run.

4. Buy your running outfit.

Wear a good running bra for support and a t-shirt that is specifically made for running, so it can breathe. For spring, summer, and fall, wear black knee-length running pants and a cap and sunglasses to keep the sun off your face. In winter, wear thicker long black running pants—with black running shorts over them—and layer long-sleeved t-shirts under a light-weight, waterproof, breathable running jacket. If it's really cold, wear running gloves, a hat, and a turtleneck long-sleeved shirt.

Buy two bras, two t-shirts, and two pairs of the running pants, all in black, and rotate them. That's all you need and black is simple and looks great. In summer, a light-colored shirt is cooler, but stick with the black pants.

5. Last but not least: tell everyone you know that you're going to start running.

One of the ways that I actually accomplish something I want to do is to tell people I'm going to do it. Then, I do it. Jason Zweig, one of our experts in *Chapter 11* told me about a website where people can make public proclamations about what they intend to do: www.stickk.com. Want to make a change? Start by telling the world. You'll have no choice but to do it.

The Run/Walk Program: You Can Do It!

This is an easy-to-follow program. There is nothing in it that the vast majority of us can't do. It'll teach you to run lightly and easily, gradually increasing distance and duration rather than speed, and alternating running with walking throughout each session. If you already run, follow Jeff's plan for safe running to reduce the risk of running injuries as you get older. If you have never run before, once you get out there with your cool new running shoes, you'll never look back.

Rules to live by when doing this program:

- **Leave your ego at the front door.** You will run slowly and gently, with liberal walk breaks. Get used to the idea of other people running past you. It's okay. They will get the injuries. You will not. They are probably gasping for breath, too. You are not. Enjoy yourself, and do your own thing.
- **Run three times a week.** You need one day of rest in between. It is not good for your body to run every day, or even two days in a row.
- **Do not huff and puff.** While running, if you can talk comfortably, you're doing fine. Are you huffing and puffing? Then you're going too fast, and you should slow down until you can breathe easily.

- **Have something to eat an hour or so before running.** Don't eat a heavy meal, but do fuel up before you exercise—even if you're trying to lose weight. A cup of coffee is a great pre-run drink.
- **Focus on your stride.** Jeff recommends a "shuffle"—keep your feet low to the ground, lightly touching, without lifting your knees too high. Slow and gentle running will help you to steer clear of aches, pains, and injuries.
- **Walk breaks are forever.** The goal is not to build up your running to a point where you no longer need walk breaks. You will always take walk breaks, no matter how many years you run, because that's what will keep you running.

How to start:

- **Schedule three runs for the week, whatever days work best for you.** Just make sure they are not consecutive days, and mark them on your calendar.
- **Walk slowly for five minutes** to warm up.
- **Walk slightly faster for ten minutes** and then try running a little to see how it feels. Pay attention to each step,

trying to move silently and slowly. **Make sure you can talk comfortably.**

- **Alternate ten seconds of running with 20 seconds of walking.**
- **Walk slowly for ten minutes to cool down.**

If you're comfortable with this, add five minutes to your workout for the second week, and try to run for twenty seconds at a time. If it's too much, cut back a bit. In a few more weeks, add more seconds and minutes to the program and slowly increase your running-to-walking ratio as outlined below.

Increase your distance and the amount of time you spend running, not your speed.

The benefits to your cardiovascular system and the number of calories you burn are determined by the distance you cover, and the amount of time you spend moving, not how fast you go. Walk breaks allow you to go further and longer without tiring out.

Are you already a runner?

Jeff knows many veteran runners who incorporate walk breaks into their programs, and improve their running times. Be open-minded. If you already run regularly, go directly to the full program outlined below, skipping over the beginner's six-month gradual build up.

Build up to the program—slowly—as follows:

Increase your Run/Walk Ratio gradually over a six-month period. Don't push yourself harder than your body tells you is alright.

- **Weeks 1 to 4:** Walk ten minutes to warm up. Alternate 10 seconds of running with about 2 minutes of walking, for a total of 20 minutes. Walk ten minutes to cool down.
- **Weeks 5 to 26:** Walk ten minutes to warm up. Alternate 20 seconds of running with 1 to 2 minutes of walking, for a total of 30 minutes. Walk ten minutes to cool down.
- **Weeks 26+:** Walk for five to ten minutes to warm up. Alternate 1 minute of running with 1 to 2 minutes of walking for a total of 45 minutes (twice a week) and 60 to 90 minutes (once a week). Walk five to ten minutes to cool down.
- **Ultimate Goal:** Try to work up to 2 to 3 minutes of running with 1 minute of walking.

The Run/Walk Weekly schedule you do for life.

Work your way up to this program gradually. Depending upon your starting fitness level, it may take you several weeks or several months to get to this stage of the program. Do not push yourself. Take the time to do this correctly.

With this schedule, you will move your body every single day, which is the goal. The days of the week and activities are suggestions—do what works for you, and what you enjoy.

For each day, start with a 5 minute walk to warm up, and end with a 5 to 10 minute walk to cool down.

Monday	Run/walk for 45 minutes or more.
Tuesday	Walk as much as possible or do some other aerobic activity like tennis, biking, swimming or a gym workout, but no running.
Wednesday	Run/walk for 45 minutes or more.
Thursday	Same as Tuesday.
Friday	Same as Tuesday.
Saturday	Run/walk for 60 to 90 minutes.
Sunday	Same as Tuesday.

Ten point review of the Run/Walk Program:

1. **Have a health check** before you start.
2. **Visit a podiatrist** and then buy running shoes.
3. **Eat something** an hour before you start a session.
4. **Start slowly,** and gradually increase your running/walking ratio.
5. **Run with your feet close to the ground,** like a shuffle.
6. **Never huff and puff,** and always be able to carry on a conversation.
7. **Eventual goal: run/walk three times a week**—twice weekly for 45 minutes (or more if you want) and once for 90 minutes.
8. **Stay active on your "off" days**—walk, play a sport, do Wii Fit, but don't run.
9. **Build distance,** not speed.
10. **Never stop taking walk breaks.**

Does it work?

Once you are really into this program, and you see how far you can go and for how long, and when you start to see your body change, and your waist size go down, you will feel really good about yourself. The 10,000 steps and run/walk combo program is our fitness foundation to keep our weight where it should be, our heart healthy, and visceral fat far far away.

It would be great if the run/walk and 10,000 steps were all we needed. But there's the other side to the fitness equation to talk about: Strength training.

Flex those muscles.

The other part of the fitness equation is strength training. You need to strengthen your muscles, so that you can do simple things like open a jar, climb the stairs, get up from a chair, or—most important of all—push yourself up if you fall. Strength training is your tool for building muscle and bone strength.

Hmmm. Heidi Klum seems pretty strong to me. I'll have what she's having.

For years I had heard about the trainer, David Kirsch, who regularly works with Heidi Klum, Anne Hathaway, Ellen Barkin, and many other celebrities (and very cool non-celebrities like my good friends Larry and Alison). This tough trainer had famously whipped Heidi into such great shape that she was the star of the Victoria's Secret lingerie fashion show only a few weeks after she gave birth. My goals were a bit different than Heidi's—to look fitter, but to also keep osteoporosis from continuing its journey through my bones.

Okay, David, make me buff (or at least stronger than I am now).

Since his best-selling book, *The Ultimate New York Body Plan* is a bit on the boot-campy side, I was expecting David to sneer in disgust when he told me to "give him ten" (push-ups) and I dropped to the floor and . . . well . . . couldn't even do one. David is sweet and patient, and he assured me that if

I did a few simple exercises, every day, I would soon be doing push-ups just like Heidi. That became one small goal, but what I really wanted David to tell me was much more comprehensive—how to get in shape, strengthen my muscles and bones, and look really great in lingerie (just kidding).

I asked him:

1. What do I need to do?
2. How do I do it?
3. How often do I do it?

First, we had to decide what needed the most work. Poor upper body strength, weak abdominal muscles and assorted flabby parts are typical for women over fifty, and I had a little of everything. After assessing the condition of my body further with a few sit-ups, more push-ups, and some time on the rowing machine, David was ready to make his recommendations.

You can do this at home.

I wanted to have a program that I could do at home or while traveling, easily, safely and quickly. It had to be a program that really worked, with clear goals and results. David created the perfect plan to meet those needs.

The "Core Strength Training in 15 Minutes" Plan:

Do this every day, or at least four times a week. Before you begin:

- **Get the green light from your doctor.** Talk to your doctor before starting any fitness program, especially if you haven't done much of anything lately.
- **Get a yoga or exercise mat.** You'll do these exercises on your back and knees, so make sure to protect your body while doing them.
- **Wear comfortable clothes that you can move in.** Wear stretchy clothes so you can check your form to make sure it's right.
- **Wear your running shoes.** It's best if you're wearing shoes, instead of going barefoot.
- **Get a stop watch.** You'll need it to time yourself.
- **Buy some weights.** Eventually, you'll want to add free weights into your program, once you've gotten the basics down. Get a pair of 3 lb., 5 lb., and 10 lb. hand weights.

The guidelines:

- **Do this at least four times a week.** Every day is ideal, but with four times a week, you will definitely see results.

- **Do these as a circuit.** Move from one exercise to the next quickly. After you've done all five, take a fifteen second break, and then do them again. The goal is to strengthen your muscles but also work your heart, so keep moving. Start with one set, and gradually build up to three sets. This will take you no more than 15 minutes, max.

- **Stretch a little before you start, and a little when you're done.** Loosen your body up a bit, but don't overdo it.

- **Start slowly.** Build up to three (or more) sets gradually. When three sets start to get too easy, put more repetitions (reps) into each set. But increase your sets and reps slowly. If you start too fast, you have a much greater chance of injuring yourself. Pay close attention to how you feel. It's good to push your body, but not too far, or it will fight back.

- **Remember to breathe.** Breathe slowly and deeply as you go into and out of each rep of each exercise. Never hold your breath.

The Exercises

- **Push-up**
- **Squat**
- **Plié Squat**
- **Plank**
- **Crunch and Sit-up (alternate)**

Exercise No. 1: Push-Up

Nothing symbolizes fitness quite like the simple push-up. It tests your entire body by engaging every part of it—arms, chest, abdomen, hips, and legs. Doing push-ups is the easiest, fastest, and most effective way to get fit. You may need to start with a modified push up and work your way up to doing full push-ups. Do it gradually and you'll get the benefits without getting hurt.

How to do the modified push-up: Kneel on mat, and put hands on floor under your chest. Keep arms almost straight but don't lock your elbows. Keep knees on the floor, raise your feet and cross your ankles. (To the count of 3, lower yourself down to 2 inches off the floor, keeping your body straight like a plank, from your heels to your head. Your arms should bend out to the sides. Then push yourself back up to the count of 3, always keeping your body taut like a plank. Pull your stomach in and do not let it drop down or you'll be putting stress on your lower back. If you are doing this correctly, your entire body will be working.) Do 12 reps. Slowly work your way up to 15 (or more if you can).

How to do the full push-up: Make your entire body straight as a plank, with your toes and the balls of your feet on the mat and hands directly under your chest. These are hard. Very hard. You have to believe you can do them. Because you can. Do 12 reps, and work your way up to 15, slowly.

Whether you're doing the modified or the full push-up (or both) David cautions you to keep your spine neutral, stomach in, and core (abdominal muscles) high. All energy should be in your chest and triceps. Don't let your hips and stomach drop down, but keep everything engaged and taut like a plank. You must visualize a string attached to your back, pulling you up

toward the ceiling, never letting your core slouch down. If you can't complete a rep by going all the way down, go partially down, but always be sure to maintain proper form. Hold the last rep for a few seconds longer, making it the most mindful rep of the set.

Exercise No. 2: Squat

This is one of David's favorite exercises for working the entire lower body, thighs, hips, and butt. The action is as if you were about to sit in a chair. If you've never done these before, try doing them with a chair behind you.

How to do a squat: Stand with your feet under your hips, shoulder width apart. Extend your arms in front of you or put your hands on your hips—whichever makes you feel more balanced. Now slowly bend your knees and stick your butt and chest out stopping once your knees are bent almost 90 degrees or, if you are using the chair, right before you sit on it. Rise up by pushing down through your heels. Repeat 15 times.

When you're comfortable with this exercise, think about adding hand weights and doing some bicep curls, as follows—as you are going down, curl your biceps, and as you're coming back up, straighten your arms. Start with 3 lbs., and work your way up to 5, 8 or 10 lbs. This is a great way to work your arms while you work your butt.

Exercise No. 3: The Plié Squat

This version of the squat focuses on the inner thigh, a problem area for many women. David believes this is one of the best moves for getting the inner thigh area strong, lean, and firm. It also works the rest of the thigh and the butt.

How to do a Pliè Squat: Stand with your feet wider than hip distance apart. Turn your toes out and your heels in. Slowly bring your body weight back onto your heels as you bend your knees out toward your toes and squat down while pushing your butt out. Keep your chest straight. Exhale as you rise to the starting position. Repeat 15 times. When you feel that you have mastered this move, you can add two things to make it even more challenging: hold a 3 lb. weight in each hand, and start by being on your toes, lifting your heels up as you go down, and then pressing into your heels as you go up, and squeezing your butt muscles the whole time. But only add these two extra elements after you've mastered the basic Plié Squat.

The two squat exercises are challenging, but extremely effective. If you need help with balancing, place your hands lightly on the back of a chair or table. It's essential that you push your butt out during these exercises or, in David's words, "Put your brain in your ass when you're doing squats!" Don't tuck your tailbone in. That puts too much stress on your knees.

Exercise No. 4: The Plank

I first did the plank when I took a mat Pilates class a few years ago. I thought it was incredibly hard, but almost Zen-like because you have to be totally and completely still for 60 seconds. It's an amazing exercise that, like the push-up, works your entire body.

How to do a plank: Hold your body in a "plank" position, simulating the "up" part of a push-up, but stay there, holding perfectly still, for 30 seconds to a full minute. Keep your abs tight and your back flat the entire time. Try to lengthen your whole body, reaching back through your heels and forward through the top of your head. Never let your abs droop down, and as with push-ups, visualize a string attached to your back pulling you up toward the ceiling.

When you do this exercise, your heart will be pounding, your arms will be shaking, and you will be waiting for the little ding from your stop watch letting you know that the 60 seconds (or 30, or 45) have passed. David recommends this version, with arms almost straight, but if you have wrist problems, you can do a variation with your arms bent so that your forearms are on the floor facing forward and your shoulders are directly over your elbows.

Exercise No. 5:
The Crunch and Sit-up

Even though our abs get a workout by doing the push-ups and the plank, it is still a good idea to spend a little time doing an exercise just for them. Strong abdominal muscles look good, of course, but they will help us maintain good posture and take a lot of pressure off of our backs as we age. Here's how

David describes a proper crunch:

How to do a crunch: Lie on your back on the mat with your knees bent and feet flat on the floor, engaging your core. Place your fingertips behind your head. Draw your navel toward your spine, tucking in your tailbone, and exhale as you lift your shoulders a few inches off the floor. Aim for 2 to 4 inches at first, and then go a little higher as you get stronger. Inhale as you lower yourself down. Focus on your form while doing this exercise. Don't pull yourself up with your hands, neck, shoulder or back. Use only your abs. Keep everything tucked in. Use a timer and do as many as you can in 60 seconds, but make sure your movement is even.

The sit-up—Alternate sit-ups with crunches and you'll be working all the abdominal muscles effectively.

How to do a sit-up: Lie completely flat on your back, hands behind your head, pull your belly button down into the floor, and using your abdominal muscles pull yourself up, and then lower yourself down. Breathe through the exercise—exhale going up, inhale going down, and keep your legs flat on the floor. Do as many as you can in 60 seconds with even movement.

Eventually, you'll be able to do one whole set in less than four minutes. Challenge yourself to three sets for a full strength work out.

- **Push-ups:** do 10 to 15 in under 45 seconds.
- **Squats:** do 15 in 30 seconds.
- **Plié Squats:** do 15 in 30 seconds.
- **Plank Position:** hold for 30 seconds to 60 seconds.
- **Crunches/Sit-ups:** do as many as you can in 60 seconds.

Feeling out of balance?

As we get older, we can start to lose our ability to balance, which can lead to falls. The best way to counter that is to keep our balance in shape. Several times a day, stand on one foot and bend the other leg up, and hold for 30 seconds. Switch legs and do it again. If you need help in balancing, hold on to a counter top or chair. This is an essential part of your overall fitness, so find the time to do it. Waiting in line at the su-

permarket? Just lift one leg slightly off the ground and no one will ever notice.(By the way, that's one of the best times to do your Kegel exercises, too, although I wouldn't recommend doing those both at the same time. See *Chapter 3* for more on Kegels.)

Want more options?

Walking, running, and strength-training are the three essential components of our new long-term fitness plan. But there are other options to explore if you want to expand your fitness horizons.

Zen=Feel-Good Exercise

Yoga offers excellent benefits for women over fifty. It's well-known as a stress-reliever, can ease arthritis, back pain, and other joint problems, and boost circulation. Holding the poses improves balance and since yoga is a weight-bearing exercise, it fights osteoporosis. It can also alleviate some menopause symptoms. There are many different kinds of yoga—gentle restorative styles that can help ease you back into exercise; stretchy styles that work well with running and strength-training; fast-paced "flow" styles that offers a cardiovascular workout and build strength and stamina. (It is famous as the fitness choice of that oh-so-toned over-fifty woman: Madonna.) Try Pilates, bicycling, hiking, dancing, aerobics, or swimming—whatever gets you burning calories, pumping your heart, and working your muscles. Just do it, each and every day.

Want to have some real fun? Work out with the Wii.

Yoga, strength training, running, Pilates, push-ups—it's all there on the Wii. A very patient voice coaches you. You get measured for weight, Body Mass Index (BMI), and how well you control your balance. You can set goals for yourself and get checked every time you do the Wii to see how you're doing. Do the Wii Fit on those "off" run/walk days, when the weather is awful, or just for fun. There are fitness activities— hula hoop, tightrope walk, ski jump— and all sorts of challenges. This is no toy, but a fun way to seriously work out your body. It's a great way to get your kids up and moving, too. I recommend it highly.

Does it work?

Everything suggested here has been well-researched, tested, and tried by high-level fitness professionals. Now I'm doing it myself—without disrupting my normal life with work, a husband, two children, and a dog. It's manageable—and it works. I've lost weight and gotten leaner and stronger. I feel better. When I recently visited David Kirsch for a check-in, he was pretty pleased with the number of push-ups I can now do. As I say with a lot of things I've pushed myself to do, "If I can do it, anybody can!"

Get on board.

Don't get sidetracked by the latest fitness craze you might see in magazines or on TV. Do these things regularly, and you'll see results:

- **Walk 10,000 steps** every day.
- **Run/walk** for 45 to 60 minutes twice a week, and for 90 minutes once a week.
- **Take long, intentional walks** or do something else fun and active on your non-run/walk days.

- **Find new ways to move your body** every day.
- **Do the core strength training routine** at least 4 times a week.
- **Do a few extra push-ups or sit-ups** whenever you have a minute to spare.

Get more information.

To get you safely started on your journey to fitness and better health, check out the following resources:

Magazines

- *More*, www.more.com
- *Prevention*, www.prevention.com

- *Women's Health*, www.womenshealth.com
- *Runner's World*, www.runnersworld.com

Websites

- www.jeffgalloway.com
- www.davidkirschwellness.com
- Shape Up America, www.shapeup.org

Books

- *Strong Women Stay Young* by Miriam E. Nelson, Ph.D. with Sarah Wernick PhD, Bantam Books 2000
- *The Ultimate New York Body Plan* by David Kirsch, McGraw-Hill, 2007
- *Women's Complete Guide to Running* by Jeff and Barbara Galloway, Meyer & Meyer Sport Publishing, 2007

Chapter 7

Love the Skin You're In

Smart and Easy Skin Care Solutions

Let's reflect.

I spent my teenage summers basking in the sun in my Brooklyn backyard—and at the beach at Coney Island—with baby oil slathered on my body, a reflector aimed at my face, and Creedence Clearwater Revival blasting on the radio. There were many bad sunburns in my youth which have finally, a few years over fifty, come back to haunt me.

Older but not much wiser.

I threw away my reflector and tried to remember to put on sunscreen, but even in my twenties and thirties, I still wasn't careful. Let's face it: tans can (temporarily) make you look healthy and glowing and I wanted a piece of that. Many of us feel fabulous as we're soaking up the sun, and a lot of us look really pretty with that pinky-peachy-glow on our faces. But that gorgeous glow lasts for, what, a day? Then it turns into brown spots, wrinkles, sagging skin, and possibly, even skin cancer. It isn't worth it. If we subject our skin to too much sun, it will not age well, and no amount of tanning will make it look better. Skin cancer is on the rise among women over fifty because we grew up thinking that tan was the way to go. Now our skin needs our attention—both for beauty and for health. We have to get informed, be aware, take control, make smart decisions, and do the right things. But what, exactly, are we supposed to do?

Let's ask Mom.

Growing up, I watched my mother perform her meticulous skin care rituals every morning and evening. She was never one for chasing a fad or buying the next new thing. She believed in the basics for two good reasons: 1) she didn't have a lot of money, and 2) she didn't have a lot of time. I've never seen her without a jar of Pond's Cold Cream in her bathroom.

Being a woman who likes her routines (it's genetic), my mother does the same thing now as she did back then, and her skin looks terrific. Her program includes the basic steps that dermatologists tell us we should do every day: wash, exfoliate, moisturize, protect. I suspected there was more I could do for my skin going forward, but also (just maybe?) reverse some of the damage I had already done.

Facing the future.

With all the scientifically-advanced options that are available these days, I figured I could make my mother's basic healthy skin routine even more effective. When I started researching exactly what and exactly how, I found too many conflicting opinions. I was getting frustrated, especially when I went into a department store and every salesperson in the cosmetics section was trying to sell me the latest and greatest "youth serum." I quickly realized that skin care could be a very expensive proposition.

Recently, I received a gorgeous catalog in the mail from a high end department store. One of the featured skin creams cost $750 for less than 2 ounces. Excuse me? That's a lot of money for a very small amount of something that may or may not work. Unfortunately, we are living in a youth-centric society and everyone feels like they have to "look young." That makes some of us desperate enough to try anything—including surgery—no matter the cost.

I don't want to "look young"; I just want to look healthy and not older than I am, and I want to protect myself from skin cancer. Is that too much to ask?

Take that question to the pros.

Seeking sensible skin care advice from an actual dermatologist, I found Dr. Doris Day, who is a frequent guest expert on TV shows like *Good Morning America* and in magazines like *Allure* and *Health*. She has written a terrific book on ageless skin called *Forget the Facelift*. I liked the sound of that.

Dr. Day's book summed up exactly what I wanted in a skin care program:

- **Low maintenance**
- **Minimal cost**
- **No surgery**
- **Lots of protection**

When I met Dr. Day, I was sure I had found my skin care mentor. She is a living, breathing example of what taking good care of your skin can do. By her own admission, Dr. Day—who is in her late 40s—made mistakes in her younger years, as we all have. She smoked, got too much sun, and didn't eat very well. But with time, patience, and an easy but committed skin care regimen, her skin is healthy and glowing. She is beautiful. It doesn't hurt that she smiles a lot and is upbeat, caring, and a pleasure to be around.

Great skin is our right!

I also spoke with the very smart Dr. Patricia Wexler, who has appeared on TV shows including *The View* and *The Oprah Winfrey Show*, in many health and beauty magazines, and is the skin care guru to some of the biggest names in show business. Dr. Wexler was happy to share her wisdom with us for a very simple reason: she thinks that the more women understand how to take care of their skin, the better we will look, and the less skin cancer we will get. She told me that we don't need expensive skin care products and we don't need a lot of products, just the *right* products. To back up her philosophy of "good skin care for everyone," Dr. Wexler has created her own line of products which are well priced and have the stamp of approval from the Skin Cancer Foun-

dation, which is one of the reasons why I called her. She is in our age group, and created this line with herself in mind.

Beautiful skin, inside and out.

Dr. Day started my skin care education by telling me that we need to take a "whole body" approach to skin care. We must take care of our skin, eat right, stay away from unhealthy food and drink, exercise regularly, refrain from smoking, get plenty of sleep, and minimize stress. The health of our skin is a direct result of our overall health, so the lifestyle choices we make every day can make our skin sallow and dull, or clear and glowing, no matter our age.

Since I had already started my new healthy eating and exercise plans, I was ready to move full speed ahead on a skin care plan.

Here's what I want to know.
- **What should I be doing?**
- **What products do I need?**
- **What results will I see?**
- **How much will it cost?**
- **What else is there, if I want to go beyond the basics?**

Mirror, mirror
in my hand.

Dr. Day handed me a 5x magnifying mirror, told me to look in it and say out loud what bothered me about my skin. I did, and this is what I saw:

- **Crow's feet wrinkles on the outside corners of my eyes (especially when I smile)**
- **Dry patches on my cheeks and on the sides of my chin**
- **Light brown spots, mostly on the right side of my forehead where I part my hair**
- **Tiny red, broken capillaries**
- **Large pores on my nose area**
- **Feathery lines under my lower lip**
- **Lines above my upper lip**
- **Deep folds from the sides of my nose down to the corners of my mouth**
- **A crease between my brows, from furrowing them when I'm knitting, I think**
- **Dull skin**

Dr. Day assured me my skin would look better in a few weeks if I followed some simple steps, using the right products for my more mature skin.

What are those products?

When Dr. Day outlined our skin care program, she also recommended some specific products. Dr. Wexler named a few more, and I tried many, many others based on their descriptions of what we should expect from our cleansers and moisturizers and sunscreens. Each of these recommended products has been tested and tried during the past year with good results. The following is not a definitive list of effective products. New products are always being introduced, so check in with your dermatologist periodically. Also useful are the information resources listed at the end of this chapter.

As for the products, use your own favorites or try different ones—just make sure that the products do what they are supposed to do. Take a look at our suggestions if you're interested in trying something new. Almost everything is available in any drug or mass merchandise store across the country or online—and at reasonable prices. Great skin does not have to cost a fortune, as long as you follow these guidelines.

Look for products with peptides.

Peptides stimulate the body to produce more collagen, which helps to restore luster to maturing skin. Collagen is a natural substance that keeps skin looking plump and line free, but we lose collagen as we age, and sun damage makes it worse. When the body makes more collagen, fine lines and wrinkles are reduced, and skin looks more radiant and less puffy. Dr. Wexler uses a very effective peptide called haloxyl in her Instant De-Puff Eye Gel (which has a huge cult following and which I love).

Look for products with antioxidants.

Exposure to sun and pollution releases substances called free radicals in our skin, which slow the production of collagen. Antioxidants stop free radicals in their tracks and preserve our supply of collagen. Effective antioxidants include Vitamins C and E, kinetin, alpha-lipoic acid, idebenone, and green tea. The most powerful one on the market today is coffee berry. The first coffee berry product on the market was RevaléSkin, but Priori and a few others are quickly moving in.

Exfoliate, exfoliate, exfoliate.

Exfoliating is the key to skin perfection. Many women are afraid to exfoliate every day, thinking that their skin will become irritated. Not so, our experts say, if you're using the right product, exfoliating gently, followed by a restoring serum, moisturizer and protection. Recommended products are below.

The Smart and Easy Skin Care Plan

Here's the program. Follow it and your skin will look better, fresher, and more clear. But that's only if you are also making healthy eating and exercise choices to nourish your skin health from the inside (see *Chapter 5: You= What You Eat* and *Chapter 6: Move that Body*).

As soon as you wake up in the morning:

1. Cleanse

Take a wet, warm, soft washcloth and slowly, gently wash your face with a small amount of a recommended facial cleanser, or just warm water. Gently scrub in circular motions, spending a bit more time on the t-zone (the area around your nose, chin, and forehead), and then rinse well with cool water. Very gently pat almost dry, leaving your skin slightly moist.

Recommended products:

- **Aveeno Ultra Calming Facial Cleanser ($8 for 6 oz.)**
- **RevaléSkin Facial Cleanser with Coffee Berry ($40 for 6 oz., available at your dermatologist's office or online)**
- **any Neutrogena cleanser ($7–10 for 5–7 oz.)**
- **Olay Regenerist Daily Regenerating Cleanser ($8 for 5 oz.)**
- **Cetaphil Gentle Skin Cleanser ($8 for 8 oz).**

2. Exfoliate

Exfoliate every day with an at-home microdermabrasion product or an exfoliating cream. Carmindy, who is one of our makeup experts in *Chapter 8*, uses plain white sugar mixed with warm water on a washcloth. She swears by it, although Dr. Wexler cautioned that sugar might be a little too rough for some women's facial skin—but she agreed that it makes a great body scrub. Try it and see how it works for you. Rinse with cool water and pat dry until skin is slightly damp.

Recommended products:

- **Neutrogena Healthy Skin Rejuvenator device with disposable pads ($32 for starter kit, $19 for puff refills)**
- **Olay Regenerist Micro-Exfoliating Cleansing Cloths ($7 for 30)**
- **Patricia Wexler Resurfacing Microbrasion System ($51)**
- **Aveeno Skin Brightening Daily Scrub ($9 for 5 oz.)**
- **or good old white sugar (free because you took it out of your kitchen, since you are no longer eating sugar—see *Chapter 5: You = What You Eat*).**

3. Moisturize the skin around your eyes

Use your ring finger (it's the most gentle finger) to apply a few dots of eye cream under your eye, but avoid getting too close to the lash line, as it could irritate your eye or clog an eyelash follicle and cause a sty. Gently dab the cream around each eye, including the outside corners where those dreaded crow's feet hang out. Make sure it's properly absorbed. During the day, consider using an eye cream with added SPF, as recommended by the Skin Cancer Foundation, and use one without SPF at night. Keep an extra bottle of eye cream in your purse for a touch up during the day. Dr. Wexler's Intensive De-Puffing Eye Gel is a great choice to revive, refresh, and de-puff all at once.

Recommended products:

- Patricia Wexler MD Instant De-Puff Eye Gel ($19 for 0.5 oz.),
- Patricia Wexler MD Intensive 3-in-1 Eye Cream ($33 for 0.5 oz.)
- Garnier Skin Renew Anti-Sun-Damage SPF 15 Daily Eye Cream ($12 for 0.5 oz.)
- Olay Professional Pro-X Eye Restoration Complex ($42 for 0.5 oz.)
- RoC Retinol Eye Cream ($22 for 0.5 oz.)
- Relastin Eye Silk ($69 for 0.5 oz.)
- DDF Protective Eye Cream SPF 15 Plus CoQ1 ($50 for 0.5 oz.)

4. Restore and brighten your face with an antioxidant serum

Take a small dollop of a lotion with antioxidants that works to brighten and even skin tone, and place dots all around your face. With gentle upward strokes, massage it into your skin. Put a little on your neck and chest area.

Recommended products:

- Choose a serum that includes coffee berry, green tea, CQ10, retinol Vitamin C or idebenone.
- Revalé Skin Coffee Berry Day Cream (SPF 15 and available at a dermatologist's office or online ($110 for 1.7 oz.)
- Priori Brightening Facial Complex ($75 for 1 oz.)
- SkinCeuticals Phloretin CF ($150 for 1 oz.)
- Prevage by Elizabeth Arden Concentrated Brightening Serum ($125 for 1 oz.)
- Aveeno Positively Ageless Rejuvenating Serum ($20 for 1.7 oz.)

- **Olay Regenerist Daily Regenerating Serum ($18 for 1.7)**
- **Olay Professional Pro-X Discoloration Fighting Concentrate ($48 for 0.4 oz.)**
- **Patricia Wexler MD MMPi-20 Intensive 3-in-1 Serum ($60 for 1 oz.).**

The whole process takes about 5 minutes.

Before going out for the day.

You've already cleansed, exfoliated, and put on an antioxidant serum or lotion to restore your skin. Now you need to get your skin ready for makeup and protect it from the elements (sun and pollution).

1. Moisturize

Carmindy convinced me to try the only moisturizer she uses: Crème de la Mer, which has been around since the 1960s and has a cult following. The basic cream does not have SPF in it, which makes it a good choice for evening and for winter months when a heavier cream is better. It's luxurious and my skin felt like velvet, but it is expensive. For days when you're out and about, wear a moisturizer with sunscreen (and a tinted moisturizer or foundation with sunscreen; see *Chapter 8: Face the Facts* for recommended products). Tap your ring finger into the jar and dab little dots all over your face and neck, massaging it in with gentle upward strokes. Let it set for a few minutes while you start getting dressed, or whatever you need to do before you add sunscreen (if needed).

Recommended products:

Rich moisturizers without sunscreen are:
- **Crème de la Mer ($230 for 2oz.)**
- **Olay Regenerist Micro-Sculpting Cream ($30 for 1.7 oz.)**
- **Olay Professional Pro-X Wrinkle Smoothing Cream ($18)**

Some of the best moisturizers with sunscreen include:
- **Olay Regenerist UV Defense Regenerating Lotion SPF 50 ($30 for 1.7 oz.)**
- **Aveeno Positively Radiant Daily Moisturizer SPF 30 ($17 for 2.5 oz.)**
- **Aveeno Ultra-Calming Daily Moisturizer SPF 30 ($17 for 4 oz.),**
- **Aveeno Positively Ageless Daily Moisturizer SPF 30 ($20 for 2.5 oz.)**
- **Bobbi Brown's Extra SPF 25 Moisturizing Balm ($85 for 1.7 oz.)**

- **Patricia Wexler MD Universal Anti-Aging Moisturizer SPF 30 ($40 for 1.7 oz.)**
- **Patricia Wexler MD Intensive 3-in-1 Day Cream SPF 30 with MMPi-20 ($43 for 1.7 oz.).**

2. Protect with sunscreen

This step is for those days when you're out in direct sunlight, or you're not wearing a moisturizer and foundation

Sunscreen Smarts

Some sunscreens now have an SPF of 100. Do we need such a high number? Sunscreens protect our skin from two kinds of harmful ultraviolet rays, UVA and UVB, that cause skin aging and skin cancer. SPF, or Sun Protection Factor, calculates how much time you can stay in direct sun without incurring UVB damage. If your bare skin could manage 10 minutes before burning, a SPF of 30 will theoretically give you 300 minutes, or 5 hours. (In reality, no sunscreen will be fully effective for much more than two hours due to skin absorption and sweating.) SPF 30 is the lowest you should go, but a very high SPF isn't as important as how much you put on and how often you apply it. The super-high SPFs are a marketing tool, since the functional difference in UVB protection between an SPF 100 and SPF 50 is marginal. Here are our experts' rules for sunscreen:

- Look for sunscreens (or moisturizers with sunscreens) with the following ingredients: ecamsule (Mexoryl), titanium dioxide, and avobenzone (Parsol 1789).
- Make sure the sun protection ingredients give you broad-based protection (broad spectrum) against both UVB and UVA.
- Use one full ounce (the equivalent of two tablespoons or a shot glass) per application to cover your whole body.
- If you use a spray sunscreen, apply two coats in case you miss a spot.
- Apply your sunscreen 15 to 30 minutes before exposure.
- Reapply after swimming, toweling off, sweating, or every two hours, whichever comes first.
- The lowest SPF you should use is 30, especially if you're out in direct sunlight, and (importantly) even if it's cloudy.

with sunscreen. After moisturizer has set for a few minutes, apply sunscreen (SPF 30 or higher) over moisturizer. Put a few dots evenly on your face, keeping away from the eye area, and very gently massage in with upward strokes. Then apply some to your hands, ears, neck, chest, and any other part of your body that may be exposed (including your feet if you're wearing sandals).

Recommended products:

- **Neutrogena Ultra Sheer Dry Touch Sunblock SPF 45 or 55 ($10 for 3 oz.)**
- **SkinCeuticals Sport UV Defense 40 ($38 for 3 oz.)**
- **La Roche Posay Anthelios W Gel 40 ($55 for 3.4 oz.).**

Okay, beautiful, now you're ready to put on a little makeup (little is the operative word) to add some extra glow to your gorgeous skin. Read *Chapter 8* for great advice from our makeup experts, Laura Geller and Carmindy.

Before going to bed.

Like your mother told you, never go to bed with makeup on. If you want your skin to look good, you've got to be good to your skin, and that includes keeping it clean.

1. Remove your makeup

Dr. Day recommended good, old Albolene cream, which has been around forever (our grandmothers probably used it), and can be found in any drug store. This humble, inexpensive product is hydrating, and effective at getting makeup off—even waterproof mascara. Massage it in all over, even your eyelids, and then tissue off or remove with a moist warm washcloth. Plain petroleum jelly is not recommended because it is too thick, can clog pores, and creates an annoying film over your eyes. Albolene, by comparison, liquefies on the skin. Dr. Day also likes Pond's Cold Cream and pre-moistened makeup remover towelettes. With these recommended products, you won't need a separate eye makeup remover. They get the job done.

Recommended products:

- **Albolene Moisturizing Cleansing Cream ($12 for 12 oz.)**

- **Pond's Cold Cream ($5 for 3.5 oz.)**
- **Neutrogena Makeup Remover Cleansing Towelettes ($8 for 25)**

2. Cleanse

Splash a little warm water over your face, take a small amount of facial cleanser in your hands or with a wash cloth and wash your entire face, including over your eyes, to remove any residue. Rinse and pat dry.

Recommended products:

- **use the same facial cleanser you use in the morning**

3. Moisturize the skin around your eyes

Use an eye cream without SPF (see above for recommendations) and with your ring finger, dab a few tiny dots all around your eye area. Keep dabbing until it's all absorbed.

4. Make sure your skin is completely dry—not damp—before going on to step 5.

Get down on the floor and do ten push-ups while you're waiting for your skin to dry before the next step. Or, floss and brush your teeth if you aren't feeling that ambitious.

5. Slough off the skin cells and work on those wrinkles while you sleep:

Retinoid products speed up your skin's natural sloughing action to smooth fine lines and wrinkles, remove brown spots, and even out skin tone. Retinoids are Vitamin A-derivatives which you can get from your dermatologist (Retin-A or Renova) or over-the-counter. Our experts recommend the dermatologist-prescribed brands, which are stronger and more effective. Other prescription-only brands include: Tri-luma, which combines hydroquinone—a retinoid—with an anti-inflammatory; Vivité, which has ingredients that both exfoliate skin and restore an even skin tone; and Atralin, a more hydrating retinoid product. Retinoids can be drying and when you first start using one, your skin may look a little chapped and may even peel, but that won't last long. Because this product is helping to remove that top layer of skin cells and uncovering the new ones underneath, your skin will be more sensitive to sunburn. Be extra vigilant about sunscreen. The products are simple to use. Your skin must be ultra dry which will help lessen irritation. Take a pea-size amount and dab it all over your face and, using gentle upward strokes, massage it in. Keep it away from your eyes but make sure that you get it into those crow's feet.

Recommended Products:

- **Renova or Retin-A (prescription only, $150, lasts 3 to 4 months)**
- **RoC Multi-Correxion Night Treatment ($25 for 1 oz.), Neutrogena Advanced Solutions Skin Transforming Complex Nightly Renewal Cream ($40 for 1.4 oz.)**
- **SkinCeuticals Retinol 1.0 ($56 for 1 oz.).**

6. Moisturize (optional):

To make sure the retinoid product doesn't dry out your skin while it's doing its job, consider a light layer of moisturizer (without sunscreen). Take a dime-sized amount of moisturizer and dab it all over your face, gently massaging it in.

Recommended products:

- **RevaléSkin Night Cream with Coffee Berry ($110 for 1.7 oz.)**
- **Aveeno Ultra Calming Night Cream ($13 for 1.7 oz.)**
- **Patricia Wexler MD Intensive Night Reversal and Repair Cream ($45 for 3.4 oz.).**

There you have it.

Our basic skin care program doesn't take long to do and, unless you opt for a few indulgences, it won't cost much. Many beauty products are priced based on perception and how much companies think they can get for their products. Spend where it matters. For example, retinoid products have been proven to be effective, so spend the money to buy the best one there is, even if it's prescription. If you have a prescription plan through health insurance, you can often get a better price or can buy a generic equivalent of the retinoid product your dermatologist recommends.

Does it work?

I spent a few weeks testing out products to decide what I wanted to use, and then I started my official eight-week trial of the program as outlined above. I followed it religiously and, when I went back to see Dr. Day eight weeks later, she agreed that my skin had improved, and would continue to improve. She cautioned me that since I was stripping away the dead skin cells, I had to be even more vigilant about protecting it from the elements with moisturizer and sunscreen. For best results, Dr. Day encouraged me to continue with this program in conjunction with eating well, getting exercise, and making smart lifestyle choices.

So, about those "other things" . . .

What if you want to do more? You know . . . "other things." Perhaps you're already doing Botox or chemical peels, or giving them some serious thought, but there are a lot of other treatments to consider, too.

First things first: will it hurt (my face and my bank account)?

While none of the following treatments are surgical, the discomfort and cost vary depending on what you're having done. Dr. Wexler explained that non-surgical medical advances in dermatology carry minimal risk, work extremely well, and are much more affordable than plastic surgery. Do your homework and find a board-certified dermatologist or dermasurgeon with a stellar reputation. Check the doctor's credentials with respected groups such as the American Society for Laser Medicine and Surgery (www.aslms.org) and the American Academy of Cosmetic Surgery (www.cosmeticsurgery.org).

Help for the Most Common Complaints

Here are a few of the more common concerns women over fifty have about their skin, and what you can do about them.

- **Crow's feet lines**—short lines that radiate from the outer corners of our eyes that show more when we laugh, and can get deeper as time goes on.
- **Mouth-to-nose lines**—also called nasolabial folds, which go from the sides of the nose to the mouth, and can often be quite deep.

- **Frown lines**—a deep line can develop between our brows that is permanent and can make us look angry, or like we're concentrating.
- **Forehead lines**—lines that occur when you raise your eyebrows in surprise or to express emotion.

Non-surgical treatments for lines:

Botox (Botulinum Toxin Type A)

As soon as it got FDA approval in 2002, Botox became the celebrity choice for removing lines, especially between the brows, in the forehead, and the crow's feet area. Botox, which is injected with a tiny needle directly into the area to be treated, relaxes the muscles and smoothes the skin for up to four months. Derived from the bacteria that causes botulism, there are no bacteria in the final Botox product. There is almost no pain, and recovery is quick. Localized pain, infection, inflammation, tenderness, swelling, redness, and/or bruising are possible but rare side effects. Cost: depending on which and how many areas, the cost can be anywhere from $400 to $900. Most women get injections every four months, but it varies. A similar drug, Reloxin, has recently been approved by the FDA, and has been available in Canada and Europe under the name Dysport. It lasts at least ten weeks longer than Botox. Alternatives: Dr. Wexler recommends products that contain the peptide GABA, which helps to relax muscles. She suggests trying them before you try Botox. Using these products after Botox injections may help to prolong the effect.

Recommended products:
- **Fastscription Advanced No-Injection Wrinkle Smoother by Patricia Wexler MD ($29.50 for 0.5 oz.)**
- **Freeze 24—7 Instant Targeted Wrinkle Treatment ($65 for 0.35 oz).**

Temporary injectable fillers

Fillers are injected into wrinkles to "fill" them, smoothing out the skin. They are often used on wrinkles that Botox can't adequately treat. Temporary fillers are absorbed into the body, so they need to be refilled regularly. Some doctors use a layering approach with

Botox first, then a filler. Possible side effects of all fillers (temporary or permanent) include temporary swelling and bruising. Multiple treatments are necessary to achieve results, and technique is critical, which is why it's essential to have it done by the right doctor. A big advantage to temporary, rather than permanent, fillers is that if you don't like the results, you are not stuck with them, but to maintain the results you must do the treatments several times a year.

Alternatives:

- **Dr. Wexler recommends using a cream with polysilicone-11, which fills wrinkles for 10 to 12 hours. It can be applied directly under your foundation in lieu of a filler, or to prolong the effect of a filler.**

She also recommends:

- **The Youth As We Know It Anti-Aging Moisture Cream by Bliss ($79 for 1.7 oz.).**

Most common temporary fillers:

Human collagen

Collagen is a protein that is naturally found in our skin. As we age, we lose collagen, and wrinkles can appear, some becoming quite deep. Collagen-replacement therapy can restore the natural collagen support layer to our skin, smoothing facial lines, diminishing wrinkles, and plumping lips. Cosmoderm (for fine lines) and Cosmoplast (for deeper lines) are two of the more popular treatments made from human collagen. Injections can be painful. The cost is about $500 per treatment, and most people get three treatments per year.

Hyaluronic acid

Some of the most popular brand names are Restylane, Hylaform, Juvaderm, Captique, Prevelle Silk, Puragen, and Perlane. All are made from hyaluronic acid, which exists naturally in all living organisms. As with collagen, our bodies will not reject this product, and the incidence of adverse reactions is very low. Cost is about $600 per treatment and each lasts from three to nine months. Some, like Perlane, have been known to last for up to a year.

Synthetic Poly-L-Lactic acid

The most well-known is Sculptra, also called New Fill. It's made from a type of sugar in the alpha hydroxyl acid family. Sculptra is recommended for filling the deeper lines of the face, restoring volume and natural contour, especially on sunken cheeks, and for filling those deep lines from the nose to the mouth. This treatment can last up to two years or longer, but two treatments is common. Cost varies, but is generally $1,200 per treatment.

Bovine collagen

Yep, you got that right: bovine as in cow. The most well known brands, Zyderm (for fine lines) and Zyplast (for deeper lines), are FDA approved have been used with success for over twenty years. These can cause an allergic reaction since they are made from a substance not found in the human body, and typically last about three to four months. Cost is about $500 per treatment. The newest entry to this category of fillers is Evolence. It costs a little more ($600) but lasts for over a year.

Calcium-based microspheres

A long-lasting filler marketed under the name Radiesse. The cost is over $1,000 per syringe, but it lasts about a year.

Fat transfer

Also known as using your own fat. This is a great concept—remove fat from your butt or thigh and inject it into your facial lines! If only I was brave enough. It comes with a hefty price tag, though: $4,000 per treatment. You would think there would be a discount since you're using your own fat, no? The results can last up to six months, but some people have reported a permanent fix.

Permanent Fillers:

These are used to treat the same areas as temporary fillers: nose to mouth lines, forehead lines, brow lines and crow's feet. It is critical that you are sure about doing this because the results are permanent. If you're very unhappy with the results, the filler can be removed surgically, but scarring is possible.

Silicone

Silikon 1000 is one of the best known

permanent fillers and is made from highly refined liquid silicone. The price varies from about $500 to $1500 per treatment.

Synthetic Material

Polymethylmetha-crylate (PMMA)is a synthetic material commonly used in hip implants, bone cement, and other medical devices. Artefill, which received FDA approval in 2006, is a mixture of PMMA microspheres and bovine collagen. It is injected in selected sites over several sessions. The cost is $500 per syringe, and how many syringes are needed depends upon the number of sites to be treated.

Out, out, damn brown spots (and fine lines, and broken capillaries).

Dr. Wexler says that one of the best ways to get rid of brown spots and other facial discolorations is to first try an at-home microdermabrasion kit— like the ones recommended earlier— in conjunction with a retinoid product. If your brown spots and red veins are too dark to be covered up with found-ation, and they just bother the hell out of you, there are other weapons in the arsenal.

What you can do at home.

At-home peels and microdermabrasion

If you have extra stubborn brown spots, shift your at-home exfoliation into high gear by using a combination of a microdermabrasion product, such as the Neutrogena Healthy Skin Rejuvenator, and an at-home glycolic peel, like Avon Anew Clinical Advanced Retexturizing Peel. Alternate the products every night until the brown spots have been diminished enough to make you happy, then go back to your basic skin care program. Do this routine once a month to keep the spots away. The key to success is sticking with the basic skin care program.

Hydroquinone bleaching cream

Hydroquine inhibits melanin production to fade brown spots and other discolorations of the skin, such as melasma, and takes three to six months. Every night—before putting on your retinoid product—dab this cream directly onto brown spots and discolored areas (including spots on your hands). Apply your retinoid product over the bleaching cream. Hydroquinone should be used for only a few months.

What your dermatologist can do.

Chemical Peels

Chemical peels speed up the natural exfoliating process and are faster and more powerful than what we can do at home. The ingredients, techniques, and strengths of the chemicals vary and should be matched to your skin type and goals by your dermatologist. The most popular approach is a series of light glycolic acid peels that are done once a month and gradually increase in strength. Medium and deep peels are not quick, easy, or painless. They can leave your skin crusty and red (much like a burn), and can require you to stay home for several days to recover. Some experts believe monthly light to medium peels help the body shed precancerous lesions before they become a problem. The American Cancer Society, however, does not take a position on face peels as a skin cancer prevention strategy. The cost for light peels is around $100 to $200 per treatment, depending upon which one is used.

Most common chemical peels:

- **Glycolic acid peel**—Glycolic acid dissolves the upper, older layer of skin to reveal the new layer and can also stimulate collagen production. They are usually done as a series of three to five peels, increasing in concentration and contact time. There are usually no visible signs of peeling, although the skin may appear red for a few hours afterward. It will feel almost instantly firmer and more hydrated. To get rid of brown spots, the dermatologist will use a higher concentration on those areas, so you can expect more redness and possibly a bit of crusting over on those spots.

- **Trichloroacetic acid (TCA) peel**—The TCA peel is considered the gold standard of chemical peels for women over fifty. The dermatologist can apply TCA in superficial, medium, or deep strengths, depending on the concentration of acid used and the number of layers applied. ou may need to plan for recovery time depending upon the strength of the peel. The skin appears frosty white after the peel, then turns a deep red, becoming dark brown and leathery. After this colorful process, the skin peels off. Within one week to ten days, your skin will look younger, fine lines will be erased, and brown spots will be greatly diminished. The cost is anywhere from $250 to $800 and up, depending upon the strength. Two treatments may be necessary for full effect.

- **Lactic acid peel**—Lactic acid works basically like glycolic acid, but is milder than other chemical peels, so it may be a better choice for sensitive skin or skin conditions like rosacea. Lactic acid peels can be done in a series, or in combination with other peels, and are sometimes used as a first peel to prepare the skin for stronger treatments.

Microdermabrasion

This is a super-charged exfoliating process, much more powerful than anything we can do at home. Fine crystals are applied to the skin to loosen the outer layer of dead cells, which are vacuumed up with a suction device. One to two treatments per month for three months, followed by maintenance treatments every eight weeks, is the recommended program. Cost is $200 to $250 per treatment.

Lasers

Dermatologists can use lasers to treat brown spots, broken capillaries, wrinkles, and can even permanently remove facial and body hair or tattoos.

- **Laser beam (V-Beam)**—This specifically treats sun-damaged skin, brown spots, broken capillaries, and rosacea. It involves intense pulsed light (IPL), which allows the dermatologist to carefully target a single spot as opposed to the entire face. It is especially effective in removing tiny red veins. Several treatments may be necessary, at $450 or more per treatment.
- **Q-switched ruby laser**—Isolated brown spots on the chest, hands, arms or legs can be erased with this laser, which emits a red light that vaporizes targeted areas of clustered pigment. A scab develops, which fades over a few weeks. One to

three treatments are required, depending on the areas, and how bad the damage is. Cost is about $300 to $700 per treatment.

- **Fraxel resurfacing**—This is one of the most highly effective treatments available and can offer dramatic improvements without surgery. The laser penetrates beneath the surface of the skin, stimulating the production of collagen while it diminishes the fine lines and brown spots. The laser digs microscopic tunnels in the skin and does its work under there, so there is no damage to the outer skin. For about two days after the treatment you will probably look as though you have a sunburn, but your skin will produce new collagen after several weeks and after the treatments are finished, skin is brighter, smoother, more radiant, and has fewer wrinkles. There's no scarring, and the risk for complications is extremely low. About 20 percent of the face is treated during each session, so about 4 to 5 sessions are normally required. Cost is about $450 or so per treatment.

- **Fractionated CO2 Lasers**—These are hard-core resurfacing treatments. Some common brand names include Fraxel Re:pair and TotalFX. If you have severe wrinkles, a lot of dark spots, or large clusters of hyperpigmentation, you may want to consider it. The laser goes much deeper into the skin than the Fraxel Resurfacing procedure, but you only need to do it once. It can take over a week to recover. Skin will peel, and look red and rough during recovery. Many beauty experts feel, however, that even this new version of the CO2 laser is very old-fashioned, and not the way to go. It is a big commitment, costing anywhere from $3,500 up to $8,000, but you only do it once, and Dr. Wexler says you can expect up to a 90 percent reduction in discoloration.

Lift your face to the heavens.

Are you feeling a little jowly lately? It's funny how it works; when you wake up in the morning, your face looks a little plumper, and the wrinkles look less noticeable. By the time night comes around, does your face looks decidedly less plump, and more, how can I put it gently . . . like it's heading south? If you're not happy with this, there is a non-surgical thing you can do (or have done to you, as it were) to counter gravity's law.

Thermage

This is a non-invasive procedure used to smooth, tighten, and contour the skin of the face (or body) and it has no recovery time, so women can usually go back to their normal lives immediately. This technology uses radio-frequency energy to heat the collagen below the skin's surface so that the collagen tightens and creates a gentle facelift without surgery. It can also be used just to treat the area around the eyes instead of having your eyes done surgically. But here's the catch: since Thermage works by heating the collagen in your skin, you need to have enough collagen to work with. If your skin is very saggy, this may not work. Talk it over very carefully with your dermatologist. It can be painful, and topical anesthesia, or intravenous sed-ation, is required. The treatments cost about $3,000 to $5,000 each and sometimes a woman needs two (six months apart). The results can last for years if you take very good care of your skin going forward.

Surgery, anyone?

If you choose the surgery route, find the best doctor available who specializes in what you want to have done. Ask around, talk to friends, consult with your own doctors, and make sure the surgeon you choose is board-certified.

All in favor, say "Eye"!

I did a decidedly unscientific survey of friends and friends of friends about what cosmetic surgery, if any, they would consider. The vast majority of them said a blepharoplasty, better known as "getting your eyes done." If you look tired when you're not; if you have little bags under your eyes that even Dr. Wexler's Instant De-Puffing Gel doesn't help; if your eyelids are hooding over to the point where it doesn't matter what color eye shadow you're wearing; then maybe, just maybe, it's something you might want to consider. There are some people who must do this out of necessity because their eyelids hood over so much it can obstruct their vision.

Body of Evidence

There are a few important things you

should do for healthy, lovely, glowing skin—all over. They are the same things you do for your face.

Cleanse

As we age, our skin tends to get dry. Short showers at cooler temperatures are better than baths or long, hot showers. Afterward, use a gentle, moisturizing cleanser.

Recommended products:

- **Aveeno Active Naturals Advanced Care Body Wash ($7 for 12 oz.)**
- **Olay Body Quench Body Wash ($9 for 23.6 oz.)**

Exfolilate

Use an exfoliating body scrub every day, or several times a week. Keep a jar filled with white sugar in your shower stall, and a washcloth, and scrub away. Add a few drops of scented oil, like lavender.

Recommended products:

- **Neutrogena Energizing Sugar Body Scrub ($10.00 for 6 oz.)**
- **good old white sugar**

Moisturize

Slather on moisturizer while skin is still moist. Plain, natural food-grade oils like olive oil or safflower oil are luxurious and highly effective. Get a plastic squeeze bottle with a good spout—like the kind used for ketchup in diners—fill it with olive oil plus a few drops of lavender or other essential oil (from the health food store), shake it up and use. It makes skin feel like velvet (and it smells good, too). Oils do not technically moisturize (meaning add moisture), but act as a barrier to hold moisture in. You can also use oil over your favorite moisturizer, especially in winter when skin is extra dry. Consider a daily moisturizer with a sunscreen built into it for day use.

Recommended products:

- **Olay Body Quench Moisturizing Body Lotion for Extra Dry Skin (I wish they would put an SPF in this, then it would be the perfect product) ($12 for 20.2 oz.)**
- **Avon Skin So Soft Satin Glow Ultimate Body Moisturizing Lotion SPF 15 ($12 for 8.4 oz.)**
- **Aveeno Active Naturals Daily Moisturiz-**

- ing Body Lotion SPF 15 ($12 for 12 oz.)
- Eucerin Everyday Protection Body Lotion SPF 15 ($12 for 13.5 oz.)
- Clarins Hydration-Plus Moisture Lotion SPF 15 ($48 for 1.7 oz.)
- olive oil (get extra virgin, so you can throw some on your healthy salads, too).

Protect

Going out? You have to put on that sunscreen. For most days, try to use a moisturizer with a built-in sunscreen. If you're going to be in the sun for hours apply a broad-spectrum sunscreen with an SPF of at least 30—and reapply every two hours.

Recommended products:

- all of the sunscreens recommended for your face are fine for your body.

Got road maps in your legs?

You may be one of those lucky women whose skin hides veins, or you may have lighter skin which shows every little vascular thing going on underneath the skin. Varicose veins could be a health concern, but other visible veins, like spider veins, are mostly a cosmetic nuisance. They're often genetic, but hormone changes can trigger them during menopause. To help prevent varicose veins, lose extra weight and exercise regularly—both will reduce the pressure on your veins and keep blood flowing. If you have a tendency toward varicose veins, compression stockings can help—there are now even brands that look just like regular hosiery with many colors and styles. Once they've appeared, there are still things you can do to get rid of these visible veins—or at the very least, hide them.

For Varicose veins

Doctors used to perform "vein stripping" which required general anesthesia and a hospital stay of several days. This is a very old-fashioned approach and rarely done today. For larger varicose veins, there are highly effective options that need only local anesthesia and minimal recovery time.

- **Radiofrequency (RF) closure**— RF closure is a minimally invasive procedure performed on an outpatient basis by a vascular doctor (vein specialist). The physician makes a small opening in the skin near the diseased vein, and inserts a tiny catheter, which uses radio-frequency (RF) energy to heat the vein wall. The vein wall shrinks until the vein seals closed. Once the diseased vein is closed, blood will re-route to healthy veins.

- **Transilluminated powered phlebectomy**—This is a minimally invasive surgical technique performed under light anesthesia for varicose vein removal. The vascular surgeon removes the vein using a small, electrical surgical device while viewing the vein with the use of a transilluminating light that passes under the skin. This method allows the surgeon to remove veins using a minimal number of small incisions and during a short amount of time. While this technique removes the vein, it is far superior to the "vein stripping" that was once the only choice. Recovery time is a few days.

For Spider Veins

These appear as tiny red, blue, and purple squiggles and are actually enlarged capillaries. With treatment, they will disappear, but new ones pop up. Spider veins are usually genetic. You'll need to deal with them every two or three years. Spider veins are not a health issue, which is the main reason why insurance companies won't usually cover the cost of treatment.

Solutions—These are the most effective solutions for dealing with spider veins:

- **Sclerotherapy**—This is considered the gold standard for dealing with spider veins. A tiny needle is used to inject the vein with a saline solution that irritates the lining of the vein, causing it to collapse and disappear from the surface of the skin. The blood will re-route through new capillaries. You might need to do the treatment again in several years, since new ones will almost definitely form. The cost is about $250-$500 per session.

- **Laser Treatment**—Laser treatments just like the ones that are used for those broken capillaries on the face can treat spider veins. Such treatments are often used in combination with sclerotherapy for maximum impact. Multiple sessions are usually necessary. The cost is about the same as for sclerotherapy.

Raise your legs
if you want to avoid surgery.

Here's a simple, effective way to prevent or reduce vein problems in your legs. Lie on the floor (on a yoga mat) with your tush up against the wall, and put your legs straight up. If that's too much for your back, then rest your legs on a chair or at an angle with your feet on the wall. Stay like that for about ten minutes, if you can. Meditate, relax, think about how good it feels to let all the blood flow back down. It's a great late afternoon pick-me-up and any swelling you had in your feet, ankles, or legs will be gone.

Or just cover them up.

You can always cover up minor blemishes with leg makeup, or a good self-tanner. One coat will deepen your skin tone enough to make leg veins less noticeable, or you can try a leg bronzer, which will help to camouflage them. Try a moisturizer that gives you a gradual tan.

Recommended products:
Moisturizers that build color include:

- **Jergens Natural Glow Daily Moisturizer**
  ($9 for 7.5 oz.)
- **Neutrogena Summer Glow SPF 20 ($10 for 6.7 oz.)**
- **Aveeno Continuous Radiance Moisturizing Lotion ($9 for 8 oz.)**

Self-tanners include

- **L'Oréal Paris Sublime Bronze Luminous Bronzer Self-Tanning Lotion (which offers self-tanning and instant bronzing; $10 for 5 oz.)**
- **L'Oréals Sublime Tanning Towelettes ($12 for a box)**
- **any of the self-tanning products from Clarins (always with an SPF) ($32 and up)**

Effective leg makeup choices are:

- **Sally Hansen Airbrush Leg Makeup ($9)**
- **Scott Barnes Body Bling (at Victoria's Secret $50)**

Hands up.

Our poor hands are overworked and they get dry from being washed (but do wash them often) and washing dishes. We rarely put sunscreen on them, and except in the winter, they are out facing the elements, alone and unprotected. It's time to get right with your hands. Protect them every day with sunscreen. To improve the look of bony or veiny hands, fillers such as Restylane or Sculptra can be used. For brown spots, apply hydro-quinone cream onto the spots, then put a dab of your retinoid product over that.

Recommended product:

- **Neutrogena Age Shield Hand Cream SPF 30 ($6 for 2 oz.)**

Don't do dishes without wearing rubber gloves and keep little pump bottles of hand moisturizer next to every sink in your house. Every time you wash your hands, moisturize.

Your feet need TLC, too.

Take time to give your feet the same treatment as the rest of your skin. Scrub them with body scrub and exfoliate your heels with a pumice stone while they're still wet. Pat dry and moisturize. If they're very dry, massage in a rich foot cream at night and wear thin cotton socks while you sleep to seal in the moisture. Get a professional pedicure every other week in the summer, and once a month during the rest of the year. Your feet will be all set for sandals . . . and running.

Beyond pretty skin, let's talk about healthy skin.

There are a few skin conditions that can happen more often after fifty.

Psoriasis

A common skin disease in people over fifty, it appears as dull red splotches the size of a dime, covered with a thin, silvery white scale. They often form a large patchy area, which is itchy, flaky, and uncomfortable. Women with psoriasis can run a higher risk of diabetes and high blood pressure, probably due to the inflammation that causes the skin condition. Treatment is generally topical.

Eczema

Eczema is a type of skin irritation that can be chronic, but temporary forms can also be caused by contact with an irritating substance, such as makeup. Skin gets red, swollen, and itchy. It is not an infection, but a reaction. It can appear anywhere on the body. Steroid and non-steroid creams are generally prescribed.

Shingles

Shingles, or herpes zoster, is an infection of the nerves caused by the chickenpox virus, which goes dormant in your body if you ever had chickenpox, but can reoccur as shingles many years later, especially in people over sixty. It starts as a burning, itching, painful eruption of tiny blisters. Treatment includes soothing skin lotions, antibiotics, analgesics, anti-viral medications, and sometimes pain relievers if the discomfort is severe. The rash will eventually go away, but the pain can last for many months or even years. One attack of shingles usually vaccinates a person against future attacks, but there is an effective vaccine that is recommended for people over sixty (See *Chapter 1: Feelin' Alright*).

Skin Cancer

Skin cancer is the most common form of cancer. The Skin Cancer Foundation gave me some facts to consider:

- **Skin cancer is the most common form of cancer in the US.**
- **Each year there are more new cases of skin cancer than breast, prostate, lung, and colon cancers combined.**
- **Contrary to popular belief, only about 23**

percent of lifetime exposure occurs by age eighteen, so sun protection is a lifelong commitment.

There are three major types of skin cancer:

Basal Cell Carcinoma

The most common of all skin cancers, it affects close to one million people every year. If caught early, the cure rate is greater than 95 percent. It occurs mostly on sun-exposed areas of the body, and is most common in people over fifty. If you have an open sore that doesn't heal, a reddish patch, or a shiny bump on your skin that won't disappear, check in with your dermatologist.

Squamous Cell Carcinoma

The second most common skin cancer in its pre-cancerous state may appear as a flaky red patch. It's also one of the most dangerous. If left untreated it can spread to distant tissues and organs, and can be lethal. It usually occurs after years of sun exposure and mostly on sun-exposed parts of the body. This cancer is 95 percent curable if caught early. Actinic keratoses are scaly patches that can be precursors to squamous cell cancer. The best thing you can do is get rid of them through treatment. Photodynamic therapy (PDT)—where the areas are painted with a photosensitizing chemical then activated with a light—is the most common treatment.

Malignant Melanoma

The third and most common and most lethal form of skin cancer is melanoma. The signs to look for are in the ABCD assessment list (below). Melanoma accounts for about 5 percent of all skin cancers, and are due to genetic factors and multiple sunburns. Melanoma often looks like a brown or blackish spot, either flat or raised. It usually has uneven borders and more than one color. It occurs more commonly on sun-exposed parts of the body, but can occur anywhere including the scalp, palms, or soles, and even on the genitals. Melanoma most often occurs in a mole that is already present, but can also appear on previously normal-looking skin.

Know your ABCDs

According to the American Cancer Society, almost all basal and squamous cell cancers can be cured if the cancer is detected and treated early. If detected in its earliest stages and treated properly, melanoma is also highly curable. The most important thing we can do for our skin is a monthly skin check in full light and in front of a full-length mirror, checking everywhere, including between toes, behind ears, and in all those little nooks and crannies where the sun don't shine. Use a mirror where you have to. Specifically, look for red or pink patches, bumps, and scaly spots, and assess moles for possible growth or change by using the "ABCD" method:

A—asymmetry: if one half doesn't match the other half

B—border irregularity: if the edges are ragged

C—color: if the pigmentation is not uniform, with variable degrees of tan, brown, black, or blue

D—diameter: if the size is greater than the size of a pencil eraser

If a mole meets any of the above criteria, see a dermatologist as soon as possible. Melanoma may not have any of these common signs, so you must be alert to any new or changing skin growths.

Get your annual skin exam, without fail.

Not only can a good dermatologist get rid of annoying broken capillaries and fine lines, but she can also check your body, from head to toe, every year, for signs of possible skin cancer. Many of these grow slowly, so it's very likely your doctor will catch them in the earliest stages.

Get on board.

We're over fifty. Growing up we thought being tan was cool, and that the best vacation in the world was sipping a rum punch somewhere in the Caribbean, on a beach chair, under the blazing sun (okay, that still sounds good). We didn't put much stock in sunscreen until damage was already done. Our job now is to make sure we are always on the lookout for signs, and minimize future damage. Our other big job is to help the next generation to see the error of our ways. Tell your daughters and nieces and granddaughters that we weren't always as smart as we look. As the ozone layer gets thinner and more dangerous UVB and UVA rays hit the earth—and all of us on it—the incidence of skin cancer will probably rise. Do what you can to prevent whatever you can prevent, and fix whatever you can fix. Here's a breakdown of what you can do now:

- **Limit time in the sun.**
- **Use sunscreen.**
- **Cover up.**
- **Avoid tanning beds.**
- **Check skin every month and report changes to your doctor.**
- **Wear sunglasses.**
- **Use a retinoid product.**
- **Exfoliate.**

Get more information.

These resources come highly recommended:

Websites

- www.cancer.org
- Dr. Doris Day's Website, www.myclear skin.com
- www.patriciawexlermd.com
- The Skin Cancer Foundation, www.skin cancer.org
- www.skincareguide.com
- www.totalbeauty.com

Books

- *Forget the Facelift: Turn Back the Clock with a Revolutionary Program for Ageless Skin*, by Doris J. Day, MD, Avery, 2005
- *The Skin Type Solution*, by Leslie Baumann, MD, Bantam Books, 2006

Chapter 8

Face the Facts

When it Comes to Makeup, Less is More

Where have you gone, Helena Rubinstein?

One of my most vivid childhood memories is sneaking into my mother's room to behold the wonders of her makeup kit: the Helena Rubinstein mascara that came in a thin gold wand, the deep red Cover Girl lipsticks, the little Maybelline eyebrow pencils, and of course, the Pond's Cold Cream to take it all off at the end of the day. Ah. Life was so much simpler then. There were only a few cosmetic companies around—and there were enough choices to make it interesting, but not so many that they drove you insane.

All you need is Love.

The very first independent beauty purchase I ever made was from a then hot, new company called Love. They first came out with Love's Baby Soft cologne, and then Love's Face Gel—a clear gel that you put all over your face and let dry. The end result was a face that was completely shiny. I still don't understand what it was supposed to do exactly, but I can tell you that when I slapped on my Love's Face Gel and went to school, I felt very cool indeed.

I still get a kick out of getting all done up, especially when my daughters are watching me in action. Even on days that I don't have any place special to go, I still take a few minutes to "prettify." As I'm incorporating other post-fifty updates to my life, I know this is a good time to find a lasting look that will fall somewhere between my Love's Face Gel experiments and my mother's trusty old makeup kit.

Let's makeup!

As much fun as it is, though, this should be the shortest chapter in the whole book, because the less makeup we wear after fifty, the better we look. I studied the magazines and copied their suggestions; I let experienced consultants at exclusive department stores "make me up"; I had some of the most practiced makeup artists in the country teach me professional techniques; and I spent hours in front of my bathroom mirror trying different products (much to the delight—and occasional horror—of my daughters). I modeled many new looks and products for my friends, and got a wide range of reactions. Guess what I discovered after almost a year of this "research"? The less I put on, the better (and dare I say, younger) I looked.

Conceal the truth.

In my younger years, I used concealer to dab over the occasional pimple, which, thanks to menopause, I no longer have. But during my makeup experimentation, I went to one of the nicest department stores in New York to talk to one of their beauty advisors. A thoughtful-looking young man offered to help me, and I told him I was doing some research. What were the daily makeup basics, I asked, for a woman over fifty? The first word out of his mouth was: concealer. Concealer is the key, he told me. Key to what? I wanted to know. To a polished face. (Polished face? Ah.)

To demonstrate, he dabbed concealer not just under my eyes, but around my nose and in places I had never thought one might put concealer. Over that he added the foundation. Then: more concealer, a little blush, some eye makeup,

a bit of powder, and voilà. He handed me a mirror.

I stared at my reflection. I looked ten years older. The concealer made a screaming announcement to the world: Wrinkle alert! Wrinkle alert! Clearly, the young man had never heard of "less is more." With a flourish, I put on my sunglasses, thanked the thoughtful young man, and left, vowing once again to keep concealer far, far away from my face.

A Better Beauty Advisor

Shortly after my encounter with the beauty advisor and his concealer, I met with Diane von Furstenberg, who advises us on ageless fashion in *Chapter 10: You Wear it Well.* If anyone knows how to pull off a polished look through the years, she does. Back in 1976, when I was still in college, Diane owned her own company, had designed one of the most successful clothing styles ever (the wrap dress), appeared on the cover of *Newsweek*, was exotically gorgeous, and was every young woman's idol. We wanted to look like her, dress like her, be her. I bought her first book, *Diane von*

Furstenberg's Book of Beauty, in which she revealed to her many fans the beauty rituals that she followed for skin care, hair, makeup, and exercise. That book stayed with me—as did Diane's advice—through many different boyfriends, jobs, apartments, and adventures. Surprised and pleased to hear that I still had the dog-eared book all these years later, Diane talked with me about some of the beauty routines that she r ecommended back then, whether they had withstood the test of time, and if they could still apply to us now that we're over fifty.

Diane von Furstenberg's Beauty Rules, Then and Now:

- **A woman is most attractive when she is being herself, being natural, and not fussing over her appearance.** Once you've put on your makeup—whether for day or evening—forget about it. If you go out, bring a lipstick and a tiny mirror to touch up after eating, but that's it.

- **Makeup should be fun.** Go to Sephora and play around with lipsticks and eye shadows. Let the department store beauty advisors make you over once in a while. Try new things and enjoy yourself.

- **Moisturize and then let your face set for a while.** Makeup will go on better if you let your moisturizer sink in while you get dressed or do something else (some push-ups?).

- **Get ready for the makeup ceremony.** Think of makeup as a ritual and prepare for it. Pull your hair back, so all your focus is on your face, then let the fun begin.

- **Start your day with a very light makeup.** You can always add more of anything and everything as the day goes on.

- **Makeup is an illusion.** The most important thing about makeup is learning the principle of light and dark: light brings an area forward, dark moves it back. Highlight your good features with light colors and play down your least favorite with darker colors.

- **Apply your makeup in good, strong light.** When you're done, check your face in other lights—especially natural light—to make sure you're not overdone.

- **Remove your makeup as soon as you get home to let your skin breathe.** Even if you're going back out for the evening, wash off your makeup, do a little exfoliating with a washcloth, maybe place some cucumber slices or cold tea bags over your eyes for 5 or 10 minutes, and put your moisturizer on again, letting it set in before you put on makeup. This not only gives you a fresh start on your makeup, it's a great way to recharge.

- **Give yourself no more than half an hour to get dressed and made up for the evening.** That way, you won't overthink—or overdo it.

- **Leave a few minutes to make corrections.** Check yourself one last time in different lights and different mirrors. Happy? Go out, have a great time—and don't fuss anymore.

Bring in the beauty brigade.

Diane's rules, which I've been following more or less for three decades, are still my general beauty guidelines, but I was ready to update the details. What colors, for instance, are most flattering to us now? Should we be wearing powders or creams? What do we do about changes in skin tone? Or, okay, wrinkles?

So I got help. Very good help.

First Stop: Laura Geller

Laura Geller is the founder of Laura Geller Studio and developer of her own successful makeup line. Her products are sold at Sephora stores nationwide, online, and on QVC, where she does frequent shows. I had seen Laura on TV a few times and was always impressed by her ability to connect with her audience. Women call the show just to talk to her. She's one of those people who can just make you feel good about yourself.

Beauty by Laura

Laura turned fifty shortly before we met, and she wanted to start off with a few big picture thoughts about beauty for women over fifty:

- **Love your wrinkles.** They're the story of your life. Makeup will never cover or hide wrinkles. In fact, certain makeup if not applied properly (concealer perhaps?) can play up wrinkles and lines. The role of makeup is to play up the health of your skin and enhance its natural beauty.

- **When you wear makeup, look like you're not wearing makeup.** If makeup is obvious or thick, it will only serve to take away from your natural beauty, and will actually make you look older.

- **Have fun with makeup, but first get a basic look.** Perfect that one basic look that makes you feel great—that you can do in five minutes—and build from there.

- **Concealer is your friend—but only where, when, and if you need it.** Two minutes after meeting Laura, I told her about my fear of concealer. She understood. Concealer has its place in our makeup kit, but less is always best, and sometimes you don't need any at all.

- **Use makeup brushes and sponges to apply all of your makeup.** Never use your fingers. Makeup brushes and applicators are as important as the actual makeup.

- **Play up your eyebrows.** Eyebrows can frame your face.

- **Do the "Three E's": eyebrow, eyeliner, eyelashes.** Filling in your eyebrows, lining the base of your lashline (top and bottom) and adding a coat of mascara are must do's. Eyebrows frame the face, eyeliner accents and enhances the shape of your eyes, and mascara makes them pop.

- **Lipstick is sheer fun.** Moisturizing, sheer lipsticks are best for women over fifty. Colors that are a little lighter and pinker are best for everyday. Avoid thick, heavy lipsticks, and keep a light hand when applying lip liner. The dark outline is totally dated.

- **Blush is a terrific tool in small doses.** No matter what shade you use—pink, mauve, peach, bronze, or a combination—it should add a light, healthy glow to your face and some definition to your cheeks.

How to Do a Simple, Everyday Look.

We want a makeup look that:

- is easy and fast to apply.
- gives skin a glowing, healthy look.
- will not look dry and cakey.
- uses colors that flatter just about anyone.
- lasts the whole day and can be intensified for evening.
- makes us look gorgeous.

That's not asking too much, is it?

These products are your foundation for a fabulous face:

Primer

This is a silicone-based gel or cream that goes on after your moisturizer and prepares the skin for foundation. Primer smoothes over wrinkles and pores so makeup doesn't settle into the lines and creates a barrier that holds moisture in your skin and makes foundation stay put.

Foundation

To avoid a heavy, "made-up" look, aim for the lightest coverage and choose a color as close as possible to your natural skin tone. Good choices are cream foundation, tinted moisturizer, mineral powders, or baked powder foundation—Laura's favorite choice for women over fifty—which is easy and fast to apply.

Concealer

There are ways and places to apply concealer that are effective.

Use it only if, when, and where you need it. What you don't want to do is use it everywhere (like the beauty advisor).

Always use it after you've put on foundation because you may not need concealer.

You need two concealers: one for under the eyes, which will be lighter and creamier, and one for covering blemishes, age spots and little broken capillaries, which will be slightly thicker to last longer and give better coverage.

Use the teeniest, tiniest amount possible and apply it with a brush that is made specifically for concealer.

Blush

For most of us a rosy pink shade of blush, applied under our cheekbones, is going to be the most flattering, but you can also use a brush-on bronzer instead of a blush for a healthy, summery glow. Laura prefers to work with powder blush and bronzer. Application is easy. Suck in your cheeks to find the bottom of your cheekbone, then brush the blush up and out along the bone to slightly above your eyebrow, almost like the letter C. After it's applied, take a sponge, dampen slightly with water or moisturizer, and dab (not rub) all over your face, blending everything together.

Eye shadow

Use matte eye shadow. Avoid anything with glitter or a little too much shimmer (It's a little too young.) Browns and creams are universally flattering shades for every day. A neutral color is best for the entire lid, with a darker color in the crease.

Eyeliner

Eyeliner is one of the keys to a great makeup look. It defines eyes, makes them stand out, and makes you look fabulous. Laura prefers liquid eyeliner, because it tends to stay put all day and not smear, but it also takes a steady hand and some practice, so try pencils first. Apply a thin line with a light hand, but be sure to follow the entire eyelash line, top and bottom. Don't start the line midway on top, as some makeup artists suggest. Black can be too harsh during the day, so chocolate brown or charcoal are better daytime colors.

Mascara

Put one or two coats of mascara on the top lashes only, but for evening do the bottom as well for extra drama. Black is the universally perfect color for mascara, but very fair-haired women might prefer brown. Some of us are born with long curly eyelashes, but most of us benefit from an indispensable beauty tool: the eyelash curler. Use lash conditioner first (it preps lashes for mascara, and helps to make them thicker, with less clumping), curl, then put on mascara. It'll make a world of difference in how your lashes look.

Eyebrows

Use a pencil, brush, or brow gel to add a little color onto eyebrows, and fill in where they are sparse. Pluck if necessary, but be aware it can leave redness.

The result?

Laura used her own products when she "did my face" and the end result was beautiful—healthy, soft and very flattering. The baked powder foundation (Balance-n-Brighten, which took less than 20 seconds to apply) covered imperfections. (Turns out I didn't need concealer!) My new favorite beauty product—Laura's Bronze-n-Brighten—gave my skin a pretty glow. These two products are now my go-to beautifiers for every day. Laura is a genius.

A woman obsessed.

Later that night, after I was able to pull myself away from the mirror where I was admiring my new polished face, I sat down with my fashion-savvy daughters, Sarah and Elizabeth, to watch the latest episode of The Learning Channel's *What Not to Wear*. In this show, someone is secretly nominated by friends and family to get a complete, head-to-toe make-over. This particular segment focused on a woman who never wore makeup. After Stacy London and Clinton Kelly were done imparting their style wisdom, it was Carmindy's turn to give her the Carmindy Look.

While the woman sat in her chair with her arms tightly folded in grim determination to keep her face un-polished, Carmindy appeared, smiled brilliantly at her, and gave her a big hug. The woman's angst visibly melted away, her arms lightly dropped to her sides, and she said that she was ready for a change. Carmindy not only gave the woman a great new look, she also taught her how to recreate it at home—and how to do it easily and quickly. Watching this makeup drama unfold, I remembered Carmindy's first book, *The 5-Minute Face*, and I knew I had found another terrific expert.

You're Gorgeous!

The first thing Carmindy said to me when I met her was: "You're gorgeous!" No, I said. "*You're* gorgeous." And it went back and forth like that for a while, until we got down to business. Carmindy is gorgeous. She has beautiful California-blonde, blue-eyed, easy-breezy looks, wears a minimal amount of makeup, and exudes warmth and sincerity.

We started talking about all the women we know who are accomplished, smart, and beautiful, but choose to focus on the negatives—the bags under their eyes, the extra ten pounds, the hair that frizzes up in humid weather, or whatever their "beauty negative" might be. We've all been guilty of that. Years ago, Carmindy noticed herself doing this too, and decided to do something about it.

She came up with the simple step of complimenting other women. She does it all the time now. Tell the next woman you see how nice her hair looks, or how well that dress fits her, or whatever it is that you think you could—honestly—compliment her about, and you'll see what it does. When one woman feels better about herself, she will be more open to complimenting another woman. And on and on and on. These are what Carmindy calls "contagious compliments." It's her grassroots effort to help women acknowledge their own beauty. The end result? More confident, sexy, feel-good-about yourself women. It's contagious.

Positively beautiful. In five minutes.

As much as I love Carmindy's attitude, I also love her easy, no-fuss approach to makeup. She has a streamlined, five-minute makeup strategy for women over fifty who want to look great in a short amount of time.

Carmindy's best tips for women over fifty:

- **Use makeup to enhance who you are now.** Don't try to look younger.
- **Don't get makeup tattooed on your face,** like permanent eyebrows or eyeliner.
- **Stay away from anything sparkly on your face.**
- **If your eyes are getting hooded, try waterproof mascara**—it won't smudge.
- **Use a magnifying mirror.**
- **Whiten your teeth,** either professionally or with one of the whitening strips for use at home.
- **Create a five-second face lift.** After applying foundation, take a light concealer (one with pink tones would be best) and dab it down the creases that run from the side of your nose to the corner of your mouth (the nasal labial folds). Do this same thing from the outer corner of each eye up to the ends of the brows, in a C shape. Blend in with your ring finger. This will "lift" the outer corners of the eyes and the folds around the mouth, and will look as good as if you've had "something" done, without the surgery, the cost, and the recovery time. Yes, it does take just five seconds. And it works.

Your Makeup Strategy:

As we get older, a funny thing happens. The less makeup we wear, the better we look—and the less time it takes. Here's how to look pretty in minutes, with combined tips from Laura Geller and Carmindy. Their advice was very similar, except Laura likes baked powder foundation and blush, and Carmindy prefers cream. I tried everything, and use both with great results.

Start the clock.

Primer

Take a pea sized amount of primer, and apply all over your face, even over lips and eyelids.

Foundation

Dip a sponge into foundation or tinted moisturizer, and dot it around your face, focusing specifically on those areas that need it the most—over red areas, around the nose, on eyelids, and under eyes. Buff and blend everywhere, with downward strokes, including down under your chin. If you need more coverage, dab more on with the sponge, gently pushing the foundation into the skin. Use an amount about the size of a nickel—or less—for your entire face. For the baked powder foundation, swirl the brush around, and then swirl it gently over your face, applying more as needed, buffing with the brush as you go. Don't overdo the foundation—less is more.

Under-eye concealer

After you've applied foundation under eyes, you may not need concealer. If you do, use a small concealer brush and dab a tiny amount of lightweight concealer next to the inner corners of your eyes and blend it downward toward your cheek by dabbing it gently with your ring finger, away from your nose. If you need more under your eye, use the brush (or your finger) without adding any more product, and gently dab along under your eye as close to the lashline as possible, without dragging your skin.

Spot concealer

To cover blemishes, brown spots, and capillaries, apply concealer to noticeable spots with concealer brush, then use your ring finger to dab and blend so that you don't see either the trouble spots or the concealer.

Highlighter

This is Carmindy's secret weapon for the 5-minute face. The highlighter should be pearly, and for older skin, a cream color is generally best. With your small concealer brush, Q-tip, or ring finger apply highlighter in these three areas only: under your eyebrows, on the inside corners of your eyes by the tear ducts, and on top of your cheekbones. Blend it all in, very gently. The end effect will be a luminous glow in all the right places. For cheekbones: place two fingers side by side under the outer corner of your eye. That's where you put the highlighter.

Blush

Apply blush (cream or powder) so that it mimics a natural flush. Apply under the cheekbones, bringing out and up. Use a special blush brush for buffing it all in. If you put on too much, put a tiny bit of foundation on your sponge, and with upward strokes, buff over the blush to soften the intensity.

Translucent Powder

Use only if you need it. You don't want to add any more color to your face, you just want to set everything so that it stays in place. Less powder is modern and leaves skin dewier. Compact powder is a lot easier to control than loose powder. Dab the brush in the powder, shake any extra powder loose, and lightly dust down your nose, across your chin, and over your eyelids, leaving your cheeks alone.

Eye shadow

Once you've added the highlighter, you could skip eye shadow during the day. It's a nice, light look. If you want a little more oomph, take an eye shadow brush, dab in it a neutral color (your natural skin tone is a good choice, or cream, or light brown), and swipe it lightly all over your eyelid, up to just about under the brow bone, slightly above the crease. Take the brush, wipe it with a tissue, and buff your lids with it. Want more drama? Add a little bit of darker color in the crease.

Eyeliner

Whichever kind of liner you use—liquid, pencil, or gel—the goal is to apply it along your upper and lower lash lines as close to the roots as possible. It's faster and easier to use a pencil. Save the liquid and gel for whenever you have a little more time (and after

Carmindy's Tips for Beautiful Brows

Grooming:

- Brush brows straight up, and trim any wild hairs with a pair of small manicure scissors.

- Find your starting point: hold a brow brush vertically, so that it touches the side of one of your nostrils. Hold the brush straight up. That's the point where your eyebrow should start—directly above the side of your nostril. Do this for each side. If you need to tweeze hairs to get this starting point, go ahead and do it.

- Find your end point: take the brow brush again, and lay against your nostril. Angle it back to the outer corner of your eye. Where the brow brush hits your brow area is where your end point should be. Tweeze hairs that go past that point.

- Recommendation: Get your first eyebrow shaping done by a pro, and then maintain it yourself.

Filling in:

- Once your brows are nicely groomed, use a product (powder, pencil, or groomer) to fill in and shape your brows. Be very careful about how you do this, so you don't end up looking like Groucho Marx.

Some tips:

- What color? Redheads: a light sable; blondes: the same shade as the darkest color in your hair; brunettes and women with black hair: one shade lighter than your natural hair color.

- What product? Powder: apply with a short, firm angled brush, using tiny, hairlike strokes; pencil: fill in bald spots and extend brow slightly if you need to using short, hairlike strokes; groomer: this looks like mascara and can be clear or tinted; use short upward strokes.

you've practiced). Keep the line thin or your eyes will appear smaller. Take a thin, soft eyeliner brush to smooth out the lines you've made, and soften and blend if necessary. Brown or charcoal are best for most days. Save black for evening.

Mascara

For day, use mascara on the top lashes only. Start by applying lash conditioner, then curl your lashes. Don't curl just in one place, because that won't look as natural. Curl them in little movements from front to back. Don't pump the mascara wand. It'll only cause the mascara to build up on the wand, and deposit big clumps on your lashes. Wipe the wand with a piece of paper towel (don't use tissue because it shreds and the little pieces will get into your eye). Start as close to the roots as possible. Put on one coat on the upper lashes only (try lifting your lid with your finger slightly, if that helps). Blinking your eyes a few times right after you put mascara on my top lashes causes a bit of the mascara to get on bottom lashes, giving them just enough color.

Lip color

Go for sheer, light lipsticks. If you have trouble with lipsticks bleeding, or with color fading too quickly, try using a lip-colored pencil (not a dark one that gives you an outline), then apply your lip balm or lipstick over that.

Add a little more for a glamorous night.

When heading out for the evening, add a little more depth and intensity to the colors you're already using.

- **Switch from eyeliner pencil to liquid eyeliner pens, and try black or a darker brown.**
- **Add a darker eye shadow to the crease of your eyelids for more drama, blending everything with a brush, and bring it up slightly above the crease.**
- **Apply black mascara to the top (two coats) and bottom lashes (one coat).**
- **If you're using a cream foundation, swipe a little translucent powder over your t-zone.**
- **Use a slightly darker lip color (but still pinky rose toned) and then add a dab of lip gloss for a little extra shine.**
- **Check yourself one last time in the mirror,**

and out you go, gorgeous! Just bring a little mirror and a lipstick and have fun.

Lighten up for summer.

In the summer, lighten up your makeup routine by making a few subtle changes and adding more sunscreen.

- **Switch to a lighter moisturizer (lotion instead of cream), with a sunscreen (See *Chapter 7: Love the Skin You're In* for recommendations).**
- **Use either a tinted moisturizer with an SPF in a slightly darker shade, or a mineral powder with sunscreen.**
- **Try Laura Geller's brush-on *Bronze-n-Balance* as a summer foundation.**
- **Switch to a waterproof mascara and eyeliner.**
- **Try using self-tanner all over your body and on your face for a bit of a sun-kissed glow, without actually kissing the sun.**

The best of the best for after fifty.

With the goal of looking great with minimal effort, here's the collected wisdom of our experts:

- **Less is more. Keep it light, keep it pretty.**
- **Use sunscreen every day, rain or shine.**

- **Have a basic beauty routine that you can do in 5 minutes or less.**
- **Use concealer only when necessary.**
- **Highlight three key areas—under the brows, on top of the cheekbones, and in the inside corner of the eyes.**
- **Powder only the T-zone, if needed.**
- **Keep eyeliner very thin line and follow your natural lash lines—top and bottom.**
- **For every day, use black or brown mascara and only on the top lashes.**
- **Use a neutral eyeshadow, bringing it slightly above the crease.**
- **Groom your eyebrows.**
- **Think rosy pink for cheeks and lips.**
- **Apply blush a little closer to your cheek bones.**
- **Use a skin-colored lip liner to keep lip color from spreading.**

Pick your Products

There are so many beauty products to choose from that the options can either make you crazy or give you endless hours of fun trying everything on. After many months of researching, testing, trying, talking, and listening to the experts (and my girlfriends), here are the best products for us, in all price ranges. Where I listed specific colors, anyone can wear them beautifully, but with others (like foundation) it depends upon your skin tone. Have fun!

Primer

- *Spackle* by Laura Geller ($25)
- *Luminizing Face Primer* by Sally Hansen Natural Beauty Inspired by Carmindy ($9)
- *Photo Finish Foundation Primer SPF 15* by Smashbox ($42)
- *Face Primer* by Laura Mercier ($40)

Liquid foundation

- *Luminous Moisturizing Foundation* by Bobbi Brown ($45)
- *Your Skin Makeup* by Sally Hansen Natural Beauty Inspired by Carmindy ($9)
- *Dream Liquid Mousse Foundation* by Maybelline ($9)
- *TruBlend Whipped Foundation* by CoverGirl ($8)
- *Simply Ageless Cream Foundation* by CoverGirl & Olay ($9)
- *Healthy Skin Liquid Makeup SPF 20* by Neutrogena ($9)

Powder Foundation

- *Balance-N-Brighten* by Laura Geller ($30)

- *Bronze-N-Brighten* by Laura Geller ($30)
- *Ageless Minerale* by Lancôme ($42)
- *Mineral Sheers Powder Foundation* by Neutrogena ($14)
- *Bare Escentuals Mineral Powders* ($25)

Tinted moisturizer

- *Imanance Environmental Protection Tinted Cream SPF 15* by Lancôme ($32)
- *Tinted Moisturizer SPF 20* by Laura Mercier ($40)
- *SPF 15 Tinted Moisturizer* by Bobbi Brown ($40)
- *Positively Radiant Tinted Moisturizer with SPF 30* by Aveeno ($14)
- *Healthy Defense Daily Moisturizer Sheer Hint of Color SPF 30* by Neutrogena ($8)
- *Healthy Skin Glow Sheers SPF 30* by Neutrogena ($8)

Highlighter

- *Color Design Blush in Freeze Frame* by Lancôme ($35)
- *Instant Age Rewind Double Face Perfector* by Maybelline (use the highlighter side) ($9)
- *Natural Highlighter in Pink Luster* by Sally Hansen Natural Beauty Inspired by Carmindy ($7)

- *Touche Éclat Radiant Touch* by Yves Saint Laurent ($42)
- *High Beam Highlighter* by Benefit ($24)
- *Wonder Wand Eye Brightener (Powder)* by Laura Geller ($27)

Concealer for under eyes

- *Crease-less Concealer* by Laura Geller ($23)
- *Skin Soothing Under Eye Corrector* by Neutrogena ($7)
- *All-Over Brightener* by Sally Hansen Natural Beauty Inspired by Carmindy ($8)
- *Instant Age Rewind Double Face Perfector* by Maybelline (use the concealer side) ($9)
- *Eye Bright* by Benefit ($20)
- *Creamy Concealer* by Bobbi Brown ($22)

Concealer for blemishes, capillaries, and brown spots

- *Fast Fix Concealer* by Sally Hansen Natural Beauty Inspired by Carmindy ($10)
- *Corrector* by Bobbi Brown ($22)
- *ColorStay Concealer* by Revlon ($9)
- *Hidden Agenda Concealer Set* by Sonia Kashuk for Target ($10)

Note: A little bit of your liquid foundation from the cap, applied with a concealer brush, then tapped on and blended with your finger, can work just as well as a concealer.

Cream blush

- *Pot Rouge for Lips and Cheeks* by Bobbi Brown ($22)
- *Sheerest Cream Blush* by Sally Hansen Natural Beauty Inspired by Carmindy ($8)
- *HiP High Intensity Pigments Blendable Blushing Cream* by L'Oréal Paris ($10)
- *Simply Ageless Cream Blush* by CoverGirl & Olay ($10)
- *Super Sheer Liquid Tint* by Sonia Kashuk for Target ($10)
- *Dream Mousse Blush* by Maybelline ($8)

Powder blush

- *Blush-N-Brighten in Pink Grapefruit or Golden Apricot* by Laura Geller ($24)
- *Cheekers Blush in Natural Twinkle* by CoverGirl ($6)
- *Blush in Orgasm* by NARS ($25)
- *Expert Wear Blush in Precious Pink* by Maybelline ($8)
- *Powder Blush in Everything's Rosy* by Revlon ($8)
- *Blush Subtil in Miel Glace'* by Lancôme ($27)

- *Mineral Sheers Blush for cheeks* by Neutrogena ($10)

Powder all-over bronzer

- *Bronze-N-Brighten in Fair or Regular* by Laura Geller ($24)

Eye shadow base

- *Skin Soothing Eye Tints in Petal* by Neutrogena ($9)
- *Eye Spackle* by Laura Geller ($18)

Eye shadow

- *Eye Shadow Quad* by Sonia Kashuk for Target ($11)
- *Sugar Free Baked Shadow in Biscotti/Toast* by Laura Geller ($22)
- *Instant Definition Eye Shadow Palette in The Mountain Palette* by Sally Hansen Natural Beauty Inspired by Carmindy ($8)
- *ColorStay 12-Hour Eye Shadow Quad in Coffee Bean* by Revlon ($10)
- *Mineral Eye Shadow* by e.l.f. ($3)

Eyeliner pencil

- *ColorStay Eyeliner Pencil in Brown, Charcoal and Navy* by Revlon (8)
- *Infallible Never Fail Eyeliner in Brown* by L'Oréal Paris ($9)

- *Forever Stay Eye Pencil in Chocolate Brown* by Sally Hansen Natural Beauty Inspired by Carmindy ($8)
- *Powder Eye Pencil in Brown Sugar and Cinnamon* by Laura Geller ($18)
- *Waterproof Eyeliner Pencil in Brown* by NYC ($7)
- *Ultra Luxury Eyeliner in Dark Brown* by Avon ($9)
- *Line & Seal 24 Eyeliner Pencil in Charcoal* by Styli-Style ($6)

Liquid/gel eyeliner

- *ColorStay Liquid Eye Pen in Blackened Brown* by Revlon ($9)
- *Artliner Felt Line Tip Pen in Brown and Ice Carob* by Lancôme ($28)
- *Long-Wear Gel Eyeliner in Chocolate Shimmer Ink and Graphite Shimmer Ink* by Bobbi Brown ($21)
- *Dramatically Defining Long Wear Gel Eye Liner* by Sonia Kashuk for Target ($9)

Eye brow grooming and shaping

- *Brow Tint/Brow Tamer* by Laura Geller ($21)
- *Tinted Brow Gel* by Anastasia Beverly Hills ($21)

- *Brow Pen* by Anastasia Beverly Hills ($21)
- *Eye Brow Pencil* by Maybelline ($5)

Eye lash curler
- *Shu Uemura Eye Lash Curler* ($19)

Eye Lash Conditioner
- *Cils Booster XL* by Lancôme ($20)

Mascara (black)
- *Voluminous Mascara* by L'Oréal Paris ($7)
- *Definicils Mascara* by Lancôme ($24)
- *DiorShow Mascara* by Dior ($24)
- *Great Lash Mascara* by Maybelline ($8)
- *Double Extend Beauty Tubes Mascara* by L'Oréal Paris ($10)

Lip color
- *Creamy Lip Color in Rose Petal or Tulle* by Bobbi Brown ($22)
- *Super Lustrous Lipstick (different shades)* by Revlon ($8)
- *MoistureShine Lip Sheers SPF 20 in Pink Splash* by Neutrogena ($7)
- *Comfort Lip Color in Perfect Pink and Champagne Rose* by Sally Hansen Natural Beauty Inspired by Carmindy ($7)
- *Moisture Plump Lip Balm in Sweet Plum* by Sally Hansen Natural Beauty Inspired by Carmindy ($7)
- *Lip Colour in Pink Champagne* by Laura Mercier ($20)
- *Colour Riche Lipstick in Tender Pink* by L'Oréal Paris ($8)

Lip conditioner
- *A Kiss of Protection SPF 30 Lip Balm* by Nivea ($3)
- *Beeswax Lip Balm* by Burt's Bees ($3)
- *Smith's Rosebud Salve* ($4)

Lip liner
- *Lip Liner in Bare* by Laura Geller ($15)
- *ColorStay Lip Liner in Natural* by Revlon ($8)
- *Outlast Smoothwear Lip Liner in Nude* by CoverGirl ($7)

Makeup brushes
Many companies make great brushes. You only need a few, so it pays to buy those that are high quality and will last. Just remember to wash them once a week with an antibacterial hand soap and hot water.

The brushes you need include:
- Blush brush
- Overall face powder brush

- **Eye shadow brush (for the entire eye area)**
- **Contour eye shadow brush**
- **Eyeliner brush for putting on gel eye liner**
- **Eyebrow brush if you choose to use powder on your eyebrows**

The companies that make some of the nicest brushes include:

- **MAC**
- **Sonia Kashuk for Target**
- **Essence of Beauty**
- **Posh**
- **Bobbi Brown**
- **Laura Geller**
- **Carmindy's tip: go to the local art supply store and get them there. It's cheaper.**

Give us a smile.

Are your pearly whites not so pearly white? Not to worry. After you've spent time and money perfecting your skin and your makeup, you don't want a mouthful of dingy-looking teeth. Teeth age. The more coffee, tea, red wine, and tomato sauce that we eat and drink, the more stained they will become, and the older they may look. This is a very easy problem to fix. First, keep teeth and gums clean and healthy by brushing several times a day and flossing daily (Glide Deep Clean is the best). Get your dental cleanings and checkups at least twice a year. You might experience a little more sensitivity after fifty, so consider a toothpaste such as Sensodyne.

Second, consider whitening your teeth. There are good options, depending on how much you want to spend. Buy the Crest Whitening Strips, which are very effective and inexpensive. Have your dentist whiten them in her office (about $500). Or you can whiten your teeth at home with a solution and a tray that was prepared by your dentist. All three work well, but the in-office applications by your dentist will work fastest, and that's what you're going to pay for. Skip the toothpastes and mouthwashes that say "whitening" on the labels. They don't do anything.

If you want to make a huge change in how your teeth look—including their size, shape and color—then you might consider a total tooth makeover: the porcelain veneer. Veneers are serious cosmetic dentistry, but if you have chipped, overlapping, crooked, or otherwise unlovely teeth, porcelain veneers will fix what's ailing them—at a price. The going rate is about $2,000 per tooth. However, they can last for decades.

Get on board.

Keep your skin healthy, your body fit, and your face free of heavy makeup, and you will love how you look. After fifty, when it comes to makeup, less is more.

Get more information.

If you want more tips, techniques, and fun makeup facts, check out the following.

Websites

- www.allure.com
- www.carmindy.com
- www.laurageller.com
- www.more.com
- www.sephora.com
- www.totalbeauty.com
- www.tlc.com/whatnottowear

Books

- *Bobbi Brown Makeup Manual* by Bobbi Brown, Springboard Press, 2008
- *The 5-Minute Face: The Quick & Easy Makeup Guide for Every Woman* by Carmindy, HarperCollins, 2007
- *Get Positively Beautiful: The Ultimate Guide to Looking and Feeling Gorgeous,* by Carmindy, Center Street, 2008
- *Crazy Busy Beautiful* by Carmindy, Harper Collins, 2010
- *Diane von Furstenberg's Book of Beauty: How to Become a More Attactive, Confident, and Sensual Woman* by Diane von Furstenberg, Simon & Schuster, 1976 (out of print, but you can get it online)

Chapter 9

No More Bad Hair Days

Time to Throw Out the Blow Dryer

No more curly girl.

I've always had uncooperative hair (until I learned to tame it with a blow dryer, but more on that later). One hot and humid day in July, 1969, when my hair was looking particularly frizzy and frayed, I made a life-changing decision: my days of being a curly girl were over. I didn't know quite how this magical transformation would take place, but it would take place. This was the era of straight hair parted down the middle (like Michelle Phillips from the Mamas & the Papas). I just had to have that straight hair.

Straighten out the problem.

A friend volunteered to iron my hair. When that didn't work, she set it with concentrated orange juice cans and Dippity-Do. When it rained, I still had unruly, frizzy, frayed-baseball-looking hair. I kept it securely imprisoned with a ponytail holder for most of the seventies. Until . . .

I discovered the blow dryer.

To get the "Farrah Fawcett" 'do, which was so popular in the seventies, I had to blow dry my hair for 45 minutes (which I did, every single day). As soon as it got even the slightest bit humid, my hair would balloon up and frizz out, and I would shove it right back into its ponytail prison, until it was safe to come out again, sometime in the fall.

In the nineties, things got easier (and more expensive). Straight, highlighted hair was in. And doing it yourself was out. Thanks to my hairdresser, for the first time in my life, my hair was silky smooth. Although because it had that little stubborn streak, I would also iron my locks straight (with a hair iron this time). Finally, I loved my hair. It was straight. It swung. But it had to be washed and blow-dried almost every single day. New technology allowed blow dryers to get to the hottest possible temperatures for maximum impact (and destruction?). Since I had started fooling around with blow dryers back in the seventies, I estimate that I blow dried my hair for over thirty-five years. Almost every day.

Damaged locks, anyone?

I won the battle with my hair, but lost the war.

By the time I hit my early fifties, the healthy head of hair from my youth was a distant memory. Years of blow drying, ironing, yanking on it with a brush, highlighting, and washing the hell out of it every day caused my hair to look like roadkill. I had managed to beat my hair into submission.

Even more profound, I realized that I had been fighting with my identity. Since 1969, I had been trying to make my hair into something it wasn't. I was tired. I was grumpy. I didn't want to stand in front of a mirror for half an hour every morning and blow dry each and every separate section of my hair. It was boring, tedious, and wasted a huge amount of energy—mostly my own. I was trying to figure out a newer, simpler paradigm for the other areas of my life since turning fifty, and wanted to figure this one out, too. But what to do?

Getting to the Experts: A Talk With A Curly Girl

I met my friend, Jill, for coffee and some chick chat. Jill had recently started going to a different place to get her hair cut, and it looked great—natural, not blow dried. She directed me to Lorraine Massey, the woman behind Devachan Salon and Jill's new look. Lorraine, the founder and co-owner of Devachan, has a mop of blonde corkscrew ringlets around her head, and a very clear idea of how hair should be treated, with no (or very little) shampoo, no blow dryer, and no brush or comb. At our first meeting, Lorraine eyed me suspiciously, wondering if I was, in fact, ready to give up the blow dryer and let my hair be free. I could see she wasn't sure. I wasn't so sure either. I knew I needed a change, and that my hair had to be rescued. But by Lorraine? And with no blow dryer?

Stop the abuse and find the buried treasure.

Lorraine explained it this way: if you've been blow drying, overwashing, and abusing your hair for decades, how can its natural beauty shine through? It's impossible. Marketers have made us believe that we need to wash our hair every day and put all kinds of products in it to make it look good. The intensive heat from blow dryers and other styling tools, and too many chemicals—sulfates especially—destroy the health and good, natural texture of hair. Take your hair off the diet of heavy duty blow-frying and detergents, and beautiful shapes and forms start to develop. It's like buried treasure. We need to give ourselves permission to let our natural beauty come out instead of trying to push it into a shape that it isn't.

Do you even know what your hair is anymore?

Lorraine estimates that over 50 percent of women have curly or wavy hair. As we get older, hair gets coarser, mostly because of the grays, so even if we started out with straight hair, some of it ends up wavy. Many of us abused our hair to the point where we no longer know what our hair really is. Think through these questions to get a sense of how much you have been working against your "true hair":

- **Do you have to blow dry your hair to make it look like something?**
- **Do you own a flat iron?**
- **Do you own a curling iron?**
- **Do you own hot rollers?**
- **Do you own a lot of styling products?**
- **Does your hair develop volume in humid, hot, or wet weather?**
- **Do you often wear your hair tied back in a ponytail?**
- **Do you often have that little halo of frizz around your head (yes, like a frayed baseball)?**
- **Do you live in fear of humidity or rain?**
- **Do you think about your hair more often than you should?**
- **Do you find yourself constantly looking for the best and newest product on the market in hopes that it will tame your hair into submission?**

If you answered yes to any of these questions, there's a great chance that you have natural movement in your hair, and that you are in fact a curly girl. If you are, go with it. Don't fight it. You'll look more beautiful, and your hair will be healthier. If you're naturally straight haired, keep reading because this program is for all hair types.

Set it free! Curly, wavy, or straight, follow this program, and you will never look back.

Edward Joseph, who has been with Lorraine at Devachan for over ten years, is one of the nicest people you could ever want to touch your hair. Ed took me through the process of cleansing, moisturizing, and styling hair, whether it's curly, wavy, or straight, long or short. It all comes down to the same simple program, and the end result is fabulous.

Your New Hair Routine:

Products you will need:

- **Shampoo without sulfates**—Sulfates, the ingredient that causes shampoo and other detergents to lather, are very harsh ingredients and should be avoided.
- **Conditioner**—This is the number one most important product for this program, and will be used for moisturizing, styling and (sometimes) cleansing. Experiment to see how using conditioner makes your hair look its best.
- **Styling Product**—You may not always use a styling product, but have a bottle of styling gel on hand, especially for super-humid days. Look for a gel that doesn't contain alcohol, has no fragrance, is clear, and has the ingredients PVP (polyvinyl-pyrrolidone) and PVP/VA (vinyl acrylate).
- **An old white t-shirt, or special hair towel**—Have something absorbent on hand to gently dry your hair.
- **Spray bottle filled with water and lavender oil**—Get a pretty spray bottle, fill it with filtered water, add a few drops of lavender oil and shake it up. This is what you'll use to refresh your hair, especially on those days when you don't put your head under the shower. Side note: lavender oil is a natural deterrent against head lice, so I often spritz it on my kids' hair before they go to school or camp.
- **Spray mist bottle filled with olive oil and lavender oil**—Same as above, but with olive oil and a nozzle that mists. Use when hair is feeling especially dry, spraying hair very lightly, especially before cleansing.
- **Hair clips**—Pick up a pack of 1" hair clips for positioning your hair, for styling and drying.

Products you will definitely *not* need:

- **Blow Dryer**—Use it as little as possible. The more "tools" you use on your hair, the more dry and damaged it will be. Use the blow dryer only when necessary, and on the lowest heat setting with a diffuser (for curly hair) or a nozzle (for straight hair). Curling irons, flat irons, and hot rollers? Give them away. You don't need them to get great style, no matter what kind of hair you have.

- **Brushes and combs**—You won't need these, so put them away. You'll get the knots out when you're in the shower (with your fingers), and you'll "position" your hair for drying with your fingers.

Rule #1:
Shampoo your hair only once or twice a week, and just use water and conditioner the other days.

1. Put some conditioner at the ends of hair before you put your head under the water.
2. Wet hair under the shower head, gently massaging your scalp with the water.
3. Take a small amount (half a teaspoon) of a non-sulfate shampoo. Using your fingertips, gently massage it onto the scalp. Rinse thoroughly.
4. Add a tablespoon of conditioner to your hair, starting from the ends, and work it through with your fingers, getting out the knots. Rinse for five seconds—to distribute it, not to remove it. This is key.
5. Flip your head over, bend down like you're touching your toes, and gently squeeze hair up from the ends to the roots to remove excess water, before stepping out of shower.

Rule #2:
Use your fingers to sculpt your hair, not a blow dryer and comb or brush.

1. Bend forward again and let your hair drop down, using your towel (or t-shirt) to scrunch your hair toward your scalp in an upward, accordion motion.
2. While you're still bent over, take a small amount of styling gel or some other preferred styling product (if you wish), and scrunch in the gel. Start at the back of the head and dis-

tribute, with scrunching movements, all around.

3. Straighten up, and you'll see how—straight or curly—your hair will fall into its natural position. You can help it along with your fingers.

4. To keep your hair from being flat on top, use a few clips to lift some of it on the crown of your head. Look in the mirror—how you position your hair at this point is how it will look when it is dry.

5. Drying curly or wavy hair: let your hair air-dry. If not possible (if, say, you are about to brave sub-zero temperatures), air-dry as long as you can, then use a diffuser on the lowest setting. The whole idea is to not move your hair while it's in the drying mode, even if you have straight hair. This will keep it from frizzing.

6. Drying straight hair: either air dry or blow dry quickly with the temperature setting at "air temperature" (no heat) and no brush. Heat from blow dryers and pulling with brushes is what damages hair the most.

You will be able to "do" your hair in under five minutes. Play around with conditioner, gels, and positioning, to see what looks best. It will take several months—or more—to see a change in the health of your hair, but your new styling regimen will yield instant results. Be patient, and stick with it.

How Do I Look, Frédéric Fekkai?

Six months after starting on the healthy hair program, I visited Frédéric Fekkai in his office for an honest evaluation, and also to talk through his own views on hair care and color. Charming and handsome as always, Frédéric gave a double thumbs-up to my new, natural look. His philosophy—in keeping with Lorraine's—is that we should never fight our texture. The nineties are a long time ago, and the blow-dried straight look is over (except once in a while for fun, but don't tell Lorraine I said that). We should all be working with what we have, going with the texture, and playing with and enhancing our natural look.

How do you make the most of what you've got?

I wanted to hear everything Frédéric had to say about how to treat and care for our hair after fifty. Many of his clients who started with him back in the eighties and nineties are now in their fifties, so he's quite plugged in to what's best for us.

Length

Age is meaningless when it comes to hair length. It's all about who you are, your lifestyle, and your personality. Hair length should enhance your silhouette (your height, shape, weight, overall size), not work against it. If someone is tall, longer hair could work. But longer hair on a woman who is short and slightly overweight, could be a distraction, creating an out-of-balance look. If longer hair is the goal, it must be healthy. Have it cut back a bit until the healthier hair has a chance to grow in. Short or mid-length are terrific options, too.

Style

The style of your hair should be dictated by the texture. It is important to look modern, fresh, and contemporary, no matter what the length. Don't try too hard. It should look sexy without being overdone. If you have layers in your hair, don't let the ends get straggly, which can detract from a healthy, polished look. If you air dry your hair (which he recommends), once you position your hair, leave it alone. Don't touch it. This will keep it from frizzing up and getting puffy.

Cleansing and conditioning

There's no need to wash your hair everyday, especially if it's thicker. Avoid putting conditioner on the top of your head at the roots. Put it at the midshaft down to the ends, where it's really needed. Run it through hair with your fingers in the shower, always going in the direction of the hair, never against it.

Styling products

Once you've cleansed and conditioned your hair, before leaving it to air dry (or even if you are using a blow dryer), work a small amount of a conditioning styling product through your hair before you position it. Frédéric's Glossing

Crème is one of the best products in the market, and leaves hair shiny, soft, and yet very controlled.

Color me beautiful.

I remember the first time I ever "colored" my hair. In 1969—a year filled with all kinds of rebellions—I decided to spritz on a little Sun In while tanning in my backyard. In a matter of hours my blonde hair turned a vibrant shade of orange, to match the Bain de Soleil Geleé I was using (without SPF, of course). My mother helped to hide it with a little of her own "home coloring kit," and it gradually grew out, but (despite the failed first experiment) I was hooked. Highlighting has been a part of my life since graduate school. But now that a few grays are sneaking in, I asked Frédéric if I need to do something else.

Shades of gray.

There are degrees of gray. We start out with a few gray hairs. More come in and we get up to 20 percent, then 30 percent, and eventually our hair is over 50 percent gray. That's the natural progression of gray hair. Gray hair mixes extremely well with highlights, and Frédéric strongly recommends using both highlights and lowlights with your gray—regardless of the natural color of your hair—instead of single process. Once you're over 50 percent gray, you need to decide if you want to:

- **Continue highlights mixed with gray (his preference).**
- **Do a single process with highlights (also known as a double process).**
- **Go with gray all the way, with no added color.**

You'll need to have a very good hair colorist to work with your graying hair, artistically blending the gray together with highlights and lowlights. Even if your hair is dark brown, which shows up the gray much more than blonde hair does, he encourages us to run the highlights and lowlights right through the brown and gray hair. Contrast is the most important trick in achieving great color. Single blocks of color can age you, draining your face. Don't get too highlighted, too blonde, too dark, or too one-color. It's unattractive. Some of the women Frédéric holds up as great hair role models include Michelle Pfeiffer, Kate Capshaw, Cheryl Tiegs, Sandra Bullock, Diane von Furstenberg, Dyan Cannon, and Sharon Stone.

Other tips for good color.

- Color-treated hair may lose some shine after coloring, so a gloss—a silicone-based product that restores shine and adds polish to the surface of the hair—is often used after treatment. Glosses are also good for helping gray hair to look more vibrant. Glosses seal the cuticle, blend your gray hair, and make it shine.
- Don't shampoo your hair the day you are having color applied.
- Always get the cut first, then the color, especially if you're getting a new style. This will allow the colorist to be more strategic when adding color (specifically highlights) to create the most contrast, in the right places.

What are some of the best styles for women over fifty?

Frédéric believes it's up to the individual woman—her lifestyle, silhouette, hair condition, height, and personality. There are many terrific options, but whatever

you choose, Frédéric suggested we keep these thoughts in mind:

- Don't let hair overwhelm you.
- Long is great, but not *too* long. Somewhere at or right below the shoulders and chin length is also flattering.
- Keep it healthy (by staying on this program).
- If it's curly or wavy, layers work best.
- If hair is naturally straight, layers are fine, but a blunt cut could also work well.
- Center parts aren't flattering on most women.
- Whatever your hair type or style, a softer look is prettier than a severe one.
- Look through magazines and bring a photo with you when you want to get your hair cut in a new style.
- Tell your hairstylist upfront that you're not going to blow dry it with hot air and a brush so she can take that into account.

Definite Don'ts

- Use a shampoo which lists sulfates as an ingredient.
- Shampoo more than once (or twice) a week.
- Blow dry on high or medium heat (must be air temperature).

- Brush your hair.
- Become impatient with your hair as you're growing it out.
- Be tempted to blow dry it straight (even if you have straight hair) with high heat and a brush.
- Hide your hair in a ponytail too often.
- Be afraid of letting your hair be its true self.

Definite Dos

- Leave some conditioner in your hair after rinsing (not at the roots). It should feel like wet sea weed.
- Experiment with going with gray and make it work for you. Don't cover it but have it be a part of the mix of colors in your hair.
- Go with highlights and lowlights instead of single process.
- Make conditioner the most important styling tool you use.
- Find a hair stylist who understands your hair, and what you want to achieve.

Recommended Products

Try the ones listed here, and see which work for you.

Shampoo— All are non-sulfate products

- DevaCurl No-Poo (non-sudsing cleanser, best for curly and wavy hair)
- DevaCurl Low-Poo (low-sudsing cleanser, best for straight hair)
- Fekkai au Naturel Weightless Shampoo
- L'Oréal EverPure Sulfate Free Shampoo
- Burt's Bees Very Volumizing Pomegranate & Soy Shampoo
- TIGI Bed Head Superstar Sulfate-Free Shampoo

Conditioner

- DevaCurl One Condition
- Fekkai au Natural Weightless Conditioner
- Fekkai Brilliant Glossing Conditioner
- Fekkai Ageless Restructuring Conditioner
- L'Oréal EverPure Sulfate Free Conditioner
- Burt's Bees Hair Repair Shea & Grapefruit Deep Conditioner

Styling Products

- DevaCurl AnGell Styling Gel
- Deva Set It Free Style Spray
- Fekkai Glossing Cream
- Fekkai Lucious Curls Cream
- Phyto, Klorane, Christophe, and Kiss My

Face also make wonderful sulfate-free styling products.

- **Goody 1″ clips**

Hair today, gone tomorrow?

There is a link between pulling hair with a brush while blow drying it and hair loss in women. Some of it can be attributed to hormone shifts, genes, and certain illnesses, but the constant tugging at your hair, over an extended period of time, can exacerbate it. I took this concern to Dr. Day, one of our experts in *Chapter 7: Love the Skin You're In*, who explained that hair loss in women is common as we age. The normal shedding of hair is about 100 to 150 strands each day. Each hair grows about one half inch per month for between two and six years (although the growth period slows down a bit as we age), and then falls out. Hair grows and sheds at very different times. Many factors can disrupt this cycle. The result can be that your hair falls out early, or isn't re-

placed at the same time as it is lost. Most thinning or loss of hair in a woman is reversible once the cause is determined. Check this out with your dermatologist.

Get on board.

It's best if you use shampoo as seldom as possible, and those without sulfates when you do. Keep your hair very moisturized, and don't use a blow dryer unless you really have to. Look at gray as a great new color to add to the mix, throw out your brushes, and be bold when it comes to length and style. Give your hair a chance to be what it really is. Give this program six months, and I promise you'll never go back.

Every day (or every other day)

- **Wash hair with water and conditioner only.**
- **Apply a small amount of styling product.**
- **Use the lavender water spray to refresh your hair.**

Once or twice a week

- **Wash hair using shampoo and conditioner.**

- Use the olive oil/lavender spray to deep condition before washing (on the days when you use shampoo).

Occasionally

- Use a blow dryer with a diffuser to dry your hair if you don't have the time to air dry.

Every four to six weeks

- Get a single process (if you take this route).

Every eight to ten weeks

- Get highlights.

Every five to eight months

- Get a hair cut.

Get more information.

The next step might be to find the right style and the right stylist. Look through magazines for ideas, and go online. One of the best ways to get to a good hair cut? Ask the next woman you see with really fabulous hair (as long as it's not blow dried straight!). She'll tell you where to go.

Websites

- www.devaconcepts.com
- www.fekkai.com

Books

- *Curly Girl: The Handbook* by Lorraine Massey and Deborah Chiel, Workman, 2001

Chapter 10

You Wear it Well

Shopping for Sensational Style

No jeans? Says who?

Ellen Barkin was interviewed a few years ago, about the time we were both turning fifty. I was eager to read what she had to say because she seemed wise and worldly to me with her sexy, crooked smile. I was absorbing her comments, frequently nodding in agreement, until I came to her "Rules for Life After 50." Specifically, this: "No blue jeans to dinner out." No jeans? Just because we're over fifty? She conceded that black jeans were okay for dinner, but not blue. I had just dished out $168 plus tax on a new pair of 7 For All Mankind jeans. They are dark blue, beautiful, and can absolutely be dressy enough for dinner out in Manhattan, or anywhere in the world. And, by golly, out for dinner they will go.

My love of jeans goes back to my first pair from Jordache in the seventies (which I wore with my Candies shoes). And nothing came between me and my Calvins. However, Ms. Barkin's declaration did make me consider that, by the time we hit fifty, a lot of us would benefit from a wardrobe re-evaluation. Our bodies, faces, and lifestyles have changed over the decades and our fashions haven't always kept up. Still, no jeans? This demanded further research.

Are there rules about what we should wear (or not) after fifty?

I've always worn whatever I pleased—including jeans—with one caveat: I try to never wear things that make me look silly for my age (my daughters might disagree). Once my knees started to take on an elephant-like quality, and the spider veins were climbing over my thighs, it was time to put away the short skirts. But is that an iron-clad rule for every woman over fifty, or just a good idea for me? I don't want to live by strict fashion commandments, but I did want some guidelines for achieving a more flattering look. I don't have the time—or interest—to devote to shopping so I want to streamline my style to look good without fussing—or going broke.

Most of all, I wanted answers to the clothing questions that have been cropping up for my friends and me lately:

- **How do we rise above the youth-centered styles meant for rail-thin twentysome-things without looking dumpy?**

- **Where can we find clothes that will help us look good and still look our age?**
- **How can we look sexy without looking like cougars?**
- **How short is too short?**
- **Are our arms—although improved by the push-ups recommended in *Chapter 6: Move That Body*—banished forever from view?**
- **What are the basics that every woman over fifty should have in her wardrobe?**
- **And: do we need to spend a fortune to get them?**

I went to a woman that I knew would have the answers.

My Fashion Inspiration: Diane von Furstenberg

Designer, successful businesswoman, and an icon of my generation, Diane von Furstenberg knows fashion. By the time she was twenty-eight, she had invented the iconic wrap dress, had hundreds of people working for her, and was featured on the cover of *Newsweek*. In her forties, she gave up her company and took a break from working for a few years. Once she hit fifty, she entered a period of complete rejuvenation. She restarted her business, bought a huge office building in the Meatpacking district of Manhattan and remarried. She has been in the forefront of fashion for decades but has remained true to her core style: easy, sexy, wearable, and affordable clothes for women of all ages. I have one of her wrap dresses, and I've also seen women in their twenties wearing it, as well as women who are anything but model-thin. Diane really understands the curves of a woman's body, and she has always worn her own designs.

No rules, except for one: be comfortable.

The day I met with Diane, I was wearing her designs—a light wool knee-length black dress with ³/₄ length sleeves and a pair of Diane von Furstenberg boots with black fishnet tights. I felt ageless and classic, not trendy. Diane swung me around, and nodded approvingly. "You look fabulous," she told me. "And do you know why?" she asked. "Because I'm completely decked out in DVF?" I suggested. "No," she said. "Because you are comfortable."

The only fashion rule Diane would offer, and the only one she believes in, is this: you must be comfortable. The number one thing that makes a woman feel strong, attractive, and sexy is being confident; and to feel confident you have to wear clothes that feel good and make you look better. Diane was wearing one of her signature outfits the day we met: black leggings under a geometric-patterned caftan. She looked gorgeous. Her outfit was in keeping with what she'd been wearing and designing for many years—elegant, easy to wear, and interesting. It can cover any "body flaw" that a woman has and still make her feel feminine and sexy.

Love yourself—even your hair.

When we met, Diane was a few weeks away from turning sixty-two and I was about to turn fifty-two (we're both Capricorns). We laughed about how we are both much more at ease with ourselves now that we are over fifty—our bodies, sexuality, careers, style, and even our hair. Like me, Diane used to fight her curls, but went natural a few years ago. She pointed out that this was another example of the progression of self-confidence, which makes us all more beautiful as we age.

The beauty of experience.

Back in 1976 when Diane was riding high from the success of the wrap dress and launching her first book, she was much more insecure than anyone realized. She doubted herself, her decisions, and was moving forward more on instinct than knowledge. Now that she's older and more confident, she says she makes decisions based on wisdom and experience, and feels that her approach to style reflects that. She takes a softer approach to most things—her makeup, hair, and clothes—even how she treats her skin and body. She stays in shape with gentle exercises like yoga, Pilates, and hiking and she gets a massage every week. She has no interest in plastic surgery because she wants her face to always reflect who she is at that particular time in her life. And it works. The overall feeling I got looking at her hair, skin, makeup, and clothes was soft, pretty, feminine, and very comfortable.

You are the priority.

Diane believes that one of the most important things that any woman can do for herself—especially after fifty—is to be her own number one priority. She loves her husband, children, and grandchildren, but she says: "My best friend is me, and I take good care of me." If you put time, energy, and effort into creating a positive relationship with yourself, from it will spring other positive relationships. For years we have been taking care of family, children, and our communities, but most of us haven't given ourselves the same love and care. Now we must. It may sound selfish, Diane said, but it isn't. If you take care of yourself as you get older, you'll be better equipped to take care of everything and everyone that comes your way. Diane is a living example of her own philosophy: she is healthy, beautiful, strong, confident and, she says, the happiest she has ever been.

What does that have to do with fashion?

Diane put it to me this way: if you are healthy and comfortable and feeling good about yourself then you'll give off an aura of confidence, sexiness, and power. Pick a look that reinforces that—clothes, hair, and makeup—put it on, and then forget about it. Go out and live your life and don't worry about what you look like. We did too much of that already in our younger—and more insecure—years. We should enjoy ourselves and not waste time over-thinking every fashion choice. Diane's advice is to get to know what makes you feel uncomfortable, and what makes you feel comfortable. Understand which clothes make you think, "Do I look okay?" and which ones let you not think about it at all. Forget rules and just wear what makes you feel good about you.

So how do we figure out what makes us feel good?

Diane had simple and excellent advice on that, too: try stuff on. Go through your closet and see how each piece makes you feel. Give away anything that doesn't make you feel good. Spend time with some fashion-savvy people who can show you different styles for your body. Go to department stores and work with a personal shopper. Try on a lot of clothes from many different designers. See what works and what doesn't. Once you understand this, the rest will be easy. And with that—plus a big hug—she sent me back into the world to go shopping.

(Oh, and by the way, Diane has seen Ellen Barkin in jeans many times.)

Help from the Professionals

I liked Diane's idea about working with a personal shopper to design my new wardrobe, but although I've lived in one of the shopping capitals of the world for over fifty years, I have never used a personal shopper. I love clothes, but I hate to shop. It's intimidating, time-consuming, and I usually get hungry, tired, and grumpy, which means that I buy all the wrong things and end up at the cosmetic counter buying stuff I don't need. And besides, wasn't personal shopping service set aside for the "ladies who lunch" crowd—those women who can drop several thousand dollars in one afternoon without batting an eye? But, when I started asking several perfectly normal women I know, they told me that they use personal shoppers.

I was still skeptical, but one friend explained how it works: she calls her personal shopper about a week or so in advance to make an appointment and describes what she's looking for (work, play, evening clothes, or whatever), and by the time she walks into the "personal shopping" dressing room, it is already filled with the consultant's hand-picked choices in the right sizes to try on—plus shoes, accessories, and even coffee. The personal shopper scouts out clothes on every floor and in every department and sends out notices to her customers when new styles are coming in from their favorite designers. The best part? There's no charge for the service, no minimum purchase, and no pressure to buy anything. Their goal is to keep you as a loyal customer. Another plus: a tailor is always waiting in the wings so that your personal shopper can help get things custom-fitted if anything needs to be altered.

Joining the
Fifth Avenue Club at Saks.

Saks Fifth Avenue was my first stop, since they are famous for outstanding customer service and carry a wide range of brands. At the Fifth Avenue Club, personal shopping department, I met Julie Hackett-Behr, who has been a style consultant at Saks for over twenty years. I explained to Julie, that while I was looking for some new clothes for myself, I needed to understand what wardrobe pieces and style guidelines (not rules, thank you) would be useful for all women over fifty. I had committed to a budget of $2,000. Quite an investment, I know, but all in the name of research.

Before the new comes in, the old must go out.

In preparation for our shopping session, Julie instructed me to do what she asks every new client to do:

- **Go home and review everything in my closet.** I had to evaluate every piece with brutal honesty to see whether or not it fit my new criteria. (I had Diane's good advice in my head the entire time.)

Did I love it? Did it make me feel good? Was I ever going to wear it again? This helped to edit my "collection" down.

- **Make a list of every category of clothing I owned**—pants, skirts, dresses, sweaters, jackets, and so on—and then itemize every piece by color, designer, and size. She also wanted a list of all my bags and shoes. This kind of inventory is important to a style consultant, but it is also a great tool for you to use in evaluating what you have, what you like, and what about your current style you might want to change or build on.

Let's shop!
Our mission was to choose items that were:

1. classic enough to be worn for more than one year.
2. easy to mix with my existing clothes and with each other.
3. the right material to wear for two or even three seasons.
4. not too young looking, but not dowdy either.

When I arrived for my shopping date with Julie, I was escorted into a huge suite with clothes everywhere. I tried on pants, tops, jackets, lots of skirts, and a few dresses. From the first batch of clothes, only a few passed muster (this is typical). While I sat sipping coffee out of a dainty porcelain cup, Julie and her assistant went back down to the sales floors. Fifteen minutes later they were back with their arms full of clothes.

Two hours later: the results.

I have never enjoyed shopping as much as I did that day. It was so much fun that had Julie pushed me even a tiny bit to go past my budget, I would have done so gladly. But she was determined to bring it all in for $2,000 or under. Nothing was on sale, but every single piece fit me perfectly (some had to be altered) and they all go with one another, like a happy little family. Here's what I got:

- **White, lined, very modern short linen jacket with a Nehru-type collar by Tahari**
- **Lime green, unlined, short ¾-length sleeved linen jacket by DKNY**
- **Geometric patterned ¾-length sleeved wrap top by Diane von Furstenberg**
- **Gunmetal sleeveless, knee-length, fitted, lined cotton sheath dress by Hugo Boss**
- **Charcoal grey stretch denim knee-length pencil skirt by Vince**
- **Black stretch pencil skirt by Diane von Furstenberg**
- **Navy lined linen pants by Tahari**
- **Dark blue denim straight jeans by J Brand**
- **Off-white colored tank top by Tahari**
- **Black tank top by Tahari**

All of the items can be worn with everything else. When I added these ten pieces to my existing wardrobe, they served to expand my base. They can be worn for three seasons, and a few of them can be worn year-round. All are classic pieces, not simply trends. They fit, they work together, the length of the skirts and pants are perfect, and I look and feel comfortable. Diane would be pleased.

Right on Target

Julie's guidance and fashion savvy definitely got me feeling put together, and I'll share all of her wardrobe planning advice a little further on. But first, I was curious to find out what kind of style we can get at a more everyday price point. Upscale shops are great for style advice and for investing in a fabulous jacket or a perfectly fitted pair of slacks that you can wear for years. But as a counterpoint to my spree at Saks, I decided to take another shopping trip—to Target. Target partners with big-name designers to present limited-run, lower-priced items. Even though I had gone through fashion basic training with Julie at Saks, and had my confidence boosted by Diane von Furstenberg, I still wanted a fashion guide—and a shopping buddy.

C'mon Ginny Hilfiger, you're coming to Target.

Ginny Hilfiger has spent over twenty years designing clothes, and fifteen of them working side by side with her brother Tommy as Senior Vice President of Tommy Hilfiger. In 2005, she started her own label. I invited Ginny to join me on this adventure (okay, I begged), and she graciously agreed. I gave her the same mission I had given Julie: to find items that would complement what I already had at home, including the new

pieces from Saks, and in styles that were not too trendy so they could be worn beyond this year. Her budget: $500.

Attention, Target shoppers.

Maybe it was the company, maybe it was the store, but Ginny and I had a blast. I was having too much fun to use the dressing room and was just zipping up and taking off dresses right and left in Aisle 3, and pulling Bermuda shorts right over my jeans in Aisle 5. Fun aside, we were definitely hitting pay dirt. Plus, after we were done shopping for clothes, I was able to pick up some refills for my Swiffer floor mop. Can't do that at Saks.

The end result?

We tried to spend $500, but couldn't. I ended up spending $350 on twenty items. (So I picked up a great Tracy Feith dress for my daughter, Sarah, with some of my extra cash.) What did I get?

- **Three sleeveless dresses—one is black with a slight flair to the skirt, very retro; another is a geometric print that reminds me of the Pucci designs from the 1960s; and** the third is a brown with a simple dark brown/black cross-hatch weave. All are knee-length, fully lined and very well made. Anyone could wear these flattering dresses and look great.

- Four tank tops—white, black, orange, and brown
- Three short-sleeved t-shirts—one black and two whites
- One white hoodie
- Two pairs of Bermuda shorts (khaki and blue/white striped seersucker)
- Four long-sleeved cardigans (black, white, cream, and green)
- Two short-sleeved cardigans (black and white)
- One stretchy, short, fitted dark blue denim blazer (fully lined—and the stitching inside was impressive)

Twenty pieces, all for under $350.

We were impressed. I loved the style and the price, but Ginny examined them through the lens of an experienced designer, and noted that every dress was lined, the stitching was solid, and the clothes had been made for real women with true human proportions, not super-skinny models. The dresses I bought fit beautifully without any alteration and the styles would look fabulous on any woman, regardless of size. The Bermuda shorts fit like Theory's "city shorts." The 100% cotton cardigans were soft, chic, and well-fitting, and the t-shirts were perfect. In less than two hours we were able to find twenty terrific pieces. Ginny held up one of the cardigans and said that if this same piece had been sold in Bergdorf Goodman's, it would go for over $200. Target's price? $17.99. We met our other goals, too—all the pieces could be worn with clothes I already had, and with each other.

Building your Basic Wardrobe

I had the building blocks for a great look, but had I covered the basics? I asked our experts to suggest the go-to pieces that every woman over fifty should have in her closet. You can dress them up or down depending upon the accessories—shoes, jewelry, bags. Here is the master list with the input from their combined years of style experience and wisdom.

Dark denim boot-cut jeans

Dark denim boot-cut jeans with no decoration, rips, or bling of any kind. The simpler and darker the better. The rise (the distance from the top of the waistband to the crotch seam) should be between 8 and 9 inches. If you need a size that fits your but and hips perfectly, but ends up being too large in the waist, that's easy to fix—have the waist taken in by a tailor. The boot cut creates a nice balance with our bodies. The best shoe with this cut is a mid-heel short boot or a higher pump for evening. Other good shoe choices are a wedge heel, kitten heel, or Mary Jane. The length of the jeans should be $\frac{1}{8}$ to $\frac{1}{4}$ of an inch off the floor, depending on the shoes you wear. If you want to switch between higher and lower heels, buy two pairs of jeans, and bring your shoes with you when getting them hemmed. Ask the tailor to keep the original hem style on the jeans.

Best fitting jeans:

- 7 For All Mankind
- J Brand
- Paige
- AG Jeans
- Theory
- Tahari
- Gap
- Levi's
- Not Your Daughter's Jeans

Dark denim straight leg jeans

Dark denim straight leg jeans (not "skinny jeans"—those are for teens and twentysomethings). This cut is more flattering than a true skinny jean but will still have a nice, sleek effect. If the leg is too skinny, it could make our butts and thighs look bigger. When hemming, you won't need to be as fussy, since the length can work with multiple heel heights. One pair is all you need as a basic. The color should be dark blue, with no decorations. Straight-leg jeans look great with shoes that are slightly more delicate than what you would wear with a boot cut, like a ballet slipper style with a kitten heel. Low-heeled moccasin style shoes or loafers are great casual options. Tuck them into boots in cooler weather. These jeans go well with tunic tops.

White jeans, either boot-cut, straight leg, or both.

You can wear them all year long. Pair them with brown or black boots and top with a sweater in the fall or winter. Wear panties that match your skin tone—not white ones—with white jeans.

Great fitting pants

Great fitting pants are staples and can be worn year-round and for different occasions. Look for a lightweight wool blend (a wool/lycra blend is best) in black, charcoal, and brown. Consider navy or white linen pants for summer. The cut of the pants is crucial and the length should be exact. Take your shoes with you when you go shopping and when the pants get hemmed. The experienced tailor will look at where the hem "breaks" on the top of the shoe and where the back of the hem is from the floor. Avoid "crop" pants, which hit your leg at the least flattering spot: between the knee and ankle (closer to the ankle).

Best fitting pants:

- **Theory**
- **Tahari**
- **Trina Turk**
- **Banana Republic**
- **Joseph**
- **Hugo Boss**
- **Piazza Sempione**
- **J. Crew**
- **Ellen Tracy**
- **Ann Taylor**

Black pencil skirt

A black pencil skirt is one of the most versatile things you'll own. It's great with tights and boots, and black or fishnet stockings and pumps for evening. Look for a wool/lycra blend so that there's a stretch in the fabric. The fit should stay close to the body but should not be tight. The right length for this (and most skirts and dresses) is in the middle of the knee—exactly where the back of your knee bends. If you have a favorite black skirt that is the right length (or could be made shorter to be the right length), but is slightly A-line, you could easily have it taken in to become a pencil skirt.

Don't wear a totally flat shoe with a pencil skirt. Instead, pair it with a mid-heel or high-heel pump (try a peep-toe pair), Mary Janes, or boots. On top, wear a blouse or a cashmere sweater with a t-shirt a bit longer than the sweater. You could also pair it with a t-shirt under a great cardigan, or tuck in a slightly billowy blouse and add a short jacket. A black jacket with a black skirt can sometimes be too serious of a look. Try a jacket in a fun color or a mix of colors, like a tweed or hounds tooth.

Best fitting skirts:

- Diane von Furstenberg
- Vince
- Kors
- Tahari
- Theory
- Club Monaco
- Hugo Boss
- Banana Republic
- Liz Claiborne
- Ellen Tracy
- Ann Taylor
- Chico's

Black, white, and cream fitted jackets

Black, white, and cream fitted jackets that fall just to the hip bone or above and are nicely fitted but not tight can be worn all year long and with all of your "bottoms"—jeans, pants, and skirts. Mix them with different colored t-shirts, camisoles, and blouses underneath. Invest in good fabrics and styles that are classic and timeless, so you're not out buying them all over again next year.

Best fitting jackets:

- Theory
- Tahari
- Trina Turk
- Hugo Boss
- DKNY
- J. Crew
- Liz Claiborne
- Ann Taylor
- Ellen Tracy
- Chico's

Light-weight short fitted jacket

One light-weight short fitted jacket in a great color will add a lot of versatility to your spring and summer wardrobes. Look for a lightweight cotton blend.

Wear with jeans, white pants, white "city shorts" or a sheath dress.

Cardigans

Cardigans are a terrific, year-round fashion accessory. Thanks to my shopping trip to Target with Ginny Hilfiger, I now have lightweight cardigans in both long and short sleeves and in several colors. They are perfect with pants, skirts, or jeans, and can be worn over t-shirts, camis, silk tops, or over sleeveless dresses. The key to getting the right look: buy a size or two smaller than your regular size, so that you aren't wearing a "Mumsy" sweater, but a very fitted, chic cardigan. You're never going to wear it closed, unless you just button the top button, so how it looks closed doesn't matter. It should just give you a cover-up for your arms, a bit of warmth, and add some color to your outfit. Try a three-quarter sleeve for the most versatility and look for a length above or at the hip. A long cardigan past the mid-thigh can look good with pants or jeans but doesn't work well with skirts.

Best cardigans:

- **Tse**
- **August Cashmere**
- **Merona or Mossimo brands at Target**
- **J. Crew**
- **Ann Taylor**
- **Chico's**
- **Banana Republic**

Tank tops

Tank tops in black, white, and cream are essentials. You'll wear one just about every day—layered under other tank tops and a jacket or cardigan, under sweaters, under long- or short-sleeved t-shirts. They act as a good old fashioned "undershirt" and, if they're long enough, are also great for tucking into your jeans, so that you don't flash any skin when you sit down. A great look is wearing a long tank top under a short fitted jacket. You want the fit to be snug, not loose, so size down if you need to. Tank tops are indispensable but there's no reason to spend a lot on them. Stock up if you find one that you really love.

Best tank tops:

- Target's Mossimo Supply Co. Long and Lean
- Banana Republic
- Gap
- Petite Bateau
- American Apparel
- James Perse

Long- and short-sleeved T-shirts

Long- and short-sleeved T-shirts are wonderful by themselves or layered over a tank top for extra coverage. Look for nicely finished jersey t-shirts with a crew, scoop or v-neck and a trim fit. A t-shirt can be made of many different fabrics, such as silk, cotton, or a cotton/lycra blend. You can create a casual or a dressy look depending on the material and style. The best t-shirts are thick without being bulky, and a long length works especially well under a short jacket or cardigan or over un-belted pants or jeans. As with tank tops, many different companies make t-shirts, so search out a brand that you love and stock up on them.

Best t-shirts:

- Merona double layer tee, and long-sleeved Merona Ultimate Tee (both at Target)
- Ginny H
- Petite Bateau
- Banana Republic
- Converse
- Gap

Dresses

Dresses will always make you feel pretty, sexy, and special. Plus, they're the fastest way to get dressed. There are two styles that are particularly flattering for women over fifty. Aim to have one of each in black, and a second in gray, brown, tan, or blue.

A sheath dress is a simple sleeveless dress that is slightly fitted and falls just to the right spot at the knee. The skirt shape can be A-line or straight down like a pencil skirt, but the whole dress should be cut or tailored to follow and accentuate your curves and waistline. Fit is key to making this look great. You don't have to spend a lot. When I gave my family a fashion show of my Target finds, my husband fell in love with the Merona sleeveless, fitted black sateen cotton sheath dress with the slightly A-line skirt. It was, as Howard put it, "a dress that every woman in America should own." But he was right. There wasn't a single body flaw (real or imagined) that this dress couldn't tackle. Tush a little plump? The A-line skirt will hide it. Arms flapping in the breeze? Throw on a little cardigan or a short jacket. It cost . . . drum roll, please . . . $39.99.

The wrap dress, made famous by Diane von Furstenberg, is now made by many designers and retail brands. One of these in basic black can be worn for many different occasions from the office to a cocktail party, depending upon how it's accessorized. The secret to wearing this dress comfortably is how the top fits. If needed, have a tailor put a snap at the place on the top where it starts to cross, or wear a tank top or silk camisole underneath. Tie it on the side, never in the front, and not as a bow. Totally flat shoes can look dowdy with skirts and dresses, so try a slingback, classic pump, or Mary Jane-type shoe with a heel at least 1½ inches high, or boots.

Best dresses:

- **Hugo Boss**
- **DKNY**
- **Tahari**
- **Merona (Target)**
- **Diane von Furstenberg**
- **Trina Turk**
- **Theory**
- **Ann Taylor**
- **Liz Claiborne**
- **Nicole Miller**
- **Ellen Tracy**
- **J. Crew**
- **GinnyH**

City shorts

City shorts are shorts that come down to that same point at the knee as our dresses and skirts are very polished-looking and not at all like beach wear. They should be fitted, not pleated or puffed out around the thigh. They should fit as if they were great-fitting pants hemmed to knee-length. A pair in black can look great in the summer, as can white and khaki. These can be dressed up with a jacket or cardigan. Pair with kitten heel slingbacks or wedge-heel sandals. You will live in these during the summer.

Best fitting city shorts:

- **Theory**
- **Merona (Target)**
- **J. Crew**
- **Banana Republic**
- **Ann Taylor**

Summer skirts

Summer skirts are indispensable in hot weather and can be a lot of fun, too. Try a stretch-denim pencil skirt in a lighter fabric and color. They are easy to wear with low-heeled sandals and a tank top with a summer jacket or cardigan. Long or knee-length peasant-style skirts look great with a fitted t-shirt (and a fitted cardigan) and low or wedged sandals.

Best fitting summer skirts:

- **Calypso**
- **DKNY**
- **Vince**
- **Tahari**
- **Milly**
- **Anthropologie**
- **J. Crew**
- **Liz Claiborne**
- **Chico's**

Winter Coats

A cashmere/wool blend coat in black or another rich color is an essential. The cut should be classic, flattering and beltless. Belted coats can be unflattering. There's usually too much material, and if you want to wear the coat open, you have two long things flapping around. A classic and versatile length is either to mid-thigh or to the knee, which looks great with pants and skirts or dresses. In places where the winter is snowy or wet, a long, water-resistant quilted coat is another must-have. Not one of those puffy down parkas that add on about twenty pounds, but a sleeker version. One that falls to the knee is a great go-to winter coat that can handle a lot of weather and still look good. Black is classic for winter coats, but so is chocolate brown. Maybe one of each?

Best fitting coats:

- **Cole Haan**
- **Calvin Klein**
- **Coach**
- **Max Mara**
- **Burberry**

- **Ann Taylor**
- **Banana Republic**
- **Soïa & Kyo**
- **Post Card**

A raincoat or waterproof spring/fall coat

A raincoat or waterproof spring/fall coat is a necessity to keep you dry and to ease you through those "transition seasons." Look for something lightweight, water resistant, and definitely not belted unless you're super-skinny and want to deal with the nuisance of a belt. It should fall to the knee, and have a simple design with some interesting details, in a neutral brown, black, or taupe.

Best fitting rain or spring/fall coats:

- **Cole Haan**
- **Trina Turk**
- **Hugo Boss**
- **Coach**
- **J. Crew**
- **Burberry**
- **DKNY**
- **H&M**
- **Target**

What about shoes?

Our experts were in complete agreement about the most wearable and versatile shoes for our closets. These will be the ones you go to every day:

- **Knee-high Boots:** with a mid- or high-heel, or one of each. Boots should come up to your mid-calf or knee; any higher is too trendy. Consider boots with a wedge heel for extra comfort. Get one pair in black and another in brown.
- **Ankle-high bootie:** These short boots (in leather or suede) should have a mid-heel and are worn under pants and jeans. Get one pair in black and one in brown, with different heel heights.
- **Pumps:** This is the classic mid- or high-heel shoe that looks great with dresses, skirts, pants, and jeans. Have a traditional closed-toe pair, but consider a second pair with a peek-a-boo toe. The most versatile pumps are black leather, black patent leather, brown leather or suede, and nude or beige.
- **Slingbacks:** With a closed toe, a slim back strap, and about a 2" heel. At least one pair in black, brown, or nude. These look fabulous and a little sexy with everything—pants, jeans, dresses, and skirts.

- **Mary Janes:** Like a pump with a single strap across the top of your foot. Just one pair in black with a medium heel is really terrific with pants, boot cut jeans, skirts, and dresses.

- **Kitten heels:** This is a low curvy heel between 1 and 2 inches high. A kitten heel is more flattering than a completely flat heel, and is usually more comfortable. If you have a pump, sling back, and sandal with this heel, you'll be covered for all seasons, and you will wear them all the time.

- **Walking shoe:** Purchase one good pair of almost flat shoes for casual outfits and for days that you need to walk quite a bit. A classic loafer is great, as is a moccasin-style slip-on, but find something that makes you look and feel put-together, not frumpy. A heel that's at least one-inch high will be more comfortable and stylish than a totally flat sole.

- **Wedge sandals:** For summer, a simple mule-type espadrille sandal with a rope bottom is really versatile, stylish, comfortable, and comes in different heel heights. There are many choices for colors and materials, but skip any with ribbons that wrap around your ankles. That's a very young look, and unflattering to your leg.

- **Sneakers:** Buy two pairs—for running and one for working out. Don't wear them as a fashion statement though. (See *Chapter 6: Move That Body* for tips on picking out good running shoes.)

- **Snow boots and rain boots:** Get a pair that's completely waterproof, stylish, and well made. (La Canadienne is the best.)

- **Flip flops:** You are not your teenage daughter. Only for the beach, running around your own backyard, or getting a pedicure.

Best shoes and boots:

- Cole Haan (with Nike Air)
- Kors (from Michael Kors)
- Prada
- Stuart Weitzman
- La Canadienne
- Anne Klein
- Banana Republic
- Coach
- Easy Spirit
- Naturalizer
- Nine West
- Jaime Mascaró

It's not just about what's
on the outside.
What goes underneath
all those fabulous clothes?

Get a bra that fits.

The majority of American women are wearing the wrong size bra, and it shows. Get fitted by a pro at your local lingerie or department store, and invest in some good new bras, including one specifically for wearing under a t-shirt or other smooth shirts. If you have a problem with nipples showing through your clothes, buy Gel Petals, which are little reusable silicone pads that you stick over your nipples before putting on your bra. Buy bras that are close to your own skin color for wearing under white or light colored tops.

Stop wearing Grandma panties.

Try on a pair of Hanky Panky thongs (made in the U.S.A. and sold everywhere), or even their boycut panties, and you will never wear anything else again. You've never worn thongs? Try a pair before you say no. You won't feel like you're wearing anything at all, and you'll say ta-ta to panty lines forever. They're incredibly comfortable. Do not wear white panties when wearing white or light colored pants. Wear panties and bras that are closest to your own skin color, and they'll blend right in. The only panties you'll ever need are Hanky Panky. Buy them in every color, for fun, but get most of them in the color that is closest to your own skin color.

Shapewear can help.

Not like our Grandma's girdles. The new era of shapewear comfortably firms you up, and keeps the jiggling at a minimum when you wear clingier outfits. All are sold in lingerie or department stores. Try Spanx, Donna Karan, and Maidenform.

What's the best overall fashion advice for women over fifty?

We don't want strict rules, but our fashion experts did have some great ideas about how to develop a polished, confidence-boosting look.

- **Find a good tailor** who's an expert in women's clothing. Fit is everything, no matter how much you spend. If you're working with a personal shopper, that person will help you get what you need from the store's in-house tailor. But also have a reliable neighborhood tailor who can alter new clothes, and can update some of your old styles to make them wearable again—turn an A-line skirt into a pencil skirt; narrow pants that are too wide; take eighties-style shoulder pads out of jackets. You might be surprised at the fashion gems you have in your closet.

- **Wear clothes that define your waist.** Even if you think your waist is large, clothing that follows your contours—even gently—will always be more flattering and attractive than garments shaped like a sack. If clothes have too much fabric or flare, they can make you look heavier.

- **Use a Personal Shopper** for pricier items and for those that demand a great fit—pants, jeans, skirts, and jackets.

- **Spend more and choose long-lasting quality fabrics** for pants, skirts, and jackets.

- **Try discount retailers** like Target, H&M, and Kohl's for basics like cardigans, tanks and t-shirts. Keep an eye out for that perfect jacket, dress, or raincoat while you're there.

- **Keep it simple.** The less bling, decoration and fussiness, the better you will look. Jackie O knew that simple elegance trumps overdoing it every time.

- **You need more than one outfit or look.** Don't keep buying jeans, even if that's what you wear most days. Every woman needs a few perfect go-to outfits for each season and for specific needs like business meetings, shopping trips, going out to lunch with friends, out for romantic dinners, and for special events. If you're in a rut, try a personal shopper or browse magazines or websites like www.What2WearWhere.com for ideas.

- **Balance the fit of your clothes.** Don't wear tight with tight or loose with loose. Pair a blousy top with a pencil skirt, or if you're wearing a tight tank with a slim skirt or narrow pants, add some volume with a jacket or cardigan. If you're wearing a full, summery skirt, wear something snug on top.

- **Prints can be aging compared to solids,** so be careful when choosing prints, especially bold, colorful patterns, which can be overpowering, and dainty floral prints, which can look too cutesy.

- **Be careful with lace.** Lace can look either too old and matronly or too young and cheap. Best is to avoid it.

- **Consider your skirt length.** Do your legs look like they did when you were twenty? Then most likely you shouldn't be flaunting them anymore. In the fall or winter, a shorter skirt can work well with tights and boots (Shorter, not short, big difference). But a short skirt with bare legs? That needs to be thought through very carefully. The perfect length is right at the middle of the knee, where the knee bends in the back.

- **Avoid ruffly, puffy, or girly.** As with lace and short skirts, clothes that are frilly, puffy at the sleeves, or stacked with ruffles don't go with our lives or bodies anymore. A single ruffle on a crisp white shirt or a tailored black dress looks fine.

- **Knot a wrap dress or top on the side,** never at the front. And don't tie a bow; it'll look too girly.

- **Avoid the matronly fit.** While tight clothes are a bad idea, those with too much extra fabric will make us look dowdy. Baggy sweaters, relaxed-fit pants, and very long skirts are unflattering.

Wide-leg pants can make us look wider. Consider having your tailor narrow too-full pants and take in skirts and hem them to knee-length for a fresher look.

- **Think "cardigan" before "jacket."** A cardigan will give you a softer, more feminine look, is easy to wash, and can become your most frequently chosen piece of clothing.

- **Consider what you're putting on your legs.** Wear black opaque tights or fishnet stockings in the fall and winter with boots or shoes. If you are comfortable, try using leg makeup (like Sally Hansen) instead of nude stockings in warmer seasons. But do what makes you comfortable.

- **Clean out your closet and keep only what works.** See if there are clothes you already have that can be revived with alterations. Everything else should be heave-hoed out the door.

- **Keep your shoes looking good.** Take care of your shoes and boots—get heels fixed and soles redone when they get worn down. You'll be able to keep them a lot longer if you do.

- **Invest in a few great bags.** Have a large, black leather bag for day; one in white leather, which can be carried over

Do you need a Personal Shopper?

I was impressed by the benefits of using a personal shopper for even one trip to a nice department store. If you think you'd be interested but aren't quite sure, Lisa Bruni, the director of the Women's Fifth Avenue Club at Saks Fifth Avenue, described what you can get from a personal shopper or style consultant. Personal shoppers can help if you:

- **are busy with your career and life, but still want to have some great clothes.**
- **have a special occasion and don't know what to wear.**
- **want to create a solid wardrobe foundation on which to build.**
- **are looking for brands that work best for your body shape, style, and age.**
- **often buy clothes that you don't wear because they aren't right.**
- **want to figure out what goes with what or how to put accessories (belts, bags, shoes, or jewelry) together with your outfits.**
- **are stuck in a fashion rut, wearing the same brands, colors, or styles year after year.**
- **need help sticking to a budget.**
- **want all of this without any obligation or fee.**

My personal shopper, Julie, helped me with all of that and more. Over time, you will establish a relationship with your personal shopper, who will know what you have in your wardrobe to work with, and will be able to determine what you need and want. You can save money using a personal shopper because you'll be less inclined to buy items that you will never wear, and more apt to buy those that fit you well and last several seasons. Personal shoppers let their clients know in advance when sales are going to happen and work with you on creating the maximum number of "looks" with the minimum number of pieces. Most large stores have in-house tailors available at a cost on par with tailors from outside the stores, and sometimes there is no charge for basic alterations like hemming. Almost every major department store offers this service, but if your favorite store doesn't have a personal shopping department, you can establish a similar relationship with a good salesperson.

three seasons; and one or two clutch bags for evening. It's also fun to add bold colors as accents—a turquoise blue bag for the warmer months and a burnt orange one for the fall, for example. If you spend wisely, you'll have a few great bags that can last for many seasons.

The best bags are:

- Prada
- Bottega Veneta
- Fendi
- Coach
- Michael Kors
- Cole Haan
- Rafe
- Isabella Fiori

Above all, be comfortable.

Get on board.

We can look great, at any age, for not a lot of money. All we need are some well-made basics, a good-fitting bra, and a few closing thoughts:

- A great black dress is an essential piece for every woman.
- Fit is everything, no matter your size.
- A tailor is your best fashion friend.
- Great clothes with fabulous style don't have to cost a fortune.
- You won't look good if you aren't comfortable.

An Online Personal Shopper?

Nosing around the web recently, I came across something that must be shared; the online equivalent of a personal shopper. The appropriately named **What2WearWhere.com** offers really smart contemporary outfit suggestions for the office, black tie dinners, traveling, and basics for everyday life. Go to the site, choose the appropriate "event," and the site's fashionistas will suggest a selection of affordable ideas, complete with accessories. When you click on your choice, you're linked directly to the retailer, so you can buy what you need online, without having to locate the store. Makes life a little easier.

Get more information.

Having a basic wardrobe is essential, but there's a world of fashion out there, and your personal style should be your guide. So get the basics in order, and then go have fun!

For style inspiration, try these websites:

- www.what2wearwhere.com
- www.more.com

And for more from our experts, visit:

- www.dvf.com
- www.saksfifthavenue.com
- www.ginnyh.com
- www.target.com

Watch this on TV:

- "What Not to Wear" on the TLC channel

Chapter 11

Money

Strategies for Simplying Your Finances

Ah . . . money.

Money. You gotta love it. Or, at least, you gotta have it. Whether you work for it, inherited it, married into it, won the lottery, or some combination thereof, once you're over fifty, just make sure you have a plan in place so there's some left over for you to enjoy. How else will we be able to pay for the clothes we just talked about?

What, me worry?

Financial issues can be complicated, frustrating, and emotionally charged, but dealing with these things now will ensure that we're not scrambling in the future. These days we're facing global economic circumstances that aren't terribly reassuring, as well as more personal financial concerns—our own health issues for starters, plus aging parents who might need our help, and maybe even college expenses for those of us with kids still in school. They don't call us the sandwich generation for nothing. But we can handle all of this if we get serious, get honest, and make a plan. The most important thing—as with almost everything in life after fifty—is to keep it simple.

No house of cards.

Life was so uncomplicated when I was growing up. We lived with my grandparents who had paid $14,000 cash for their little attached house in which they raised five children before they took on the job of raising my sister and me while my mother worked as a secretary in Manhattan. My grandfather was a cement mason and every Friday night when he came home with his weekly pay, he handed it directly over to my grandmother. Grandma was the manager of the house and of the money. The monthly utility bills were paid in cash. No mortgage, no department store credit cards, no Visa, MasterCard, or Amex, and no debt. We paid cash for everything we bought, which, under Grandma's control, wasn't much. "Never buy what you don't need," she would say, and most things she figured she could make herself. She kept the cash locked in a small metal "strong box" along with the few stocks they owned, the deed to their house, and all other important life documents. That box could withstand an earthquake, fire, flood, and an attack by a swarm of locusts. And Grandma was the only one who knew where the key was.

Take a card, any card.

Why didn't I pay attention to my grandmother when she tried to teach me how to make the perfect turkey gravy, to speak German, or manage my money so I would never have debt? She was brilliant, and I was a smart-alecky kid who morphed into a smartass teenager who evolved into a know-it-all adult. Cards? Oh, I had many. You name the store, it was represented in my wallet. Amex? My closest friend. Cash? Why bother when plastic is so much neater? Luckily, I was earning enough to cover my monthly payments, but using them was just too easy. And the rates? Outrageous! But that didn't stop me (and most Americans) from using those cards and racking up the debt. It's the American way.

The American Dream

For decades, we've all been working hard at building the American dream— buying a home, getting mortgages, having kids, refinancing our mortgages, taking out lines of credit on our homes, using the plastic, and buying, buying, buying. Credit cards, which didn't exist before the late 1950s, were born with our generation and multiplied faster than we did. The credit was irresistibly easy to get (which maybe should have made us a little less eager and a little more wary) which led to our country's current problems. For many Americans in the 80s, 90s, and last decade there didn't seem to be any way—or even any need—to stop borrowing, so the debt just kept building with no thought about saving anything for later. Later seemed too far away.

Some New Realities

What I just described has been the financial reality of many people in this country. But even those of us who were more like Aesop's fabled ants who spent the summer busily gathering up food for the winter while the grasshopper basked in the sun saw our personal savings drop when the financial freefall started in 2008. The grasshopper lives for today; the ant plans for tomorrow. Most of us have both the ant and the grasshopper fighting it out inside our heads. But at fifty, tomorrow is fast becoming today. So how do we stop the battle and take charge of our finances? Call in the experts.

First Stop:
A Great Financial Planner

Michael Axelrod became our financial advisor a few years back after Howard and I realized that we hadn't updated anything—insurance, wills, and other parts of our financial plan—in a very long time. Highly recommended by people we trust, Michael is a fee-based wealth management advisor, associated with Northwestern Mutual Investment Services. We originally met with him to review our insurance needs, but now Michael is helping us with much more. I asked Michael to offer advice on how to plan for our financial future.

The State of the Union

Michael started us off with a reality check about the financial world that we are now dealing with. Between October 2007 and March 2009, the U.S. stock market lost over seven trillion dollars (it's so big, I'm not even sure how to write that as a number). Housing values are down, and the unemployment rate for workers over fifty is up. Some experts believe it will be years before the U.S. economy comes back. One of the major reasons is that we 79 million baby boomers are aging. The first wave of the boomers are getting ready to retire, and as we do, we're going to tighten up our wallets, as we should. We are such a huge financial powerhouse that if we stop spending, we could slow the economy for years to come. That happened in Japan in the 1990s, and the Japanese economy still hasn't fully recovered. It's a Catch-22—how else can we have enough to live on comfortably, if we don't stop spending and start saving? But if we do stop spending, how will the economy start growing again?

Plan of Action

Michael's good advice—have a plan.

Determine where you are financially, decide where you want to be, and create a plan to get there. You're not alone, and you can do this.

Jane Bryant Quinn Takes You Back to Basics

Despite Michael's reassurance, and his wonderful way of holding our hands through some of the more complicated financial stuff, I freaked out, convinced that my husband and I would be homeless and starving on the street in a few years, given all of our current and future expenses (like college). So I called Jane Bryant Quinn. Jane was a contributing editor at *Newsweek* for years, reports for Bloomberg, has been a key advisor for AARP, was named one of the "25 Most Influential Women in America," and is a best-selling author of many books on finance. My breathing slowed to normal just knowing that I was going to meet her.

Put down the financial reports, and start using common sense.

Every morning I get up at 5:30, wash my face, make coffee, and wait patiently until I hear the plopping sounds of the *Wall Street Journal* and *New York Times* hitting the floor outside my apartment door. While I do my best to wade through the financial reports, I quickly feel my eyes glazing over, and my fingers itching to turn to the sections on culture, world news, or health. When I confessed this to Jane, she said: "You don't need to read the financial reports to manage your money. You don't need to be a financial expert to get the job done. You just need to be sensible."

Jane's Reality Check:

> **The stock market won't be back to its former level for a number of years.**

When the stock market tumbled in 2000, it didn't come back up to that same level until 2007. We don't know what will happen this time around, but we can assume it won't restore all your losses.

The real estate market isn't coming back too quickly, either.

The real estate market will hit rock bottom, then will do what it always does: go up slowly, roughly in line with the rate of inflation. In recent years, we had access to easy cash through home equity loans. Now that so many homes have lost their value and credit is harder to get, this may no longer be an option. The advice is to pay off home equity loans and as much of your mortgage as possible before you retire, because you'll need whatever money you have left to live on. You might want to consider downsizing by trading in your home for something smaller and more manageable.

Plan on working longer than expected.

This generation hasn't saved enough to retire, and part of the money that we did save disappeared when the stock market crashed. The reality is that many of us will be forced to stay in the work force longer, possibly lifting the new "normal" retirement age as high as seventy. On the upside, if we work longer, and therefore have more disposable income, we'll be putting more money back into the market, which might help our savings to recover faster. We'll also defer the day we start taking Social Security, which can increase our future benefits.

What does this mean to you?

Jane is viewed as a conservative thinker when it comes to financial planning and in 2003, she wrote a *Newsweek* article with good advice for people pushing fifty. In it, she said that if we haven't started saving yet, she hopes that we'll inherit a bundle of money. But if that still hasn't happened, then we have to get very tough with ourselves, starting immediately.

After fifty, as we're heading toward retirement—which we now understand probably won't happen until we're closer to seventy—we ask ourselves how we're going to afford to live. This is where the simple part comes in: you need to save more, and spend less. There's no magic involved. Just basic common sense.

Jane's Smart Advice:

- **Tighten your belt**—Stop spending and don't live above your means (channeling Grandma?).

- **Stash it away**—Put as much money into your 401(k) or other retirement plan as you possibly can and invest in a conservative mix of stocks and bonds, preferably through mutual funds. (Jane does not recommend individual stocks for most people. Too risky.)

- **Hands off the house**—Don't tap your home equity for cash.

- **Cut the cord**—Stop helping your (adult) kids. Put money into your retirement fund first, then the college fund.

- **Stay healthy**—If you're going to work for many more years, you must stay healthy, so stop smoking, exercise and eat right.

I know, I know. You're just going to keep on working. But what if . . .

You may have decided that you are going to solve your money problems by just not retiring. But what if you are laid off? What if you were planning to work until you hit seventy, but your company lets you go when you're fifty-three? No matter what your plans are, you could very well lose your job unexpectedly. Being prepared for that possibility is essential to your overall financial (and mental) health.

Insure the Future

In addition to creating a sensible monetary strategy and building our savings, Jane and Michael both pointed out that as we pass fifty, we need to pay attention to the other critical part of long-term financial planning: insurance.

Our Essential Insurance Needs

Health Insurance

Without health insurance, your health, savings, and standard of living are at serious risk should you or a member of your family develop an illness or become injured. Having no health insurance is a much greater financial risk than almost anything else. If you lose your job, or choose to leave, you'll need to find a way to stay insured until you're sixty-five, at which time you'll be eligible for Medicare. If you have a choice, don't retire until you know you can fill the insurance gap. Here are some ways to stay covered if you do leave or lose your job:

- **Get on your spouse's plan. There is a short amount of time after you lose your coverage when you can sign up, so don't wait on this.**
- **COBRA will let you keep your previous insurance coverage for up to eighteen months, but it's very expensive, so isn't usually the best option.**
- **Look for a new job specifically for the benefits it offers even if it means a pay cut.**
- **If you're starting your own business, talk with your local chamber of commerce to see if there are group policies you can join. In some states, "group" policies can be a group of one.**
- **Investigate individual policies with the help of a health insurance agent; it will be more costly than a group plan, but it's worth checking out the options.**
- **If you move, make sure to find a new doctor before you turn 65, because doctors often refuse to take on new patients if their only insurance is Medicare.**

Life insurance

If you have dependents—children, a spouse, a partner, or even aging parents—you want term life insurance so they can live the same life they are currently living if anything happens to you. If you don't have any dependents, there's no reason to have it. The rule of thumb: the total policy amount should be six to eight times your annual salary. If your partner earns an income, that person should also have life insurance proportionate to his or her income. According to Michael Axelrod, you should buy the maximum amount of insurance you can afford because while you can always cut back later, it can be hard to increase coverage as you get older and more prone to health problems.

Disability insurance

If you're in your fiftiess, you are most likely in your peak earning years. If you become disabled, your disability insurance will protect your assets. Check to see if your employer offers a plan or work with an insurance broker on finding an individual disability policy. Never put your assets in jeopardy.

Long term care insurance

This is a relatively new type of insurance and something that we should consider once we're in our late fifties.

- **What is long term care insurance (LTC)?** LTC policies cover the cost of custodial care or nursing home facilities for people who become ill or disabled, or just live to a very ripe old age.

- **What's the best age to get LTC insurance?** The ideal time is when you're in your late fifties or early sixties. Typically people in their late fifties will pay an average of $2,250 a year, and the cost generally increases with each decade of age. Don't put this off past your early sixties because the longer you wait, the more likely it is that you'll develop a medical condition that could disqualify you from getting coverage.

- **Who needs LTC?** Very wealthy people don't need LTC insurance because they have enough money to handle anything that comes along. People in the lowest tax brackets probably don't want LTC insurance either because 1) it can be prohibitively expensive, and 2) Medicaid will cover the cost of care for an ill spouse, while protected or exempt assets (IRA, car, home, term life insurance, healthy spouse's personal income, part of the ill spouse's income, and a specified amount of the savings) are left with the healthy spouse. If you have no dependents, you may not need it, because you could sell all your assets to pay for your long-term care needs and, if your money runs out, Medicaid will kick in and continue to cover your costs. LTC is critical for married couples in the upper middle class because while the healthy spouse can keep the protected assets (listed above), any additional savings or investments will be taken and used to cover the cost of care. Medicaid will cover the costs only after the money has run out. In this case, having LTC insurance will help you to preserve your standard of living. If you get LTC insurance, get a policy that adjusts to inflation.

- **How do you get LTC?** It's best to find a specialist agent who is experienced in long term care policies. Contact the American Association of Long Term Care Health Insurers (www. aaltci.org) for a list of local agents.

Guidelines for Your Financial Plan

Jane's advice is simple, straightforward, and has withstood the test of time. These are her general recommendations for getting your finances in order and keeping them there—and they are the same guidelines that she follows in her own life. The specifics will vary according to our specific lives, circumstances, needs, and goals. But these guidelines will help you create your Life Plan, which should include some version of all of these components.

- **Save more**—This is the top priority. Set up your banking so that a portion of your salary is deducted from your paycheck and put into your retirement account. Put as much as possible into your 401(k), your IRA, and every retirement fund you have going.
- **Pay off debt**—Pay more than the minimum monthly amount every month, and once you've paid off your debts, don't build them up again.
- **Borrow less**—Live below your means and you'll rarely have to borrow. Try hard not to take out a home equity loan on your house to pay for bills.
- **Pay bills electronically**—Take advantage of online banking and autopay options; it will help you to pay bills on time, which will help keep your credit score in good stead. You'll also save on checks and postage.
- **Pay attention to taxes and tax breaks**—Find a good accountant and financial planner and ask for their help.
- **Invest regularly,** especially in your retirement funds.
- **Have a diversified portfolio** with a mix of bonds, stocks, and liquid assets, and review your portfolio at least once every three months, preferably with your financial advisor.
- **Have cash available**—Make sure you have some money in liquid assets or cash that can be easily accessed; this includes CDs and money market funds from stable companies. The point of this money is not to give you a great return but to earn a small steady return while still being available for your regular bills.
- **Limit your risks**—Now's not the time to go crazy trying to maximize returns; stay focused on protecting what you already have.

- **Get all of the insurance that you need, and keep it current**—health, auto, home, life, disability, and long term care. If you miss a payment, you may lose your insurance (though companies will often work with you to get your payments up to speed).

- **Hold down fees**—Pay attention to fees from mutual funds, banking, credit cards, and other transactions, and minimize them. It doesn't hurt to call in and ask for lower fees or rates.

- **Get your will and estate planning in order**—Don't leave your heirs with a mess to clean up after you're gone. This is important for anyone, but it's especially key for "blended families" with stepchildren and the like.

Get Started!

To make a truly actionable Life Plan for going forward, you need to know where you are right now. The following steps will take you a few hours to complete, and they will be a great investment of your time. If you do it right, you'll only have to do it once and then update it occasionally.

1. **Gather all of your current financial statements, including:**
   - Bank accounts: checking and savings
   - Debts: mortgage, Home Equity Line, credit cards, and so on
   - Insurance: life, homeowner's, auto, disability, LTC, health savings accounts
   - Retirement accounts: IRA, 401(k)—their value and how much you contribute
   - College savings plan
   - Brokerage house and mutual-fund statements
   - Real estate holdings
   - Any other investments

2. **Make a list of all your debts,** including the balance, interest rate, and how much you pay every month (keep breathing).

3. **Make a separate asset list** of all your savings, investments, and insurance polices, and include their current value and monthly contribution.

4. **Next to each item—both debts and assets—write a brief note about why you have that particular item.** As you go forward with your master plan, you may find that some of

these items are keepers, some are no longer necessary, and others may need some adjusting. By doing this, you'll be giving each item the attention it deserves, and you'll be moving forward on decisions about each one. Chances are good that not everything on these lists will appear in your final plan.

5. **Review your checkbook and credit cards and make a list of average monthly expenses.** It's important to know where your money goes every month.

6. **After you've completed all of the above, start a new list called "Goals."** This will help to create a concrete list of financial goals and life goals as well. If you have a partner, this can get really interesting as you create your own separate lists of goals and then compare lists. You may have specific financial objectives such as: buy a new car, get rid of credit card debt, help an aging parent, or all of the above. Whatever your goals are, put them in writing, and then review your lists together, merging and purging as you go.

7. **Prioritize your goals.** Life can change, and so will your goals. But you need a clear idea of what your financial and life goals are so that you can plan how to get here. Whether you are solo or working with a partner, prioritize your goals, decide when you want to reach each goal, and try to realistically estimate how much money you will need for each goal to be met. Some of your goals will be "wish list" items like traveling around the world. Most will be pretty down to earth, like paying off your mortgage. Prioritize which are most important, and then figure out what you need to save and what you need to invest to reach each one.

8. **You've laid your foundation, now get a financial planner and build your Life Plan.** Once you've gotten all of that information in order, you'll be able to very clearly see the following:

- Your monthly income
- Your monthly bills
- The total amount of your debts
- What is in your retirement fund(s)
- What some large looming expenses might be
- How much you will have left each month for investing

- **Which of your items could be dropped**
- **Which of your items must stay, but might need adjusting**
- **What changes, if any, should be made in your will to reflect your actual assets and debts**
- **Exactly what you need to do to reach your goals**

Do you Need a Financial Planner?

Not everyone needs one. Planners are effective, though, if you need help in getting started, setting a budget, and figuring out the tax implications of your decisions. They're also helpful if you've been widowed and are trying to get your head around you finances. If you're nearing retirement, Jane thinks it is critical that you seek the advice of a financial planner. The right expert can make genuine improvements in the quality of your life and can ensure that you benefit from and comply with the staggering complexity of tax laws and retirement rules. Don't think that

Stocks, Bonds, and Money Market Funds: Where should you invest your money now?

Jane gave me a simple rule of thumb when deciding how to allocate my investments: subtract your age from 110. The resulting number is the percentage of your investment funds that should go into stocks; the remainder should go into bonds. Another way to consider it is to ask: when will I need this money? Put the money that you won't need for a while into bonds. Bonds are good in a down market and for liquidity, and bonds are great for balancing out your portfolio. For cash that you need to be easily accessible should an unforeseen expense arise, put money into CDs and money market funds. If you have money you won't need for a long time and can truly invest, put that into stocks. Lastly, diversity: it's best to have both stocks and bonds in your portfolio.

financial planners will only work with people who have lots of money to manage—there are excellent planners who will help you with your plan, regardless of your net worth. But how do you find a really great financial advisor who is going to help you with your Life Plan, and not just try to sell you another product?

Ask the Intelligent Investor.

Turning your financial future over to a stranger can be scary, and so I asked one of the best minds in financial journalism how to get the right financial advisor. Jason Zweig is a best-selling author and the columnist behind the *Wall Street Journal*'s "The Intelligent Investor." Jason specializes in smart, sensible strategies for making and keeping money. He believes most people don't invest the time it takes to find the right advisor. How, he asks, could you place your financial future in someone's hands without due diligence? Beyond just technical qualifications, Jason says that you and the advisor need to like, trust, and respect each other. You should feel that you would seek out all

kinds of advice from this person, not just financial. To find the right advisor, first create a short list of people you know well and trust. Ask each of them to recommend an advisor. When you have a few names, then you can start the vetting process. If you come up empty-handed, search for a fee-only advisor through the National Association of Personal Financial Advisors (www. napfa.org) or the Garrett Planning Network (www.garrettplanningnetwork. com). Both organizations are great and highly recommended, but planners associated with the Garrett group will work with you regardless of your income.

Jason offered the following list of interview questions for each candidate:

- **Why do you do what you do?** You want to feel the advisor cares about what she does and is sincerely interested in helping her clients.
- **How are you compensated?** Jason and Jane feel strongly that a financial advisor must be a fee-only professional. This means the advisor will charge only for her advice, not for any financial products she sells. A really good financial planner

will cost about the same as a really good lawyer. Some charge an hourly fee. Others charge by the plan, which could end up being $2,000 to $3,000 or more. If your financial advisor also manages your money, she may take an annual fee of up to 1% of the assets she oversees. If the total bill or estimate is more than 1% of your assets annually, find another advisor. Jason suggests you should consider lower-cost alternatives, such as Garrett Planning Network (a highly regarded international network of fee-only financial advisors and planners who offer their services on an hourly, as-needed basis) and similar firms, who charge considerably less.

- **Do you focus solely on asset management, or do you also advise on taxes, estate and retirement planning, budgeting, setting up trusts, debt management, and insurance needs?** At this point in our lives, we need the expertise of someone who can help with our overall life plan, not just asset management.
- **How many clients do you have and how often do you communicate with them?** You want to know this up front so that you can manage your own expectations. It is also useful to know how long the average client stays a client, and whether you will be speaking directly with the financial planner or with a member of her staff.
- **How do you choose investments?** You want to suss out how the advisor chooses investments, and how she deals with those that aren't performing well.
- **How high an average annual return do you think is feasible on my investments?** Lest we forget about Bernie Madoff, Jason offers this advice: if her answer is anything over 10 percent, walk away.
- **Once we've developed a Life Plan, how will you work with me to monitor the implementation of the plan?** You want to feel that you're in control of your financial strategy, and that your advisor doesn't just create the plan, take your fee, and then leave you to fend for yourself.

Like money, good financial advisors do not grow on trees. The really good ones are probably so busy already that it might be tough to get an appointment. However, if you do get in the door, they'll want to check you out, too. An advisor who is really on top of her game will want to know the following:

- **Why do you need a financial advisor?**
- **What are your financial and life goals?**
- **What has your experience been with financial advisors?**
- **Do you have a budget?**
- **Can you live within your means?**
- **A year from now, what should I have accomplished so that you can say you're satisfied or even happy with me?**
- **What are your worst financial fears?**

A few more tips from Jason:

- **Don't commit.** Never commit to signing on with the financial planner during your initial meeting. Wait until you've reviewed everything.
- **Divide and conquer.** If you're married, your husband should come to the selection interview on time, and you should arrive five to ten minutes late. Here's why: in the first few minutes of a meeting people talk about social things to create a connection. If your husband gets there first, he will establish a relationship with the financial advisor. When you come in a few minutes later and they're already laughing and joking, you can watch the interaction between the advisor and your husband, and will be able to pick up on nuances that your husband is no longer able to see because his guard will be down—as will that of the advisor. You will pick up more about the advisor because research has shown that women are better observers than men, and are much better at reading people's faces to see if they are lying or deceitful. This is a helpful strategy when interviewing lawyers and other service professionals as well.

- **Tell all.** If you're going to hire a financial advisor, you must trust her enough to tell the truth. Advice is only as good as the information it's based on.

- **Be specific.** Spell out exactly what you want the advisor to do to help you achieve your Life Plan, and what her part will be in setting and managing your comprehensive financial plan (including insurance), your investment policy (especially if she will be managing your investments), and your asset-allocation plan (do you want her

to set up a trust?). Be sure you understand how she will charge for each of those items.

How can you be smarter about money every day?

Getting expert advice and making a solid plan will help us prepare for a financially stable life after fifty. Just as mportant is learning to break bad financial habits and establish a healthy relationship to money in our everyday lives. In Jason's recent book, *Your Money & Your Brain*, he explores neuroeconomics, an interesting new discipline that combines psychology, neuroscience, and economics to explain why even smart people make bad investment decisions, procrastinate, avoid planning for tomorrow—and why so many people continue to mistakenly think that money buys them happiness.

We're only human, after all.

When we're making decisions about money, our brains often drive us to do things that make no logical sense— but make perfect emotional sense. That doesn't make us irrational, Jason says,

it makes us human. He offered observations and tips to help us be less emotional, more rational, and more in control of our money.

> **Whatever our plan is for the future, the only way we're going to get there is to save more.**

If you want your money to grow 10 percent a year, the best way to do it is to save 10 percent of your money. Over the last ten years or so, many people got the idea that if they needed more money, they should buy more stocks or investment property. But the stock market doesn't exist to provide you with the rate of return that you want. Amid the new economic reality, the personal savings rate has gone from zero to more than four percent in record time. That's a good thing, but we still aren't saving enough.

What's the deal with 10 percent anyway?

During the last few years, if you asked anyone in America for the expected rate of return on any investment, including real estate, the answer was 10 percent. Why? Ten is a nice round number and we live in a base-ten world, so it sounded good. But while the historical rate of return on stocks is close to 10 percent (including inflation), the rate over any given period varies widely and the rate of return on real estate was never anywhere near that high. Historically, the after-inflation return on residential real estate is 2 to 3 percent. It's not a bad investment; it's quite stable and a good way to keep pace with inflation, but it does not return and never has returned 10 percent every year. Some people still have the idea that stocks and houses should and will give us a 10 percent return. Now both of those myths have been taken away from us. Only saving your money will give you more money.

Borrowing is the opposite of saving.

If you have debt, then you are paying interest on that debt, which is going to work against any return you might be accruing on your savings or investments. The best thing to do right now, before you even think about saving, is pay off your debt. Steer clear of home equity loans. They build up your debt, and lower the equity in your home.

Leave the cards at home.

Credit card debt makes up a huge chunk of personal debt, and adds to it with high fees and interest rates (even more so now that low-interest cards have disappeared). They are addictive because you get the pleasure of buying things now, but the pain of having to pay for it is delayed.

Carry large bills.

Carry hundred dollar bills instead of tens and twenties when you shop. People are reluctant to break such a large bill, because it feels like they're parting with the whole hundred dollars.

The "Eight Good Reasons" rule.

The next time you're thinking about making a totally discretionary purchase (like a great pair of patent leather slingbacks), write down eight good reasons why you should. Most people can't come up with more than three reasons for anything. Don't make that purchase unless you come up with eight good reasons. Chances are you won't be buying those shoes.

Steer clear of temptation.

If you know you're going to pass that shoe store (you know, the one with the great pair of patent leather slingbacks) because you have to get from point A to point B, change the route.

Resist big temptations by giving in to little ones.

If you know you're going to confront a big spending temptation, yield to a minor one. If you're headed for the shoe store and someone puts Godiva chocolates in front of you, take the chocolate. It may very well stop you from buying those shoes.

Don't take on any more risk than necessary.

This financial crisis has been particularly painful because many people lost money on risks that they didn't need to take. For example, consider the 529 College Savings Plan. Many people our age opened these accounts when their kids were born. A 529 plan is a long-term savings vehicle for short-term spending and is generally used to fund undergraduate education. You have up to twenty-two years to save, but usually only four years to spend. Many plans are designed so investors can make different asset-allocation configurations between stocks, bonds, and so on—with stocks being the riskiest but potentially most lucrative investments. Since all that money has to be spent in a four-year window, as the window approaches, you want to take less risk with the money. When you're in that window, you don't want to take any risk at all. Unfortunately, when stocks were up, a lot of people left their plans heavily weighted in favor of stocks—up until and even while their kid was in college—rather than shifting to safer investments. When the stock market went down 60 percent, people who had 60 percent of their money in stocks lost 36 percent of their total capital. Because they had to withdraw that money during the four-year window, they had no time to recoup their loss. Don't get greedy looking for the biggest reward. Figure out exactly how much risk you need to take and don't take any more than that.

Don't plan to change things later, because chances are, you won't.

One of the challenges with 529 plans is that they offer a broad spectrum of choices. When confronted with so many options, people tend not to research them carefully, but instead say, I'm just going to pick something now and then later, when the time is right, I'll fix it. That's a big psychological mistake because once you choose a course of action, it becomes the one you prefer over all others simply because it's the one you chose. It becomes hard to reverse the decision.

Be mindful of your mood.

Your emotions impact financial behavior in predictable ways. Asking yourself "what mood am I in?" should be at the top of your decision-making checklist. If you're generally happy and calm, chances are you'll make an informed decision. Negative moods can cause you to make risky decisions or deci-sions that attempt to fill a void—often an unconscious one. When you're angry or ashamed, you feel more aggressive. Someone who is angry is much more inclined to buy untested stocks or junk bonds, for example, than she would be otherwise. Similarly, if you're sad, you often feel as though you've lost something, and the only way you can fix that feeling is to get something new.

Stop procrastinating and start publicly proclaiming your intentions.

Are you a grasshopper or an ant? If you procrastinate with your financial planning and related decisions, you probably procrastinate in every aspect of your life. While most people struggle privately with the things they procrastinate about, we would be more successful if our goal was publicly proclaimed— even to just one person. This concept works for a lot of different things: losing weight, quitting smoking, housecleaning, saving money, and getting out of debt. This is not an attempt to get a group of people to join you in your goal. It is simply a way to make yourself accountable for your personal effort. If you tell someone, or many people, what your intent is and then you will be more likely to do it. There's a website—www.stickk.com—where you can make a public proclamation online, so the whole world can see your plans.

Can money make you happy?

There are many small steps you can take, and a few big ones, to get the maximum enjoyment out of your money, with a minimum of effort. Some of the small, doable things that can help you manage your financial happiness are:

- **Take a deep breath**—Spend a few minutes every day without a cell phone, TV, other people, or the computer, and just breathe in and breathe out. (This is a perfect time to lie down on the floor and put your legs up against the wall to help with the veins in your legs, as suggested in *Chapter 7: Love the Skin You're In*), and be grateful for what you have.
- **Thou shalt not covet**—Don't pine for something that someone else has, and stop comparing your financial situation to theirs. It's hard when we're constantly bombarded with images of wealth. In a culture based on keeping up with the Joneses, the best remedy might be to stop trying to keep up with the Joneses.
- **Do something nice for someone else**—Consider buying a surprise gift for someone, for no reason. People get a greater sense of satisfaction from giving someone a gift than from spending the same amount of money on themselves.
- **Have a fun goal**—The more specific it is, the easier it will be to plan and save for. And if you put a specific date to it, it'll make it easier still.
- **Make your own good luck**—You can make your own luck. Reach out way past your comfort zone, be curious, be interested and engaged, be willing to talk to people, visit new places, and open your mind and your horizons.
- **Stop procrastinating, already**—Procrastination is a major enemy of wealth and happiness. See *Chapter 12: Lose the Clutter, Find Your Life* for some good ideas on combating the habit.

Get on board.

Sage words from Jane Bryant Quinn:

You can't see the future.

If you're saving money steadily, that doesn't matter.

All that really matters is getting more out of life.

So true.

Get more information.

Websites

- www.garrettplanningnetwork.com
- *Money Magazine*, www.money.com
- National Association of Personal Financial Advisors, www.napfa.org
- www.stickk.com
- www.wsj.com
- www.jasonzweig.com

Books

- *Making the Most of Your Money NOW* by Jane Bryant Quinn, Simon & Schuster, 2010
- *Smart and Simple Financial Strategies for Busy People* by Jane Bryant Quinn, Simon & Schuster, 2006
- *Your Money & Your Brain: How the New Science of Neuroeconomics Can Help Make You Rich* by Jason Zweig, Simon & Schuster, 2007
- *The Little Book of Safe Money: How to Conquer Killer Markets, Con Artists, and Yourself* by Jason Zweig, Wily, 2009

Chapter 12

Lose the Clutter, Find Your Life

Everything In Its Place

Got mess?

I like to think of myself as a naturally organized woman, but I can still hear the voices of my mother, grandmother, and sister yelling—in unison—for me to go back and pick up the clothes that I dropped on the floor of the bedroom I shared with my sister. No amount of scolding, cajoling, or bribing ever broke me of my slovenly teenage habits. When I got my own apartment, everything changed. Suddenly, I had a place for everything, and everything was always in its place.

Now that I have two daughters of my own, I hear myself trying the same scolding—even bribing—to get them to be organized. It's working with one of them, but the other (no names, please) is a carbon copy of me at that age. I tell myself that one day she, too, will emerge from the clutter and see the light. But really, how organized am I now? After all, our apartment is clean, but it's also chock full of schoolbooks that we imagine will come in handy some day, art projects dating from before the girls could even talk, every science fair project they ever made (except the one

that exploded), bike helmets that are too small, clothes that don't fit any of us, boxes of wires that even my husband can't identify, knitting yarn for projects I never started, too many "junk" drawers filled with—you guessed it—junk, and so much more. The stuff we've acquired over the years has started to quietly chip away at my sense of being totally on top of everything.

How can I move forward if I'm stuck with my stuff?

By the time we hit fifty, most of us have developed some kind of management system for our lives. We had to. How else could we balance school, work, play dates, doctor appointments, walking the dog, making dinner, shopping for groceries, washing laundry, paying bills, remembering after-school activities, working out, and still find time for our partners and friends? If we didn't have some organizational skills, nothing would ever get done. As organized as I was, the stuff still accumulated, and the clutter grew. It's just normal clutter, nothing unusual. But after I turned fifty, I started to realize that the clutter—

not just physical clutter but mental clutter as well—was pulling me down. I look around at everything and sometimes I feel a bit paralyzed. The more clutter there is, the more stuck I feel. I am now entering a new phase of my life, but I'm still carrying all this stuff from the past. I want to unencumber myself, pare back, and streamline. But where to begin?

Make Room for What's Next

At first I thought the best way to start would be to tidy up my files, rearrange the kitchen, and clean out the sock drawer. I assumed that by creating new systems and controls I would become more efficient in my life. But I didn't have a lot of motivation for the process.

One morning, I was listening to NPR, staring into space, and mulling over which pile on my desk to attack first when Julie Morgenstern came on the air. A *New York Times* best-selling author and internationally-known organizational consultant and time management expert, Julie is a frequent guest on TV and radio shows, and is a contributor to *Redbook* magazine and other publica-

tions. On the radio that day, she was talking about life transitions, feeling stuck, managing change, and decluttering your life to make room for the next big event. I perked right up. She said that you shouldn't even try organizing anything until you have gone through a process called "shedding." Organizing is great and useful, she said, but to assume you can just tidy up what you have without thinking about why you have it and what you really want is setting yourself up for failure. It just won't work. I wanted to talk to Julie Morgenstern.

Forget the sock drawer. Do you want to transform your life?

Right away Julie told me what I already suspected: Women over fifty don't need to be taught how to organize. We've spent decades managing households, jobs, families, kids, and social lives—we have that down pat. What we need to do now is something much bigger. Julie described it in terms of our life cycle. Starting in our twenties, we go through a period where we acquire:

property, people, experiences, marriage, children, and other relationships. As we age, we organize and integrate everything we acquired. By the time we reach fifty, we should step back and evaluate our acquisitions. We need to focus on where we are now, figure out where we want to go, and get rid of anything that isn't going to help us get there, but it can get overwhelming. It's very easy to lose yourself—especially at this stage in our lives when there are so many potential changes. Maybe kids are moving out, parents moving in, or you are changing jobs, retiring, or moving into a smaller house. We can confront these life events, seize the moment of transition, and push ourselves out of the clutter, or we can get stuck in the mire. Once you're over fifty, you have the wisdom and experience to know who you really are—apart from what you do or what you own. The unnecessary possessions, unhealthy relationships, and bad habits that wear you out and drag you down are all a kind of clutter.

Julie warns that this kind of decluttering won't be as quick or easy as rearranging your bookshelves. It's a lot of work, but it will transform your life.

So how can we get ready for the rest of our lives?

Julie gave us a straightforward process to objectively evaluate where we are in our lives and decide where we want to be next. To start the process, she suggests the following steps:

1. Acknowledge that change is happening.

Your fifties can be loaded with events that can affect how well you prepare for the rest of your life. Understanding and managing these events can make the difference between having fabulous, meaningful lives as we move forward, or not. Some of the more common life-altering experiences that can happen after fifty include:

- **The "I'm really fifty?" moment—** When Julie entered her fifties, she had a profound and cathartic experience. She realized that she was past the mid-point, and her life wasn't going to go on forever. The experience was deep and powerful and brought out many different feelings.

When Julie came out of that moment, she decided that this was also the time in her life to explore the new and potentially wonderful opportunities that were ahead.

- **Your children are leaving home**— If your life has been organized around your family, you might feel lost when your children become independent and less in need of your involvement—and then even more so when they finally move out of the house. This can be a hard transition for many women. Some welcome this new, freer phase of life, but others seek to fill the void—often with more stuff.

- **You've focused on your work, and now you're going through a change, whether you want to or not**—Perhaps you've been laid off due to downsizing. Or maybe you're changing jobs, going back to work, or doing something completely different (see *Chapter 13: What's Next?* for ideas). Perhaps you're happily planning your retirement but aware that your life will change significantly once you do. Anytime you change roles, your identity can feel threatened, which can disrupt your view of yourself.

- **Your marriage is ending, or you're starting a new one**—If you've been married for many years, or even a few, a shift in this area of your life has profound implications. Even if it is something you wanted, it still can create big changes in your life and sense of self, as does starting a new life with a new person.

- **If your spouse or another family member becomes ill or disabled, or passes on**—Illness and death are natural occurrences in life, especially as we get older, but we are never fully prepared. If a spouse dies, your life is irrevocably changed on many levels, and this kind of change can stop you from creating your new life. Caring for an ill spouse or parent can also affect your ability to open up the next chapter in your life. But it can also make you more aware of what you truly value.

2. Create a personal theme that defines what your life will be.

A personal theme is a guide that states what you are reaching for and moving toward. It lets you focus on the bigger picture (I want to move out of my comfort zone; It's time to focus more on me and less on others; I want to give back and serve others; I want to make more money; I want to be creative), not just the specifics (Should I change my job? Should I get a divorce?). Ask yourself what you want your life to look like over the next few years, and you'll come up with a vision for your future, which will be your personal theme. Once you have a theme, you can work on getting rid of everything in your life that doesn't fit that theme, and you will be much better prepared to let go of the clutter.

My personal theme is "Simplify my life," because I was starting to feel overwhelmed. I decided to simplify every aspect of my life: hair, health, makeup, home, food, finances, everything. That theme is driving me forward in everything I do. It's part of the reason I wrote this book. Adopting the "Simplify my Life" theme has made it much easier for me to get rid of things that no longer fit. It has made a tremendous difference in everything I do, has freed up my time, and has given me more energy.

3. Identify the different kinds of clutter that exist in your life.

Clutter can take many different forms, but all of it can make you feel weighed down and stuck. Clutter is anything that is obsolete, time-consuming, and de-energizing. If you can call it clutter, then chances are good that it doesn't belong in your life anymore. For me, that means anything that doesn't help me to "simplify" my life. The major kinds of clutter are:

- **Objects**—It could be the boxes that you haven't opened since you moved five years ago, the jewelry that you don't wear, the old business cards in your purse, or the stacks of magazines or books that you've never read. If looking at it brings you down, it probably should go.

- **Obligations**—Obsolete roles and responsibilities can be the hardest to get rid of because they often involve other people—like boards, committees, and clubs. You need to be sensitive to others but you can't let other people's needs dictate your decision. Don't let anyone make you feel guilty about your decisions, either. Look for ways to share some obligations.

- **Habits**—If you are a perfectionist, a chronic procrastinator, or a workaholic you are doing yourself a great disservice.

These habits waste time and energy, and are stressful and draining. People who have these habits often waste additional time and energy by beating themselves up about having them. Once we're over fifty, we don't need to be perfectionists or workaholics anymore. We've proven ourselves. Maybe in the early days we felt like we had to do everything better than the next person, but now we can let our experience serve us instead of our constant effort. We don't need to be defined by what we do anymore. Let's focus on who we are as people. It is enough to be interesting, engaged, and involved.

- **People**—I know it sounds awful to refer to people as clutter, but people can be just as de-energizing and depleting as the boxes of old magazines that are piling up in your den. If there's someone in your life who drains you every time you get together because she whines and complains about her life, but she never listens to your advice or asks how you're doing, then maybe it's time to shake her loose. It's not easy to remove people from your life, so think through the ramifications very carefully before you take this step. You want to be kind, but you also have

to be honest with yourself about which relationships feed you and which deplete you. As you get older, you can be more selfish with your time. If releasing someone completely isn't an option, then figure out ways to limit the amount of time you spend together.

Once you've gone through those steps, you will have a clear idea of where you are, where you want to be, and what is holding you back. Now you're ready to shed the stuff you no longer need. Your goals during the process are:

- to create a theme that defines your vision of your future self.
- to decide what's important.
- to acknowledge and manage the transitions that are taking place.
- to declutter your life.
- to be ready for what's next.

Get Ready to Get Rid of Your Stuff

The process of shedding, as Julie calls it, has a few steps which provide a framework for managing change, and helps us to get rid of objects and obligations that make us feel stuck.

- **Find the treasures, and keep them.** A treasure is a useful object, activity, skill, habit, or person that fits in with your theme. They can be meaningful or sentimental things that bring you joy, energy, and inspiration. Systematically go through every room, closet, drawer, box, engagement calendar, and address book. Don't expect to wrap it up in one weekend. Your life has a lot of parts. Break the task into specific, doable chunks and be patient but firm with yourself. Consider each item and take time to understand the emotional attachment you have to it. You may hold on to only about 20 percent of what you have. That's why these objects, people, and activities are called "treasures."

- **Give the stuff you don't want the "old heave ho."** Once you've gone through the process of choosing what stays, you have to get rid of the rest. Say goodbye and let it go. Decide what you will give away, sell, recycle, or donate (see the end of this chapter for ideas on how to get rid of your stuff) and then get it out of your space. Don't let bags of stuff sit in the hallway or closets. If stuff is physically around, then you haven't really gotten rid

of it. It's also time to let go of bad habits, unhelpful feelings, and possibly even people. Declutter every part of your life, and keep your theme in your head while you're doing it.

- **Move forward.** You've created a theme, you've gotten rid of those things that no longer fit in your life, kept those that do, and you're ready to move forward. You can now use your space, time, and energy for people, activities, objects, and experiences that will move you closer to your vision.

This is a continual process, and a way of life.

When you organize a space—your hall closet, for example—there's a starting point, and an ending point. When you get to the end, you're done. When you go through the shedding process, there is often no obvious ending point. How do you know when a transition is complete? If you no longer feel stuck, you can safely say that you've done it. Don't be afraid of setbacks. When you're in your fifties, it's very tempting to shrink back into your familiar clutter. So many things can happen all at once—aging parents, illness, divorce, job setbacks, or opportunities—it's easy to get overwhelmed. Focus on how far you've come, and always keep your eye on your theme. If you start to slip back into some of your old habits, and piles of clutter start building up again, just do it all over again.

What do you do with all of the stuff you've decluttered out of your life?

Something that is stagnant in your life might be a treasure for someone else. Julie suggests these ideas for getting rid of your clutter in a positive way. (And you could get a tax deduction, too.) Check with your local schools, libraries, churches or synagogues, and volunteer organizations too.

Donate office and art supplies

- **I Love Schools** (www.iloveschools. com) posts wish lists from schoolteachers who need classroom supplies; donations are sent directly from the donor to the specific teacher.

Donate books and magazines

First call your local library. Or try:

- **Adopt a Library** (www.adoptalibrary. org) gets books to people who need them in schools, libraries, prisons, and hospitals across the U.S. and in other parts of the world.
- **The Darien Book Aid Plan** (dba. darien.org) is a nonprofit, all-volunteer organization that donates reading material all around the world to many different kinds of places (schools, hospitals, and so on).
- **The Global Book Exchange** (www. bookexchange.marin.org) is a nonprofit organization that fosters literacy programs world wide, and has delivered hundreds of thousands of books and journals to Africa and other developing countries since it was started in 2000.

Donate clothing, furniture, and housewares

- **The National Furniture Bank Association** (www.nationalfurniturebank. org or 1-800-373-2835) provides used furniture to families in need around the U.S. Every item must be in good shape.
- **Dress for Success** (www.dressfor success.org) gives work-appropriate clothing to low-income women to wear during job interviews and when they first begin working.

- **Habitat for Humanity ReStore** (www.habitat.org or 1-800-422-4828) accepts furniture, tools, appliances, building, and remodeling supplies to be resold or used in constructing housing for low-income families.
- **Salvation Army** (www.satruck.com or 1-800-95-TRUCK) makes it very easy to donate many items. Simply go on their website or call to schedule a pickup.
- **Goodwill Industries** (www.goodwill.org) is a worldwide organization that will accept clothing, housewares, furniture, and other items. It has many local drop off locations.
- **Animal shelter or rescue groups** gladly accept used towels and blankets. Check out www.pets911.com to find local shelters.

Donate computers, cell phones, and other technology

- **PCs for Schools** (www.pcsforschools.org or 1-800-939-6000) accepts all quality used or unused computer equipment, which is then refurbished for school use.
- **The Wireless Foundation**—Call To Protect (www.wirelessfoundation.org/ CalltoProtect) is a national program that recycles and refurbishes used wireless phones to benefit domestic violence shelters and to fund campaigns against domestic violence.
- **Humane Society of the United States**—My BoneYard (www.humane society.org) recycles and refurbishes desktop and laptop computers, digital music players, cell phones, and accessories to benefit animal welfare.

Sell your stuff

- **Checkout eBay** and other online auction sites—they're easier than you might think, and you'll get a good idea of how much to sell your items for.
- **Garage sale**—Do it by yourself or with neighbors.
- **Consignment stores**—It's a convenient and quick way to make money from items that are no longer useful to you.
- **Or . . . just give it away**—You may also want to give things to people you know, to friends, or to family members. Ask around. Someone could probably use what you have to give.

Recycle whatever isn't usable

- **Earth 911** (www.earth911.org or 1-800-CLEAN UP) is the largest environmental recycling and conservation database for locating a recycling or re-use center near you.
- **Reuse Development Organization** (www. reuse.org) is a national partnership of organizations that promote the concept of re-use as a responsible means for dealing with discarded stuff.

Got real, honest-to-goodness junk?

- **1-800-GOT-JUNK** (www.1800gotjunk.com) is a national service that carts away just about anything for a fee, as long as it's non-hazardous.

Get on board.

Once you have a clear picture of what your future will be and you systematically get rid of the clutter that's keeping you from getting there, you'll be ready for just about anything. Lose the clutter, find your life. (For more on what's next, see the next chapter.)

Get more information.

Once you get started, you may need a little help in keeping everything that is staying in your life a bit more organized. Here are the most helpful resources to help you put everything in its place:

Websites

- www.containerstore.com
- www.juliemorgenstern.com

Magazines

- *Real Simple*, www.realsimple.com
- *O, The Oprah Magazine*, www.oprah.com

Books

- *1000 Best Quick and Easy Organizing Secrets* by Jamie Novak, Sourcebooks, 2006
- *Organizing from the Inside Out: The Foolproof System for Organizing Your Home, Your Office, and Your Life* by Julie Morgenstern, Macmillan, 2004
- *The Organized Life: Secrets of an Expert Organizer* by Stephanie Denton, Northlight Books, 2006
- *Shed Your Stuff* by Julie Morgenstern, Simon and Schuster, 2008

Chapter 13

What's Next?

Get Ready 'Cause Here We Come

What will you do with the rest of your life?

Our generation has always been known as adventurous and ready for whatever's next. So it is natural that at this point in our lives, a lot of us are reflecting on what we've done, and thinking seriously about what we're going to do next. We've spent decades accumulating skills, experiences, knowledge, and wisdom. What do you want to do with yours?

I can't quit now.

While fifty is about the age that our parents started firming up their retirement plans, I've always believed that I would die with my boots on—working either for money or psychic rewards, or both. The concept of "retiring" seems quaint to me, as if it's from another time and place. It's a good thing I feel that way because I may not have a choice. A lot of us cannot assume that we will walk off into the sunset in our late fifties or early sixties, but probably can count on working into our seventies. In 1935 when Social Security was established, the average life expectancy was sixty-one. Today, most of us can expect to live many years beyond that. Let's make those years worthwhile.

Maybe you love your career and plan to keep doing exactly what you're doing until you're ninety. Maybe you've been a lifelong homemaker or are busy as a full-time grandmother. Maybe you're poised to retire. Or you already did retire but you've decided to get back into the work force because you're feeling a little financially vulnerable or you miss working. Maybe you've been thinking about making a whole new start, like leaving investment banking to join the Peace Corps or become a teacher. Maybe you don't need to earn money anymore, but you want to stay active. Even if you never work again, it is in your own best interest to stay engaged in life. We all need to feel wanted, productive, and involved—especially as we age. While some of us find our late-life passion in reaction to something out of our control (like getting laid off), it's usually better if we take the initiative in planning our own futures. Don't go another twenty years only to realize that you never pursued your big dream.

Does the world need me?

It's easy in our youth-centric society to convince ourselves that once we are over fifty, we are obsolete and should sit quietly, out of sight. But that is the wrong thing to do. Read today's paper and you'll see a growing list of problems and issues that would benefit from your experience, knowledge, skills, and compassion—all of which are the result of your years on this planet. One of the most important aspects of healthy aging is being involved and active. Yes, the world most definitely needs you.

Start Where You Are

Wherever you're going, your path depends on where you are now. So start by taking stock.

Assess your finances and update your financial plan.

Your current financial status and obligations will affect your future. How much money you have, how much you owe, and how much you will need all factor into your decision about whether you work full-time, part-time, volun-teer, start your own business, go back to school, or play tennis all day. Review *Chapter 11: Money* and consider this:

- **Social Security benefits will be reduced the earlier you start receiving them. Wait to collect as long as you can before you officially retire.**
- **If you are still working, or return to work, be aware of your employer's medical insurance benefits, because they could compromise your Medicare benefits after you hit sixty-five.**
- **Discuss your plans with your financial advisor to make sure you're taking advantage of tax breaks and other benefits.**

Once you've gotten your finances straight, you're ready for the exciting part.

- **Name your passion**—Start by thinking about what gets your juices flowing, your brain cells percolating, makes you want to jump out of bed in the morning. What can you see yourself doing for many years to come? This is your passion, and being able to name it will help motivate you to formulate your plan.
- **What will your legacy be?**—By

the time you're fifty, you understand that life is not unlimited, so if you haven't left your stamp yet, maybe now's the time. Answering the question "How do I want to be remembered?" can help to clarify your deepest priorities.

- **What's your motivation?**—Money is one motivator for engaging in work, but ideally you can find work that will make you happy as well. This could mean helping others or supporting a cause you believe in.

- **Who are you anyway?**—It's important to have a good understanding of who you really are—your character, your nature, your true self. How hard do you want to work? Do you want to sit behind a desk or work with tools? Would you like to chat with people or be outdoors all day?

- **List your skills**—We've all got something that we can offer. Every one of us. We need to take stock of our talents, skills, experiences, knowledge, and contacts. Can you speak another language? Are you patient enough to train others? If you don't feel like you're using your skills now, what could you do that would let you really shine? Perhaps it's time for a major change, or maybe you'd

be happy where you are but with a re-defined role that better uses your talents. Once you've made your list, you'll have a better handle on what you are uniquely qualified to do.

- **Do you need new skills?**—It's always smart to keep your skills up to date, but if you're switching careers or moving within your field, you might need to add new skills to your list. Once you've figured out what they are, find out how and where to get them.

- **(Re)think your theme**—Think about where you are now, decide what your vision is going forward, and then declutter your life of all the stuff that doesn't fit into this vision—but hold onto everything that does. Review *Chapter 12: Lose the Clutter, Find Your Life* and put those principles into place. Make sure your passion is firmly implanted in your brain and be willing to re-evaluate your priorities once in a while.

Once you take time to consider all of these—your passion, motivation, true nature, skills, and intended legacy—you'll get some ideas about the right path for you.

Many paths can lead you to what's next.

Looking for inspiration about what to do with the rest of our lives, I met with a few incredible women over fifty. They each had different backgrounds, financial situations, passions, goals, and talents. They each took different paths, but had one thing in common: they took charge of the rest of their lives.

Here are a few ideas.

The New Radical Path

Julia Moulden's dream didn't materialize until she was almost fifty. At that point in her life, she figured that, barring some unforeseen disaster, she had over thirty productive years left in her. She had gone through a divorce in her late forties and made the transition from "do I want to work" to "I have to work." But after twenty-five years as a successful speechwriter, Julia was getting restless. She found herself thinking about an earlier time in her life when she was still in college and talked with friends about changing the world. She realized that the other women she knew—most of them in their early fifties—had the same questions. She decided to combine her expertise with her dream of making a difference, and created a new business. The New Radicals movement was born. Julia's book, *We are the New Radicals: A Manifesto for Reinventing Yourself and Saving the World*, encourages individuals to turn their passions into meaningful and financially rewarding work. Julia consults with companies who want to foster more creative thinking, especially as it pertains to integrating public service with corporate profits. Recently, she told me, "There are endless possibilities for experienced women to use their well-earned skills to support the things that matter to them, whatever that is."

If you are looking to make a change and share Julia's commitment to changing the world, you might be a New Radical. Julia describes three different categories of New Radicals: activists, entrepreneurs, and innovators. Your vision, needs, temperament, and financial situation all factor into deciding which of these paths you might follow.

- **Activists** seek out work which will let them serve others or promote a cause, and often put a greater emphasis on doing good than on their own personal finances, working pro bono or at a lower salary.
- **Entrepreneurs** start new enterprises to address a problem, but are also interested in making a profit. Entrepreneurs recognize an opportunity to use their skills, knowledge, experience, and contacts to help make the world a better place. Suzanne Seggerman, for example, was a documentary film producer before she founded Games for Change, a company that develops entertaining digital games that teach players about social issues.
- **Innovators** stay within their current firms or industries to initiate change and innovation from within. Lawyers who convince their firms to take on pro bono cases or corporate employees who search for environmentally sustainable ways of doing business are examples of people who do good within the work they do. Julia feels that more companies are looking for ways to meet two objectives: 1) long-term profitability instead of short-term quarterly results, and 2) ways to contribute to the public good. These shifts will create enormous opportunities for workers to develop more meaningful jobs.

The fastest growing sector of Julia's business is working with corporations to introduce programs and initiatives that will add value to the company, increase profits, and contribute to the betterment of the world in meaningful and sustainable ways. We can do the same things in our own lives.

The Back-to-School Path

My friend Peggy was almost fifty when she asked herself the "Alfie Question": What's it all about? A very successful media advertising salesperson, Peggy felt she wasn't contributing anything to the world. A good income and many other perks had kept her trapped in a career she no longer loved—especially after she had a baby at age 40 and felt she needed to be responsible to keep things stable. After twenty-five years in the business, she had built her reputation and contacts, and it was too hard to just walk away. Then came 9/11. The crisis had such a profound impact on her that she quit her job without knowing what she would do next. For the year it took her to figure it out, Peggy became one of the most involved parents her daughter's school had ever seen. She volunteered for so many things that people sometimes mistook her for a teacher. But the time she spent at the school led her to "what's next." Peggy went back to college to get her master's degree in psychology, and then earned her PhD in Educational Psychology, coming up with fresh ways of looking at how children learn. Peggy says, "I've never worked harder, felt more tired, made less money, or been more passionate about what I'm doing."

Peggy had enough money saved that she could go to school full-time. Another woman I know went to school at night for several years while she worked full-time during the day. She got her master's degree in accounting and now runs a successful business, taking care of the books for small firms. There are myriad ways to kick-start a new career or add value to an existing one by going back to school—no matter how you do it.

The Business Owner Path

Sometimes necessity really is the mother of invention. Let's take my good friend Wendy who loves chopped salads. Her way of making a chopped salad used to be that she'd throw everything into the bowl all at once—chicken, lettuce, tomatoes, dressing, whatever—and then she'd take out her scissors and cut it all up. The scissors didn't do the best job, and she'd still need to take her salad fork and spoon to mix it all together. One day she thought: there's got to be a better way to do this. With her husband Michael, Wendy invented the now-famous "Toss-n-Chop," which is sold in stores all over the country, and is a best-seller on QVC. They formed a successful company that continues to grow. All it took was a need, some creativity, and the courage to put it into action.

You don't have to invent something to start a business. You could turn a personal passion into a service or a storefront. Perhaps you're great with animals, and your area has a lot of dogs which need to be walked and played with while their owners are at work or on vacation. If you don't want to start a business from scratch, consider franchising opportunities like the ones profiled every week in the *Wall Street Journal*. Most of them require an upfront financial investment, but some of this country's millionaires got their start with a franchise. If you want to start your own business—however you do it— you have to fill a need. What you have to offer, people must need or, at least, they must be convinced they need it.

The Sabbatical Path

If you're burned out, or not sure of what to do next, and you think a little time off will give you some perspective, then take it. With enough advance notice, many companies will let their employees take an unpaid—or sometimes paid—leave for extended periods of time. If that's not possible, roll over your vacation time until you have a good block of time. Use your sabbatical to write a book, take classes, volunteer, spend time with an elderly or sick parent, do some serious soul-searching, travel, or relax. Time away from your work routine can help you prioritize and give you a better understanding of your goals. You might

not return to your job at all, but instead do something completely different. A sabbatical can be a smart way to help crystallize your vision.

The Volunteering Path

One of the most inspiring people I have ever met is Gretchen Buchenholz. Gretchen saw inequality and injustice in her own backyard of New York City and decided to do something about it. She started the Association to Benefit Children to help educate disadvantaged children and their families with programs and services, with the hope that these children would be placed on a level playing field. I know many people who volunteer at ABC, including my daughter, Sarah, and the sheer joy they get out of knowing they might be making a difference in one child's life is priceless. Organizations such as ABC have a huge impact on those who need their services most, but with the downturn in the economy, it's becoming increasingly difficult to raise the funds that are necessary to keep programs and facilities like ABC going strong. But, there is something you can do, even if you don't have a lot of money to donate—give yourself. Even if it's a few hours a week or month, giving your time and skills to others who are in much greater need than you are, is rewarding, and could possibly help you figure out what your next career path should be.

According to a recent government report, almost 62 million Americans volunteered at least once in 2008. There's a lot to be said for volunteering your time and services—you feel good about yourself, you get to do something you believe in, you get out there, and you help people. But there are other perks, too. Non-profit organizations benefit by tapping into a talented pool of educated, experienced, and highly skilled workers. If you're job hunting or considering changing jobs, volunteering offers impressive benefits. You can:

- **test the waters for a possible career move into a new field or into the non-profit sector.**
- **learn new skills, and keep current skills up to date.**
- **build your resume, especially if you've been out of the work force for a while.**
- **network with other volunteers, adminis-trative leaders, members of the board, and employees at related organizations, any of whom might lead to something new.**
- **stay engaged and active, and feel really good about the fact that you're working to help others who are likely in greater need than you.**

There are many different volunteer opportunities with a range of time and talent needs. Here are a few ideas that run the gamut from a few hours a week to two full years:

- **Peace Corps (there is no upper age limit for Corps volunteers)**
- **Senior Corps (for Americans over 55)**
- **National, state and local parks**
- **Zoos and botanical gardens**
- **Hospitals**
- **Public libraries**
- **Arts and cultural groups**
- **Schools and educational organizations**
- **Boys and Girls Club**
- **Boy Scouts and Girl Scouts**
- **Mentoring**
- **Charitable organizations**
- **Soup kitchens**
- **Animal shelters**
- **Your church, synagogue, or mosque**

These organizations can use your skills for everything from home construction to teaching English, from ushering concerts to public relations, from being a foster grandparent to an advisory board member—and lots in between. If you find yourself out of work, if you aren't sure what your next move should be, or if you have some free time and just want to give back, consider becoming a volunteer.

Get on board.

The future is unknown, but it's nothing you can't handle. The important thing is to decide what you want to do, and then stay healthy and fit so you can do it for a very long time.

I'm excited about what's next for me, and I have a zillion ideas. Far too many of them involve living in Italy, so I'm not sure how soon I'll be pursuing those. I'm a bit of a New Radical in spirit, with my path somewhere between starting a new business and doing good work while I earn money. In time, I hope to be a pure Activist, working to end all kinds of cruelty that exists in the world,

specifically violence against women and children. To that end, I will work hard, stay engaged, and be ready for whatever comes next.

Get more information.

The following excellent resources can help you to define your goals, and get you on your way to wherever you're going.

Websites
- **www.a-b-c.org**
- **www.encore.org**
- **www.retirementjobs.com**
- **www.serve.gov**
- **www.vitalvoices.org**

Books
- ***Don't Retire, REWIRE!* by Jeri Sedlar and Rick Miners, Alpha, 2007**
- ***Encore: Finding Work that Matters in the Second Half of Life* by Marc Freedman, PublicAffairs, 2007**
- ***We Are The New Radicals: A Manifesto for Reinventing Yourself and Saving the World* by Julia Moulden, McGraw-Hill, 2008**

Chapter 14

Putting it all Together

The Plan

We've covered a lot of ground to-gether—from our heads to our toes and everything in between. This chapter is a comprehensive overview of the ideas, products, and resources that are exceptional or exceptionally important. There's also a master plan for turning all of your new knowledge into your best possible life after fifty.

The Best of Everything After 50

Ideas:

These are some of the ideas and con-cepts that really changed my thinking, and could change your life.

- **Prevention is the most important way to keep disease and illness out of your life.**
- **Fitness and exercise are essential to good health.**
- **Heart disease is the number one killer of women.**
- **Being a woman over fifty puts you in the "at risk" category for heart disease, so work on all the other potential risk factors even more aggressively.**
- **10,000 steps every day is one path to a better life.**
- **Running with walk breaks will keep you moving for the rest of your life.**
- **Strength training is even more important than taking calcium for keeping osteo-porosis at bay.**
- **Visceral fat (the fat around your waist) is a key factor in a woman's health.**
- **Vitamin D is the "little vitamin that could".**
- **You can eat every couple hours, enjoy food, and still lose weight.**
- **Certain skin problems are reversible.**
- **Skin care after fifty is not as complicated as the cosmetic and pharmaceutical companies want us to think.**
- **Exfoliate, exfoliate, exfoliate.**
- **You can put on makeup in five minutes and look great.**
- **Highlighting a few areas of your face is like magic.**
- **You only need three products for your hair: shampoo, conditioner, and gel.**
- **Sulfates in shampoos should be avoided.**
- **Blow drying your hair is unnecessary.**
- **Spontaneous sex is a myth—good sex takes planning.**
- **Desire can be cultivated in many ways.**
- **You don't need to spend a lot of money on clothes to look wonderful.**

- "Save more, spend less" should be your financial mantra.
- Creating a theme is the guide to your future.
- You can't get rid of stuff until you've figured out where you're going.
- There are a lot of different paths to what's next.
- Women over fifty are beautiful—really, really beautiful!

Products:

I tried many products in the name of research, and a few stand out as "must haves." It's a big world out there, with lots of makeup, skin care products, foods, clothing, and hairstyles to try, so have fun, but consider these while you're experimenting.

Skin care:

- Renova
- RevaléSkin (coffee berry)
- Patricia Wexler MD Instant De-Puff Eye-gel
- Aveeno Ultra Calming Foaming Cleanser
- White sugar (for exfoliating)

Makeup:

- Lancôme Definicils Mascara (in black)
- Revlon ColorStay Eyeliner Pencil (in Charcoal)
- Maybelline Instant Age Rewind Double Face Perfector (highlighter and concealer)
- Laura Geller Balance-n-Brighten baked foundation
- Laura Geller Bronze-n-Brighten all over face bronzer
- Shu Uemura Eye Lash Curler
- Aveeno Positively Radiant Tinted Moisturizer (SPF 30)
- Natural Beauty Inspired by Carmindy Lip Color (in Perfect Pink)

Hair:

- DevaCurl One Conditioner
- Fekkai Glossing Cream

Fitness:

- Apple iPhone—You should always have a cell phone with you when you're out running and walking, and this one gives you music, too. You can even add applications like a pedometer so you only need to bring one device along
- Wii Fit—It's one of the most fun ways to stay fit, and keep tabs on your progress.
- Omron basic pedometer to count your 10,000 steps every day.

Fashion:

- Hanky Panky lace thong panties

- **Merona brand from Target**
- **7 For All Mankind jeans**
- **Cole Haan Shoes and Boots with Nike Air Technology**
- **La Canadienne boots**
- **Long tank tops for under just about anything**
- **Diane von Furstenberg black pencil skirt**
- **Diane von Furstenberg wrap dress**

Healthy eating:

- **Fage Total 0% Greek Strained Yogurt**
- **Organic blueberries**
- **Bionaturae organic whole wheat pastas**
- **Women's Bread by French Meadow Bakery**
- **Lundberg's organic brown rice**
- **Organic kale mixed with dried cranberries and sliced almonds**
- **Quinoa**
- **Almonds**
- **Olive oil**
- **Red wine (in moderation; Pinot Noir reportedly has the highest levels of reservatrol)**
- **Organic dark chocolate (a little piece every day)**

Sex:

- **AstroGlide lubricant**

All the books listed at the end of each chapter—including some by our experts—are highly recommended. But a few others are also worth your attention and time.

- *You—Staying Young* by Mehmet C. Oz, M.D. and Michael F. Roizen, M.D., Free Press 2007—It offers a very interesting and thorough examination of our bodies, and what happens to each part as we age. This is one of several books in the "You" series, all of which are recommended reading.
- *In Defense of Food*, by Michael Pollan, Penguin 2008—He has made the following statement a mantra: "Eat food. Not too much. Mostly plants." A truer line was never written. Great book.
- *Skinny Bitch* by Rory Freedman and Kim Barnouin, Running Press 2005—The authors take you through the process of going vegan. I learned a lot about what some of the "bad" foods can do to you, although it didn't change my mind about having a good steak once in a while.
- *Outliers* by Malcolm Gladwell, Little, Brown 2009—An interesting take on why some people succeed, from the author of

two other best sellers: *Blink* and *The Tipping Point.* I think this is his best book—it's worth a read as you think about who you are, where you've come from, and what you want to do next.

If you're already a fan, great. If they're new to you, even better.

- *More*—a magazine aimed at the forty and over crowd. It's a good resource for everything covered in this book. The writing is intelligent, the information is up to date, and the ads are age appropriate.
- *Allure*—This is like a fun girls' night out with your best buddies. The Reader's Choice Awards and other lists of products that they feature regularly are especially entertaining. It's a good resource for the latest news in skin care and cosmetics.
- *Real Simple*—I thought I had this whole organization thing down pat and then another issue of *Real Simple* comes along and shows me a better way. I'm always impressed, amazed, and engaged when I read *Real Simple.*
- *O, The Oprah Magazine*—There's a lot of enthusiastic encouragement each month to do your best, be your best, and

sometimes when the going gets tough, a little extra boost can help. Their contributing editors are impressive, and Oprah herself is over fifty, so she gets it.

- *Prevention*—The magazine and the website are extremely useful, engaging, and they cover many of the health (and some beauty) concerns that we are most interested in. It's not geared specifically to women over fifty, but a lot of the info can apply.
- *Reader's Digest*—It's been around forever, and continues to entertain and educate with inspirational stories, health updates, and articles to keep us informed on what's going on in the world.
- *AARP*—*AARP* is the magazine from the AARP organization (and yes, AARP is that group formerly known as the American Association of Retired Persons, and yes they start sending you membership invitations a few months before you turn fifty). Guess what? Their magazine is amazing. Its target audience is more on the "well over 50" side, but I always find useful and actionable information in every issue. You can only get the publication if you are a member, so I urge you to become one. AARP, in its defense (and I do feel it needs

defending), has our best interests at heart—health care, employment, taxes, everything for people over fifty—and they lobby in D.C. on our behalf. They are now over 40 million members strong. AARP views its mission as enhancing our quality of life and helping us to age with dignity and grace. I like that, and I really like them. And that's not even mentioning all the discounts you can get on travel, financial services, insurance, and many other things once you join. Nothing would make me happier than to see AARP get a little bit of the hip factor happening. Check them out on their website.

- *Wall Street Journal*—It's probably the most well-written, intelligent newspaper in this country. You can skip the hardcore financial reports (although always check out Jason Zweig's "Intelligent Investor" column) and it'll be well worth the investment.

Websites:

Some of these are listed in the "Get More Information" sections at the end of certain chapters, but they all deserve special attention:

- **WWW.WOWOWOW.COM**—A group of very well-established and savvy women, including Lesley Stahl and Liz Smith, started this news/ trends/opinions website for women over forty (most writers are in their fifties). Soon other women, like Candice Bergen and Lily Tomlin, joined as contributors. What they've created is a terrific site where smart older women can discuss everything from politics to health to sex to fashion. It's very engaging and you'll find yourself checking in a few times a day.

- **www.webmd.com**—Woke up with a weird reddish welt on your arm? Plug into webmd. Your husband has a stomach ache and a sore throat? No problem, webmd will help you figure it out. It's one of the best health websites I've used, but don't let it be a substitute for your good common sense or seeing your doctor.

- **www.freerice.com**—This is a terrific site that challenges your brain with vocabulary, math, language, and other questions. Every time you get the answer right, rice gets donated to countries which need it. It keeps your brain cells working, lets you do good in the world, and it's fun.

- **www.devaconcepts.com**—This is the official website of Devachan, the hair salon that was created by Lorraine Massey. It leads you to a You Tube video demonstration of how to achieve the Devachan look in your own home. It's the epitome of streamlined hair care, and so easy. You can also find the name of a salon in your area that has stylists who were trained the "Devachan Way."

- **www.what2wearwhere.com**— It's brilliant: an online personal shopper. Need an outfit for a job interview? They'll give you great options—complete with ideas on jewelry, bags, and shoes, all in different price points—with links to get it sent to you in 24 hours. For a non-shopper like me, this is a little slice of heaven.

- **www.americanheartassociation** —It's so important for us to keep up with the latest information about heart disease, so why not go right to the source of some of the best information you can get?

Your Master Plan

Here's the big-picture checklist of what to do every day, every week, every month, every year, as you go forward.

Every Day

- Get at least seven hours of sleep.
- Wake up early enough to think about your day and your life for a few minutes.
- Drink one or two cups of coffee, if you like, and definitely some green tea.
- Drink lots of water.
- Always eat breakfast, and have it early.
- Eat something healthy every two to three hours.
- Eat more nuts and beans and less animal protein.
- Eat lots of green vegetables.
- Eat whole grains, especially brown rice.
- Eat blueberries and other berries or fresh fruit.
- Steer clear of "white foods" like sugar, white flour, regular pasta, white potatoes, white rice.
- Use salt sparingly (and sea salt when you do).
- Keep an "Eating Journal" and write down every single thing you eat and drink for a few weeks to reach your healthy eating goals.
- Take a multi-vitamin.
- Take 1,500 IU of Vitamin D.

- Take 1,500 IU of calcium (not all at once).
- Take 1 gram (1,000 mg) of Nordic Naturals Fish Oil.
- Take 1 gram (1,000 mg) of flaxseed oil.
- Try to have as many meals with your family as possible.
- Floss and brush your teeth several times a day.
- Cleanse your hair with a non-sulfate shampoo or no shampoo at all, use lots of conditioner, position your hair with your fingers, and let it air dry (or do this every other day).
- Exfoliate your skin (face and body).
- Use a little makeup, but don't spend much more than five minutes on it.
- Wear sunscreen (face and body).
- Wear sunglasses with UV protective lenses.
- Use a retinoid product (such as Renova or Retin-A) at night.
- Walk and/or run 10,000 steps or more.
- Do the strength training exercises (most days, if not all).
- Lie on your back, on the floor, and put your legs up against a wall for five minutes; breathe deeply and slowly; and think about all the reasons you're happy to be alive.

- Do twenty Kegel exercises.
- Dress comfortably, and with style.
- Keep your eye on your theme and plan your day accordingly.
- Read.
- Listen to music.
- Laugh out loud.
- Talk to your girlfriends.
- Spend time doing something that you really love to do.
- Send your partner some flirty emails.
- When your partner comes home (or when you get home) smile at him. Give him a hug.
- Use cash, not credit.
- Buy only what you need, and not everything you want.
- Push yourself out of your comfort zone: read something new, speak to a stranger, or take a different path home from work.
- Be aware of the environment: use less energy, recycle, and walk instead of using the car.

Every week

- Use VagiFem (prescription) twice a week to combat certain symptoms of menopause, if necessary.

- Have planned, fun sex as often as you want it, and try AstroGlide if you need extra lubrication.
- Take a 60-minute run/walk twice a week.
- Take a 90 minute run/walk once a week.
- Make a special plan just with your partner to make dinner together, see a movie, go for a long walk or bike ride or anything that lets you just be a couple.
- Have a special dessert once or twice a week.
- Have a glass of heart healthy red wine several times a week.
- Check your body for any unusual symptoms and don't ignore them.
- Volunteer your time as often as you can.

Every month

- Check your skin for anything unusual.
- Check your breasts for lumps or changes in the skin.
- Check your blood pressure with your home BP machine.
- Get a pedicure and a nice foot and leg massage.
- Pay your bills (online if possible).
- Stash some money in your retirement funds.

- Put receipts in their correct folders, especially those for tax purposes.
- Go out for dinner somewhere special (with healthy food).
- Check your waist to make sure it's still where it should be, and if it isn't, make changes to your eating and exercise plans.
- If you get single process color, get a touch-up every 4 to 6 weeks.
- If you keep a shorter haircut, get a trim every 6 to 8 weeks.

Every three months

- Check your financial plan to make sure you're on target.
- If you highlight your hair, get highlights every 8 to 10 weeks.
- Buy a new mascara every 3 to 4 months.
- Revisit your theme and see if you need to shed anything (or anyone), and then declutter, especially when seasons are changing.

Every Year

- Get a complete pelvic examination.
- Get a Pap smear and HPV DNA screen for cervical cancer.

- Get a breast mammogram and, if needed, a sonogram and/or MRI.
- Get a skin cancer screening.
- Do a fecal occult test (non-colonoscopy years).
- Get a complete physical examination with blood work, measurements, and any special tests you might need.
- Have your blood pressure checked.
- Update your doctor about any changes in your life, lifestyle, health, or family health.
- Get a good hair cut two to three times a year.
- Get a flu vaccine.
- Do something new: travel to a place you've never been, take a class, or learn a new skill or craft.
- Take a "financial day" and sort through all of your financial documents—tax receipts, insurance, bank accounts, everything—and discard those you don't need, deal with things you need to tend to, and file everything that must be kept.
- Go through your calendars and address books and transfer the birthdays and other special event days onto the new calendar, and update addresses.
- Have a meeting with your accountant and your financial advisor to check on the status of your financial plan, and to update and revise if need be.

Every few years:

- Get a colonoscopy every three to five years, depending upon your health history.
- Get a Bone Density Test (DEXA), usually every two years.
- Revisit and retool your vision for the coming years.

And for the rest of your life:

Love yourself, love your life, stay as healthy as you can, move your body, be informed, stay engaged, use your mind, keep a handle on your finances, be bold, be brave, walk with confidence, live with style . . . and you will always have the best of everything.

Appendix

Meet the
Experts

Chapter 1: Feelin' Alright

Gregory M. Pitaro, MD

Murray Hill Medical Group, PC

317 East 34th Street

New York, NY 10016

212-726-7400

www.mhmg.net

Dr. Pitaro specializes in internal medicine and is an instructor of Clinical Medicine at New York University School of Medicine. Dr. Pitaro is a published physician who is interested in the integration of acupuncture and traditional Chinese medicine with Western medicine. He was awarded the Lowell E. Bellin scholarship to study health care in developing countries.

James A. Underberg, MD, MS, FSVM, FACPM, FACP, FNLA

Murray Hill Medical Group, PC

317 East 34th Street

New York, NY 10016

212-726-7400

www.mhmg.net

Dr. Underberg is a clinical assistant professor of Medicine at New York University and the NYU Center for Cardiovascular Disease. As the director of the Bellevue Hospital Primary Care Lipid Management Clinic, Dr. Underberg's clinical focus is preventive cardiovascular medicine. He is involved in several clinical trials in the areas of hypertension, lipids, diabetes, and cardiovascular disease prevention. Dr. Underberg is on the education committee for the North American Menopause Society, and is a fellow of the National Lipid Association, the American College of Physicians, the American College of Preventive Medicine, and the Society for Vascular Medicine.

Chapter 2: Keep the Beat

Jennifer H. Mieres, MD, FACC, FASNC, FAHA

Director of Nuclear Cardiology

The Leon H. Charney Division of Cardiology

New York University School of Medicine

550 First Avenue

New York, NY 10016

212-263-7300

www.med.nyu.edu

Dr. Mieres, a leading expert in the fields of nuclear cardiology and cardiovascular disease in women, became the first female president of the American Society of Nuclear Cardiology in 2009, and is an active spokesperson for the American Heart Association. She is an associate professor of medicine and the director of nuclear cardiology at NYU, and is a fellow of the American College of Physicians, the American College of Cardiology, the American Society of Nuclear Cardiology, and the American Heart Association. Dr. Mieres frequently appears on programs such as *20/20*, the *Today Show*, *Good Morning America*, *Today in New York*, *CBS Early Show*, *CNN*, and many others. She was nominated for an Emmy for Best Documentary for producing *A Woman's Heart* which was shown on PBS, and recently co-wrote a book, *Heart Smart for Black Women and Latinas: A Five Week Program for Living a Heart-Healthy Lifestyle*.

Mark McEwen

www.markmcewen.com

Mark McEwen was the face of CBS morning television for over fifteen years as weatherman, entertainment reporter, and eventually serving three years as anchor of *CBS This Morning*, and then *The Early Show*. Mr. McEwen, voted one of the most trusted people in America, was a fixture on CBS until 2002, before launching a new career at the CBS affiliate in Orlando. While at CBS, he regularly interviewed prominent newsmakers, including former U.S. presidents, and major film and recording stars. In 2006, Mr. McEwen experienced and survived a major stroke, which was detailed in his book, *Life After Stroke: My Journey Back to Life*.

Dr. James A. Underberg

(see Chapter 1 Experts)

Dr. Alexandra Stern, MD

Murray Hill Medical Group, PC

345 East 37th Street

New York, NY 10016

212-726-7455

www.mhmg.net

Dr. Stern is a board-certified internist and cardiologist, who performs and interprets the cardiovascular testing for all of the practicing physicians within the MHMG group. She is a clinical assistant professor of medicine at New York University School of Medicine, has served as chief medical resident for the Department of Medicine at NYU Medical Center/Bellevue Hospital, and focuses on non-invasive cardiology.

Chapter 3: Changes Down Under

Clarel Antoine, MD, FACOG

New York University Langone Medical
    Center
530 First Avenue
New York, NY 10016
212-263-6541
www.nyu.med.edu
www.RxCompassion.org

Dr. Antoine is board certified in obstetrics and gynecology, and in high-risk pregnancy. He is an associate professor of obstetrics and gynecology at New York University School of Medicine, and has also been a past president of the New York Perinatal Society and Chief of Obstetrics at Tisch Hospital. He has been recognized by *New York* magazine as one of the "Best Doctors" in New York for several years, and has been honored as a "Super Doctor" by the *New York Times*. In 2009, Dr. Antoine founded the non-profit organization Rx Compassion, which is committed to compassionate patient care.

Margaret J. Nachtigall, MD

251 E. 33rd Street
New York, NY 10016
www.nyu.med.edu

Dr. Nachtigall, a board-certified reproductive endocrinologist in private practice, is assistant professor of obstetrics and gynecology in the Division of Reproductive Endocrinology at New York University School of Medicine. The recipient of many awards and honors, Dr. Nachtigall's clinical specialties include menopause, polycystic ovarian syndrome (PCOS), and infertility. She is a founding member of the North American Menopause Society, and is a fellow in the American College of Obstetrics and Gynecology, the American Society for Reproductive Medicine, and the New York Society of Reproductive Medicine. Dr. Nachtigall is involved in clinical trials in the areas of hormone therapy and management of menopause, and has published many articles relating to hormonal management and women's health.

Chapter 4: Sex

Esther Perel, MA, LMFT

Individual, Couple and Family Therapy

245 Fifth Avenue

New York, NY 10016

212-889-8117

www.estherperel.com

Ms. Perel is the author of the best-selling *Mating in Captivity*, and is a licensed marriage and family therapist in private practice. Ms. Perel has been featured in many international publications, such as the *New Yorker*, *Vogue*, *More*, *Elle* and newspapers around the world. She has appeared multiple times on the *Oprah Winfrey Show*, the *Today Show*, *CBS This Morning*, *CNN*, and many other television and radio programs. A frequent keynote speaker, Ms. Perel regularly addresses both the medical community and laypeople through workshops, conferences, and other forums. She serves on the faculties of the Department of Psychiatry of New York University School of Medicine, the International Trauma Studies Program, and the Columbia University Mailman School of Public Health. Ms. Perel is a member of the American Family Therapy Academy and the Society for Sex Therapy and Research.

Chapter 5: You=What You Eat

Stuart Fischer, MD

The Park Avenue Diet Center

133 East 58th Street

New York, NY 10022

212-893-8478

www.parkavenuediet.com

Laura J. Lefkowitz, MD

Nutrition and Health Counseling

817 Broadway

New York, NY 10003

917-318-2325

www.LauraLefkowitzMD.com

Dr. Fischer is the founder of the Park Avenue Diet Center, which provides a comprehensive approach to weight loss and self-image management. Dr.Fischer worked with the late Dr. Robert Atkins for over nine years as the associate medical director of the world-famous Atkins Center. Dr. Fischer regularly appears on *Inside Edition*, *FOX and Friends*, *CNN*, *CBS This Morning*, and other television and radio programs. He's been interviewed in many publications such as the *New York Times*, *USA Today*, *Star Magazine*, and the *Sunday Times* of London. An author of several publications, Dr. Fischer effectively laid out his successful plan for weight loss and self-image management in the best-selling *The Park Avenue Diet*.

Dr. Lefkowitz is a physician and founder of a nutrition and health counseling practice in Manhattan. She left traditional medicine, where she was a surgical oncologist, to focus on preventing and reversing disease by educating her patients on proper nutrition, maintaining a healthy weight, and simple modifications in exercise. In addition to studying traditional medicine at the Stony Brook School of Medicine, St. Vincent's Hospital, and SUNY-Downstate, Dr. Lefkowitz received her nutrition training at Columbia University's Institute for Integrative Nutrition in New York City.

Chapter 6: Move That Body

Jeff Galloway

Jeff Galloway Productions
4651 Roswell Road
Atlanta, GA 30342
800-200-2771
www.jeffgalloway.com

Mr. Galloway is a U.S. Olympian (1972), best-selling author of many books on running, monthly columnist for *Runner's World* magazine, and founder of Galloway Training Programs and Fitness Retreats. Mr. Galloway's quest for an injury-free marathon training program led him to develop the Run-Walk-Run method in 1978, which is now followed by millions of people around the world. In 1984, Mr. Galloway published *Galloway's Book on Running* which continues to be one of the best-selling books on running in North America. *Marathon: You Can Do It!* is considered the state-of-the-art information source for training for a marathon.

David Kirsch

David Kirsch Wellness Co.
210 Fifth Avenue
New York, NY 10010
888-683-1836
www.davidkirschwellness.com

David Kirsch is the celebrated trainer and founder of the Madison Square Club, and has sculpted celebrities such as Heidi Klum, Faith Hill, Ellen Barkin, Anne Hathaway, and many others. Credited with getting Heidi Klum ready for the Victoria's Secret lingerie runway show weeks after she had a baby, he is a popular guest on many television shows, worldwide, including ABC's *Extreme Make-over*, *CNN*, *Access Hollywood*, *Extra*, *E!*, *The View*, and *FOX and Friends*. He is also frequently featured as an exercise expert in prestigious publications, including *Time*, *Vogue*, *W*, *Allure*, *Shape*, *Fitness*, *People*, *US Weekly*, national and local newspapers, and many others. Mr. Kirsch is an author of several books on exercise and nutrition, including *The Ultimate New York Body Plan*.

Chapter 7: Love the Skin You're In

Doris Day, MD, FAAD, MA

Cosmetic, Laser and Surgical Dermatology

135 East 71st Street

New York, NY 10021

212-772-0740

www.MyClearSkin.com

Dr. Day is a board-certified dermatologist who specializes in laser, cosmetic, and surgical dermatology. She is affiliated with Lenox Hill Hospital in NYC and is a clinical assistant professor of dermatology at the New York University School of Medicine. Dr. Day often appears on *Good Morning America, GMA Health, CNN,* the *Today Show, The Tyra Banks Show* and many others television programs. She is regularly featured in major publications, including *In Style, Allure, Vogue, Glamour, W, Redbook,* and *Health,* where she has a regular monthly column. Her most recent book, *Forget the Facelift,* is an important resource book for proper and effective care of aging skin. Dr. Day is a member of the American Society for Dermatologic Surgery, the Women's Dermatological Society, and the American Medical Association.

Patricia Wexler, MD

Wexler Dermatology PC

145 East 32nd Street

New York, NY 10016

212-684-2626

www.patriciawexlermd.com

Dr. Patricia Wexler, featured in *New York* magazine's "Best Doctors" issues, is a board-certified dermatologist specializing in dermatology and dermatologic surgery, including state-of-the-art cosmetic surgical procedures. Dr. Wexler is a published author of medical research and has appeared on national television shows including the *Today Show, The View, The Oprah Winfrey Show,* and *20/20,* among others. She is regularly featured in major magazines, and is the recipient of many awards. In 2005, Dr. Wexler formed a partnership with Bath & Body Works to launch her own acclaimed and affordable skin care line. She is a member of the American Board of Internal Medicine, and the American Board of Dermatology. She is a fellow of the American Society of Dermatologic Surgery.

Chapter 8: Face the Facts

Laura Geller

Laura Geller Makeup Studio

1044 Lexington Avenue

New York, NY 10021

212-570-5477

www.laurageller.com

Ms. Geller's mission is simple: to teach women how to apply makeup so they look fabulous. She started in the makeup business by bringing her expertise to the theater. From there, she worked with the on-air talent at CBS, ABC, NBC, and HBO. Ms. Geller is frequently seen on QVC, where her brand of cosmetics is one of QVC's bestsellers. Laura Geller Makeup is also a top-selling brand at Sephora. Her exceptional ability to connect with her viewers and customers has been a key to her success and has led to a cult following of her brand. She is a sought-after beauty expert and is often interviewed in major women's magazines.

Carmindy

www.Carmindy.com

Every week, millions of viewers count on Carmindy to show them the latest makeup tips and tricks on TLC's hit show *What Not to Wear*. Carmindy's work can be seen in the pages of leading magazines such as *Cosmopolitan, Elle, In Style, Essence, Self, Lucky, Seventeen, Marie Claire,* and many others. She has created a natural line of cosmetics called Sally Hansen Natural Beauty Inspired by Carmindy, available in drugstores nationwide. Carmindy is the author of three books on beauty—*The 5 Minute Face, Get Positively Beautiful,* and *Crazy Busy Beautiful.* She writes a monthly e-newsletter featuring answers to questions submitted to her website by readers, viewers, and customers.

Chapter 9: No More Bad Hair Days

Frédéric Fekkai

Fekkai Salon (Flagship)

712 Fifth Avenue

New York, NY 10019

212-753-9500

www.fekkai.com

In 1989, Mr. Fekkai opened his first salon in New York. He soon saw a niche in the marketplace—to create high-end, luxury hair products—and proceeded to create a global business. Frédéric Fekkai products are now sold in over 40 countries. There are seven salons around the country, but for over twenty years, the Fekkai New York City flagship store on Fifth Avenue has remained the highest grossing salon in the world. Mr. Fekkai has been featured in nearly every major magazine and newspaper, has appeared on countless television programs, and continues to be the clear leader and visionary in the luxury hair care industry.

Lorraine Massey

Founder and Co-Owner, Devachan Salons

560 Broadway

New York, NY

212-274-8686

www.devachansalon.com

www.devachanconcepts.com

A staunch advocate of setting your hair free, Ms. Massey is the best-selling author of *Curly Girl*, the how-to manifesto for women who want to bring their hair back to its natural and healthy state, whether curly, wavy, or straight. With several salons in New York, and a collection of products that are sold in the salons, specialty stores and on-line, Ms. Massey and her team are helping women to put down the weapons of mass destruction (blow-dryers, straighteners and harsh detergents) and embrace their beautiful hair. Ms. Massey and her team travel around the country training other stylists in the "Devachan Way" of cutting, coloring and caring for hair. The stylists—nationwide—that have been trained are listed on the website.

Edward Joseph, Colorist

Devachan Salon

560 Broadway

New York, N.Y.

212 274 8686

www.devachansalon.com

www.devachanconcepts.com

Mr. Joseph is a lead colorist at Devachan Salon in New York City, and has worked with Lorraine Massey, the founder of Devachan, for over ten years. He is expertly trained in pintura—a highlighting technique where strands of hair are painted with the dye in the exact places where the sun would naturally create highlights. These highlights are expertly blended with the natural hair color for maximum effect, minimum amount of damage, and the most natural look. Mr. Joseph also trains other colorists at salons around the country in this technique.

Chapter 10: You Wear It Well

Diane von Furstenberg

Diane von Furstenberg Studio
440 W. 14th Street
New York, NY 10014
212-741-6607
www.dvf.com

Diane von Furstenberg arrived in the fashion world in 1972 with the introduction of her iconic wrap dress. By 1976, Ms. von Furstenberg had sold millions of her dresses, coming to symbolize female power and freedom to an entire generation. In 1997, after a hiatus from fashion, she reemerged on the fashion scene with the re-launch of the dress that had started it all and began building her company into the global luxury lifestyle brand it is today. In addition to the over 30 Diane von Furstenberg stores around the world, her line of clothes and accessories are sold in specialty stores in over 70 countries worldwide. In 2005, she was awarded the Lifetime Achievement Award from the Council of Fashion Designers of America (CFDA), and a year later was elected the CFDA's new president, an office she continues to hold. A firm believer in the power of women, she sits on the board of Vital Voices, a women's leadership organization that empowers emerging women leaders and social entrepreneurs around the world.

Ginny Hilfiger

Founder, Ginny H by Ginny Hilfiger
www.GinnyH.com

Ginny Hilfiger has been designing clothing for over 20 years. Ms. Hilfiger was a top designer for her brother's company, where she helped launch Tommy Hilfiger menswear, Tommy Jeans, Tommy Girl, and women's sportswear. After leaving Tommy Hilfiger, Ms. Hilfiger independently established her own line, Ginny H, which is sold online and in specialty stores. While her main focus is designing ready-to-wear for stores nationwide, she also creates customized fashions for clients. She is in the process of developing a new mid-priced line of clothing which will be sold in stores nationwide.

The Fifth Avenue Club Personal Shopping Service

Lisa Bruni Vene, Director

Julie Hackett-Behr, Style Consultant

Saks Fifth Avenue

611 Fifth Avenue

New York, NY 10022

212-940-4657

www.saks.com

Lisa Bruni Vene has been the Director of the Fifth Avenue Club—Saks Fifth Avenue's personal shopping service—since 2004. She supervises a team of expert associates who offer style consultations in the New York flagship store. Julie Hackett-Behr is one of the top Style Consultants in the personal shopping service group and has been advising Saks customers for over twenty years.

Chapter 11: Money

Jane Bryant Quinn

Jane Bryant Quinn has been one of the country's most successful newspaper columnists, publishing twice-weekly for 27 years, and syndicating to more than 250 newspapers. For over 30 years, Ms. Quinn wrote a bi-weekly column for *Newsweek* magazine. She has also written columns for Bloomberg.com, *Woman's Day*, and *Good Housekeeping*. Working extensively in television, she co-hosted an investment series that ran on PBS, and hosted her own program, *Take Charge!* Ms. Quinn worked ten years for CBS News, has been a regular on many other shows, as well as a frequent guest on *Good Morning America*, *Nightline*, *The News Hour with Jim Lehrer*, and many other programs. She has written several best-selling books, including *Making the Most of Your Money*, and *Smart and Simple Financial Strategies for Busy People*. Her newest book is *Making the Most of Your Money NOW!* Ms. Quinn is the recipient of many awards, including an Emmy Award for outstanding coverage of news on television, and the Gerald Loeb award for distinguished lifetime achievement in business and financial journalism. She was instrumental in the development of the top-selling software program, Quicken Financial Planner, and is currently on the board of Bloomberg LP and is a member of the Council on Foreign Relations.

Jason Zweig

The Wall Street Journal
1155 Avenue of the Americas
New York, NY
212-597-5600
www.wsj.com
www.jasonzweig.com

Jason Zweig is the investing and personal finance columnist for *The Wall Street Journal*. He is the author of *Your Money and Your Brain*, on the neuroscience of investing. Mr. Zweig is also the editor of the revised edition of Benjamin Graham's *The Intelligent Investor*, the classic text that Warren Buffett has described as "by far the best book about investing ever written." From 1995 through 2008 he was a senior writer for *Money* magazine.

Before joining *Money*, he was the mutual funds editor at *Forbes*. Mr. Zweig has been a guest columnist for *Time* magazine and CNN.com. He has served as a trustee of the Museum of American Finance, an affiliate of the Smithsonian Institution, and sits on the editorial boards of Financial History magazine and the Journal of Behavioral Finance.

Michael I. Axelrod

Wealth Management Advisor

Bleakley, Schwartz, Cooney, & Finney, LLC

Northwestern Mutual Investment Services, LLC

100 Passaic Avenue

Fairfield, NJ 07004

973-244-4223

Mike.Axelrod@nmfn.com

Michael Axelrod has been with Northwestern for almost 20 years, and is currently a fee-only wealth management advisor, specializing in managing money for women who are retired, or close to retirement age. His focus is on helping his clients accumulate and protect assets, and generate revenue streams during retirement. Mr. Axelrod also advises clients with estate planning, and all aspects of insurance needs.

Chapter 12:
Lose the Clutter, Find Your Life

Julie Morgenstern

Julie Morgenstern Enterprises

850 7th Avenue

New York, NY 10019

212-586-8084

www.juliemorgenstern.com

Julie Morgenstern, crowned the "queen of putting people's lives in order" by *USA Today*, is an organizing and time management expert, business productivity consultant, and sought-after speaker. Several of Ms. Morgenstern's five books, including *Never Check E-Mail in the Morning* and *SHED Your Stuff, Change Your Life*, are *New York Times* bestsellers. She has been featured in publications such as the *New York Times*, The *Wall Street Journal, O, The Oprah Magazine, Men's Health*, and has a monthly column in *Redbook* magazine. Ms. Morgenstern is frequently on television programs including the *Today Show* and *Rachael Ray*, and many radio programs as well. Her first two books have been made into popular one-hour PBS specials, and several others have evolved into training programs used at Fortune 500 corporations around the globe. Ms. Morgenstern is the recipient of many awards and has been honored by the White House.

Chapter 13:
What's Next?

Julia Moulden

Founder, The New Radicals

www.wearethenewradicals.com

Julia Moulden coined the phrase "New Radicals" to describe people who are leveraging their expertise to take on some of the world's toughest challenges. Her book about this movement, *We Are the New Radicals: A Manifesto for Reinventing Yourself and Saving the World*, is an international bestseller and introduces the reader to the many opportunities and paths one might take to help the world while re-inventing one's career. Ms. Moulden has a weekly column on the Huffington Post, and writes for many other publications.

Acknowledgments

My gratitude goes first and foremost to the wonderful experts who graciously shared their knowledge with me, spent hours answering questions, took my calls when I needed something clarified, and who have become valued friends.

Jennifer Kasius, my editor at Running Press, enthusiastically embraced this project and brought it to life. I thank Jennifer for her wisdom, exceptional insights, for being as excited about this book as I am, and for being such a pleasure to work with. A special thank you goes to Craig Herman, Corinda Cook, Nicole DeJackmo, Sarah Gibb, and the entire edit, design, sales and promotion team at Running Press.

Jenni Ferrari-Adler, my agent at Brick House, saw the potential in this book from the first day we met. Her support, encouragement, and calm, guiding hand through the entire writing process was invaluable.

My heartfelt thanks go to Joe McGinniss, one of this world's greatest writers, for having the good sense and wisdom to lead me to Jenni. I am forever in his debt.

Andrea Lynn Galyean's expertise in proof reading and editing, and her frequent reminders to stay true to my vision, helped me turn this book into more than just a good idea.

Many friends helped me in so many ways. My special thanks go to Dr. Margaret Nachtigall-Giordano, Alison and Larry Wolfson, Maura Brickman, Jill Sacher, Laura Higgins, Karen Goodell, Sue Weiner, Mort Zuckerman, Peggy Engel, Heidi Axelrod, Rhonda Alexander-Abt, Karen Klopp, Lisa Plepler,

Maria Turgeon, and Patti Stegman.

Extra special thanks go to Beth Klein, Denise Davila, M Crespi, Jay Sternberg, Amy Heilgeist, Catherine Pierpoint, and Ellen Levinson Gross, who were gracious and helpful, always.

I give my sincere gratitude and love to my wonderful extended family—Pauline Chou, Lillian Grufferman, Carole Soler, Danny Soler, Emily and Joseph Marino, Michael and Erika Marino, Barbara and Robert Haspel, Julieth Baisden, Mandy Jones and Joe O'Rourke—for always encouraging me, and for counting the days until they have the book in hand.

Gunther, our amazing dog, never left my side when I was writing. He is the perfect assistant.

I have saved my biggest and deepest thanks for my husband, Howard, and daughters, Sarah and Elizabeth. While I was writing this book, (and during our entire marriage), Howard was unwavering in his support, encouragement, love and pride in me. His steadfast and constant belief that I can do anything I set my mind on, has given me the courage that we all sometimes need. And, I thank him for letting me reveal that he walks around the apartment wearing his pedometer. I love him with everything I have.

Our oldest daughter, Sarah, was the first person who heard my idea, and she urged me to make it happen. I thank her for helping me to believe, once again, that dreams really do come true (by never giving up!). Sarah's quiet confidence and generosity of spirit inspire me to do more, and to do better.

I thank Elizabeth, our youngest, for knowing exactly when I need a hug, for being so proud of her mom, for making sure that music and dance are always in our home, and for living her life in a simple state of joy and happiness. She makes me laugh every day.

I am so proud of the beautiful, confident, caring people my little women have become.

Howard, Sarah and Elizabeth: you are my family, my joy, my life, and I love you with all my heart.

You are the best of everything.

♥ ♥ ♥